A History of Political Thought: 1785 to the Present

A History of
Political Thought:
1789 to the Present

BRUCE HADDOCK

polity

First published in 2005 by Polity Press

Polity Press
65 Bridge Street
Cambridge CB2 1UR, UK.

Polity Press
350 Main Street
Malden, MA 02148, USA

ISBN: 0-7456-3102-9
ISBN: 0-7456-3103-7 (pb)

A catalogue record for this book is available from the British
Library and has been applied for from the Library of Congress.

Typeset in 9.5 on 12 pt Utopia
by Servis Filmsetting Ltd, Manchester
Printed and bound in Great Britain by MPG Books Ltd, Bodmin, Cornwall.

For further information on Polity, visit our website: www.polity.co.uk

Contents

Acknowledgements

Some of the issues in this book have been with me throughout my career. I am grateful for help, advice and encouragement over many years to teachers and colleagues, especially at Leicester, Oxford, Swansea and Cardiff. Christopher Hughes, John Day and Maurice Keens-Soper have had an influence on my work that grows with the years. David Boucher, Peri Roberts, Peter Sutch and Paul Furlong have been wonderfully supportive colleagues. I am grateful, too, to Ovidiu Caraiani, who has worked with me on other matters, but whose contribution to my thinking has been immensely important. I was able to do some of the preparatory work on this book in the delightful surroundings of Emory University, where Don and Molly Verene ensured that I enjoyed ideal working conditions. Anonymous reviewers at Polity Press offered helpful advice. Louise Knight and her colleagues at Polity Press have been unfailingly encouraging. An author could not ask for a more painstaking or sensitive copy-editor than Jean van Altena. My principal debt is to my family. Simon, Jessica, Lizzie and Nellie have always helped and supported me. Without Sheila I could not have done anything at all.

I have drawn on some of my earlier essays and articles in this volume, in radically revised form. My thanks go to the editors and publishers of the following: *Themes in Modern European History: 1830–1890* (Unwin Hyman, 1990); *The Political Classics: Hamilton to Mill* (Oxford University Press, 1993); *The Political Classics: Green to Dworkin* (Oxford University Press, 1996); *History of Political Thought*, 20 (1999); *The Edinburgh Companion to Contemporary Liberalism* (Edinburgh University Press, 2001); and *Multiculturalism, Identity and Rights* (Routledge, 2003).

1 Introduction

The impact of 'politics' on basic aspects of our lives is now obvious to any reflective citizen of a modern state. But it was not always so. Competition for status and power have been qualitatively transformed as the modern state has been seen as a primary vehicle for the pursuit of a host of social, economic, cultural and political goals. This book begins with the eruption of this new style of politics in the French and American revolutions. Both may be seen as the culmination of an aspiration to manage and control political life in accordance with publicly justifiable principles.

Much more was at stake, however, than political power in any narrow sense. Political orders were now portrayed in terms of starkly opposed ways of life (monarchy, aristocracy and established hierarchy on the one side, equal rights for all on the other). The middle ground between these positions appeared (at least for a time) to be non-existent. It seemed to combatants that everything was at stake, no matter where you stood on the political spectrum.

Political argument, of course, was not conducted in a vacuum. The tensions of the modern state reflected profound changes in economy and society, as emerging national and international markets, population movements and growth demanded political management and control. The industrial revolution would unleash productive potential that would disrupt social and economic practices on a continental (and finally global) scale. Just how far these forces can be controlled and contained by political orders remains a moot point to this day. What is certain, however, is that citizens and subjects began to make demands on their political leaders, driven by ambition and desperation, that have sometimes proved to be irresistible.

Modern states have been shaped by conflicting (and often strictly incompatible) demands. The initial opposition of revolutionary and reactionary movements and arguments in 1789 has been followed by (more or less effective) efforts at political accommodation. The modern constitutional state has sought to establish terms of reference that most (if not all) citizens can regard as acceptable in the pursuit of their multifarious interests. It has in fact proved to be extraordinarily resilient, despite crises provoked by war and economic collapse that have tempted political elites and citizens to adopt more direct means of public management and control. What we see at times of crisis is very much argument about terms of reference. Not everyone will profit from any political scheme. In difficult and dangerous times, discussion has often focused on the very real costs to political losers.

Liberty and welfare, for example, have often been presented as if they could not be reconciled as goals of public policy. A state focused on maximizing the liberties of its citizens would be hampered in its efforts to redistribute resources to the poor. Yet political theories stressing one or the other goal had necessarily to accommodate at least some opposing positions. Again we see painstaking efforts to find middle ground, coupled with (sometimes dramatic) shifts in policy as states confront crises.

The state as we know it is very much a discursive construct, striving to reconcile institutional demands with wider ambitions and values. It remains coercive even in its benign forms, and thus challenges us to justify massive intervention in the lives of individuals. It has been treated as a vehicle for cultural, social and moral reform, in addition to economic and political management and control. As functions of the state have expanded, so have occasions for citizen complaint and controversy. The tiniest practical detail (what a child may be allowed to wear in a classroom) can become an occasion for heated political debate. We need to ask ourselves why this should be so; and, indeed, why public stances should be so pervasive in our lives.

Political thought invites us to see ourselves in relation to a public realm that is contested and controversial. Even our focus on the state as the embodiment of public life and responsibility has been challenged in recent decades, as political elites struggle to manage (especially economic) affairs against a backdrop of financial and technological interdependence. The thought that as citizens we share a responsibility for our affairs looks precarious in relation to the dominance of private capital in international markets. In the circumstances we may be forced to revise our conceptions of a public domain. What remains, though, is the need to sustain social co-operation among strangers in unimaginably diverse situations.

Political thought over the last 200 years has thus had to respond to unprecedented situations, often with deeply disturbing results. Stress on what is 'modern' about political thought since 1789, however, should not blind us to fundamental features of political thought in any organized society. Political thinking has a public dimension, no matter how a public domain may be specifically characterized. Arguments about social co-operation have necessarily to be projected to whomever might be expected to engage in or be subject to a given set of arrangements. It does not follow that everybody in a community would be entitled to the same sort of consideration. Consensual persuasion may be reserved for a select few, while a majority may be coerced or manipulated. The point remains that the effective exercise of political power presupposes minimally shared objectives and values among relevant groups. And these objectives and values can be challenged by the disgruntled, excluded and disappointed.

Terms of reference in political argument shift over time. Yet we can detect two contrasting themes from early Greek political philosophy that have continued to dominate political thought. On the one side, advocates of a universal and eternal standard of justice have sought to measure actual political institutions and practices against a notional ideal. On the other side, emphasis has been placed on the conventions which human beings devise to meet their needs in particular circumstances. We can picture this as an argument between Plato and Protagoras, or between advocates of utopia confronting defenders of tradition. How these arguments have worked out in practice has depended upon complex contingent circumstances. As historians of political thought, what we see are not variations on fixed themes so much as iterations of arguments adding layers of complexity in highly specific contexts. Philosophical abstraction can help us to understand the form of arguments. But it should not blind us to the distinctive features that make particular arguments and crises unlike any others in detail.

Political philosophers have never been entirely detached from the concerns and controversies of their communities, though they sometimes touchingly address posterity rather than actual opponents. In the course of their work, however, they also challenge conventional assumptions about the appropriate form of arguments. Substantive debates about who should get what in a scheme of distribution can spill over into disputes about what could possibly count as a defensible argument. Trumps in discourse that may be unquestioned in one period may be regarded as distractions in another. In the history of political thought we thus find arguments conducted at a variety of levels. We cannot assume that terms of reference will remain stable. Yet neither can we ignore the wider implications of specific arguments that may initially be addressed to very narrow audiences.

History of political thought is thus history of a very special kind. It requires sensitivity to context and occasion, in addition to mastery of formal argument. Specific philosophers and theorists must also be read in relation to the wider story of political thought. Problems here are peculiarly difficult, though unavoidable. We cannot isolate texts or periods, because our criteria of selection will be informed by the larger story we may have to tell. And that story will in its own way be a matter of theoretical controversy. There are no neutral or innocent perspectives. We cannot separate effectively our concerns as political philosophers or theorists from our concerns as historians.

Managing social co-operation in contingent circumstances has always been a basic feature of political thought and action. What has changed in the last 200 years is that the theoretical response to contingency has become central to the way we see ourselves. That theoretical staple of seventeenth- and eighteenth-century political thought, 'human nature', is no longer much in evidence in modern political thought. The term carries the suggestion that human beings are everywhere and always so fundamentally alike that the fortuitous circumstances in which they live can have only a superficial effect on their essential natures. The fact that human life is conducted in time and depends upon received understandings that are passed on to future generations is then accorded only secondary significance. Yet from Vico's *New Science* in 1725, if we must specify a starting point, a succession of texts has defended the view that the human world as a whole is a historical product.[1] Even knowledge itself is portrayed as historically relative, reflecting the particular circumstances in which communities have found themselves. From this point of view, judgements of value, which were once confidently cast in a universal form, should be seen more properly as expressions of the preferences of particular cultures and communities.

The detailed story of the emergence of historical consciousness in modern times is too complex to be told here.[2] What needs to be noticed, however, is that all modes of thought that had presupposed universal standards are rendered problematic. It could no longer be assumed that we meant what we said when we asked ourselves how human beings might ideally live together in communities. Precisely how political theorists over the last 200 years have sought to respond to this dilemma is a central concern of this book. Here we simply need to note that, in so far as it ever made sense to talk about an unproblematic tradition of political philosophy, it can now no longer be assumed that the contingent contexts in which political arguments are formulated constitute a secondary issue.

The view of ourselves as culturally and historically embedded in specific ways of life now colours all our experience. But at the same time we are impelled to respond to dilemmas and atrocities that invite universal forms of description and judgement. Political thought since 1789 has oscillated uncomfortably between these positions, with little prospect that either perspective can be permanently set aside. This poses acute problems for us as we reflect on our ordinary experience of making judgements and adopting moral and political stances.

The year 1789 also thrust theory to the forefront of political debate. The events of the American and French revolutions challenged conceptions of political order profoundly. The simple thought that failure to meet certain objective normative standards might justify popular revolution threatened all established polities in 1789. And the failure of the revolutions themselves to generate consensus and stability meant that political orders began to look like temporary holding operations, maintaining a framework of institutions and practices until the next theoretical or ideological challenge. Justification, which had always been central to political philosophy, was thus transformed into *public* justification, though arguments raged about whose opinion should count, how accountability should be secured – indeed whether or not human ingenuity was sufficient to assess the daunting complexity of a modern polity.

As political philosophy became public, so it was exposed to the demands of mobilization and polemical contention. What we may think of as an *ideological* style of political argument began to emerge, where rhetorical force became quite as important as formal consistency, with modes of argument being adapted to the requirements of different audiences. Political philosophy lost its innocence as ideological and cultural hegemony were recognized to be major factors in effective governance.

A clear criterion of truth was an early casualty. Fashioning arguments to meet the demands of particular occasions challenged the presumption of universality in political philosophy. Commitments to state, nation, community or class were more readily intelligible in public controversy than a perennial conception of the good life. Yet fraught normative issues remained. Commitments may have become more limited in scope, but they were none the less deeply contentious and problematic. Values across spheres of activity would clash. One could not see oneself exclusively as a member of a state or class. Ordinary experience continued to throw up normative dilemmas, though it was by no means evident that the challenge could be met within the new terms of reference.

Theoretical concerns about the status of moral and political principles can have a massive impact on political activity itself. The twentieth century has thrown up examples that are deeply troubling. The thought that (say) principles are merely rationalizations of interest (however conceived) undermines the credibility of (at least some) schemes of social co-operation. If we assume (for theoretical reasons) that ideological controversy is merely an indirect means of pursuing power struggles, then one possible inference is that we should dispense with discursive politics altogether. Early fascist doctrine in Italy addressed this issue directly. And from there it was a comparatively easy step to embrace a view of politics as naked power struggle.

The fascist glorification of the state is an extreme example, to be sure. Yet it would be a mistake to refuse to consider fascist doctrine seriously because we find it politically disagreeable. Deep questions are raised about the very possibility of a discursive politics. We should not assume that a discursive model would ever be sufficient to describe political life as a whole. But discounting the idea of a reasonable political consensus is perilous.

The same dilemma can be viewed from the more benign perspective of democratic theory. A possible response to the ambiguous status of normative judgements is to try to ensure that as broad a base of a population as possible is engaged in the political process. Utilitarian theory, for example, at least in the Benthamite model, accepts that judgements are rationalizations of interest, and concludes that everyone's interest should count. A universal franchise is regarded as a defensible solution to the ineradicable plurality of perspectives in political life. But, of course, democratic politics cannot guarantee that people's interests will be treated equally. We know that democratic politics is easily manipulated by powerful interests. Marx and his followers have given us plausible reasons for not trusting all the outcomes in democratic politics. In these circumstances, we have to confront the possibility that democratic politics will generate normatively indefensible policy. This should not surprise us, even in the best-managed democracies. The point to stress here is that it forces us back to a style of political theorizing that we have learnt to mistrust.

This book takes seriously the contention that normative arguments are problematic. It also accepts that they are unavoidable. Wishful thinking cannot help us here. The rich literature of the last thirty years on the social construction of identities should serve as a warning to moderate our normative ambitions. Some theorists even claim that normative judgements are a species of logical confusion.[3] Yet, despite these very real difficulties, we are led irresistibly back to normative argument. And normative arguments can be well or ill conceived.

Assessing the adequacy of normative criteria in a context in which relevant criteria are regarded as contingent is, of course, a highly complex matter. It cannot be reduced to anything as clean and neat as a 'method'. We should not expect to encounter ideal or stable solutions in a rapidly changing world. What we can do, however, is focus on the kind of thinking we are committed to in complex situations. Problems for a modern historian of political thought are thus not different in kind from those confronting modern citizens in multicultural contexts, though practical urgency will not be felt in the same way.

This book deals with political theorizing addressed to a variety of audiences, pitched at different levels of generality, responding (more or less) self-consciously to changing political conditions. Political theories are all concerned with persuasion, though not necessarily with overt mobilization. All make claims to our attention as formal responses to problems of co-operation, co-ordination and control in circumstances where we have limited knowledge and resources at our disposal. We might thus expect them to be tentative and conditional, despite the confident (sometimes dogmatic) mood in which they may be couched.

Yet we also find currents of thought that treat a tentative and conditional understanding of politics as a problem to be overcome. Following the scientific achievements of the seventeenth and eighteenth centuries, it has remained a standing temptation for theorists and politicians to try to transcend the limitations of a political condition, as if the frustrations and imperfections of conventional politics could somehow be overcome if we are bold enough. The first half of the twentieth century, in particular, is witness to the consequences of striving to establish schemes of social control and co-ordination that are beyond ordinary politics. Attempts to put utopia into practice have proved to be universally disastrous. As historians and citizens we can learn from these experiences, though not in any straightforward fashion. It would not help if we were simply to congratulate ourselves on our wisdom and self-restraint. The temptation to try to transcend or evade politics remains a factor in theory and practice, even in benign forms of withdrawal from public life. These positions must be understood theoretically and historically, whatever we may choose to make of them as citizens. In different theories they have formed focal points for agents anxious to orientate themselves in a (potentially) hostile public world. They are attempts to do things in public, but they also raise questions about the way the public sphere should be understood. And as key contributions to crucial debates, they have helped to shape wider understandings of public life.

Our position as students of political thought is different from that of citizens striving to do the best they can for themselves in difficult circumstances. But we deepen and sharpen political understanding precisely because we take seriously the shifting contexts in which political thinking is conducted. In an important sense, how we think changes the political world, at least to a minor degree. And if we want to grasp the drama of political life, we have to picture political thinking against a backdrop of uncertainty. As agents, we do not know what will happen next. Serious consequences can follow from our folly. Setting seminal thinking in historical context heightens our awareness of the raw dimension in political thought and action.

This book takes seriously the existential predicament of agents making choices in complex social situations. We know that we cannot flourish alone, and that we depend upon the co-operation of distant strangers whom we cannot hope to control. In an important sense, these are limiting conditions for citizens and political leaders. Political philosophy is a response to this dilemma, even when it purports to go beyond these terms of reference. At the very least, we have to picture agents making judgements which may be general in scope. Judgements may begin as rationalizations of interest, but they will become broader in range as the complexity of interdependence is recognized to be a factor in our flourishing.

Normative judgements are thus being made in a context of radical contingency. We know that our values may not be shared. For the most part, we may be able to rely on local understandings that do not oblige us to dwell on foundational questions. But our cultures and forms of life are not self-contained. Values will clash, priorities may differ, yet we still have to maintain schemes of co-ordination and control. The use of force has always been a possible option for the rich and powerful in these situations. Even the most powerful, however, depend upon the co-operation of strangers. And no one can ensure that their power and resources will be sustained permanently. Our priorities and values can always be challenged. In these circumstances, we have to give reasons for our choices that extend beyond the values we happen to have.

Something like political philosophy is forced upon us by circumstances. Public justification is a corollary of social co-operation among strangers, though sensitive questions are necessarily raised about the configuration and identity of relevant public spheres. Fellow citizens may have stronger claims on us than the inhabitants of the Amazon rain forest; yet we cannot deny indirect involvement with the life prospects of any individual or group absolutely. We simply have different priorities. But interdependence obliges us to think hard about the wider implications of our positions.

These arguments are often handled very crudely in public life. The fact remains, though, that difficult dilemmas commit us to thinking in broader and more imaginative styles. Philosophers in the quiet of their studies are certainly detached from the urgent business of co-operation, co-ordination and control, but they are nevertheless responding to issues that are thrown up in ordinary political experience.

The range of historical responses to these dilemmas is an integral part of our education as political theorists. Even if we set ourselves the task of explaining political choice in terms of 'ideal' models, our models are necessarily informed by ordinary experience of argument, manipulation and control. Abstraction presupposes experience. And in the context of modern political thought, that experience has been shaped by our developing awareness of historical change.

From the perspective in which we find ourselves, a political education must involve theory and history. We interpret our political world in terms of (more or less adequate) received understandings. In order to think effectively ourselves, we have to see political theorizing in relation to the press of circumstances. It is hedged around by limitations, both conceptual and cultural. Hard thinking of this kind requires immersion in contexts, and at the same time awareness of continuing efforts to grasp transient situations. Our thinking, in this sense, is never over.

How the universal and particular dimensions of political theory should be understood is a vexed question. The problem has arisen in a variety of contexts, and has been handled more or less effectively. Our thinking is torn in different directions. History of political thought can equip us to address some of these difficulties, without furnishing definitive solutions. We have to do the best we can for ourselves as thinkers, in the light of the most cogent and arresting treatments of recurring issues that have come down to us. It is a challenging and frustrating exercise; but we disregard it at our peril.

2 Revolution

The year 1789 is a momentous one in modern political history. The outbreak of revolution in France and the inauguration of the federal constitution in the United States symbolically mark the beginning of an epoch in which human beings in the round (regarded as citizens) sought to wrest control of their political lives out of the hands of hereditary or imperial elites. Documents and propaganda from both countries reflect an optimism about possibilities for political improvement that may strike us today as utopian or even naïve. Yet they ushered on to the political stage normative and constitutional criteria that continue to serve as points of reference in our political discussions.

The tone is captured in the first of *The Federalist Papers* (1788), a series of newspaper articles written by Alexander Hamilton, James Madison and John Jay in New York in defence of the ratification of the federal constitution under the pseudonym 'Publius'. Hamilton remarked in the opening paragraph: 'it seems to have been reserved to the people of this country, by their conduct and example, to decide the important question, whether societies of men are really capable or not, of establishing good government from reflection and choice, or whether they are forever destined to depend, for their political constitutions, on accident and force.'[1]

The challenge is dramatic and remains unfulfilled in our own age. What it highlights, however, is the simple thought that political arrangements are the concern of each and every one of us, though we may differ profoundly among ourselves about how these responsibilities may best be fulfilled. We cannot shrug our shoulders in resignation and assume that fate, chance, or a dominant elite will shape things no matter what we think. To be sure, none of us can dictate the pattern of events or institutions. Yet the fact remains that institutions are man-made conventions to meet the demands of circumstances and the need to establish terms of co-operation for our engagements. This is true even if we choose to acquiesce in the entrenched customs and conventions of our day. To choose to carry on as we have in the past is a daily endorsement of a co-operative scheme. And if things go wrong for us, or those in authority make unreasonable or odious demands on our time and resources, in the last resort we have a responsibility to raise our voices. These responsibilities have become ingrained in our public consciousness in democratic polities, even if they are honoured merely passively. But it was not always so. The rhetoric of the revolutionary period threw down a challenge that continues to haunt us, no matter where we stand on the political spectrum.

The *Declaration of the Rights of Man and of Citizens* (1789), proclaimed in Paris as representatives sought to establish themselves as a National Assembly, served as a clarion call to the political world. In the *Declaration* matters that were previously assumed to be ordinary misfortunes are treated as consequences of human contrivance and neglect. The political world was turned upside-down. Whereas monarchy and aristocracy had been regarded as guardians of order and civilization, they are now seen as the perpetuators of the 'ignorance, neglect, or contempt of human rights' that are 'the sole causes of public misfortunes and corruptions of government'.[2] The clear implication is that human lives over centuries have been blighted by the wanton denial of conditions that could (and should) be made available to everyone. These conditions are 'natural, imprescriptible, and inalienable rights' (p. 132). There is nothing obscure about them. They are based on 'simple and incontestable principles'; yet they have almost everywhere been denied to people (p. 132). The only obstacle to their enjoyment is the ill will and malice of those in authority. Hence governments everywhere must be held responsible for the baleful consequences of their neglect.

Rights apply universally. Thus it is asserted that 'men are born, and always continue, free and equal in respect of their rights' (p. 132). Any 'civil distinctions' introduced into a citizen body should 'be founded only on public utility' (p. 132). The point of government is simply 'the preservation of the natural and imprescriptible rights of man' (p. 132). And 'the source of all sovereignty' (p. 132) is said to reside in the nation collectively, acting on behalf of the people as a whole. As things stood in 1789, no political authority would meet the stringent requirements of the *Declaration*. Hereditary monarchy would be ruled out as a matter of course, but so too would any representative system based on the prerogatives of particular classes or estates. There is no hint in the text that these claims may be controversial, or that their political implementation might generate intractable difficulties.

Yet it was unclear at the time, and became less clear as the French Revolution progressively unfolded, precisely how these principles might be translated into viable political institutions. And because the principles were held to be self-evident, it could be concluded that dispute on points of detail was in bad faith. To contest the meaning or justification of a self-evident principle might be to declare oneself a political enemy. The text proclaims that 'no man ought to be molested on account of his opinions' (p. 132), yet by 1793 reservations about the latest incarnation of revolutionary principles could lead a sceptic to the guillotine. Freedom and equality (so it seemed) were compatible with extreme political intolerance.

Within the terms of the *Declaration*, what can we say if men of good faith disagree? The nation may be the collective expression of the people's will, yet various interpreters of that will may have radically different views. If people are all born with rights, when do they acquire the right to represent their interests? And if individuals cannot speak for themselves, who should be authorized to speak for them? We should not expect a revolutionary proclamation to resolve these difficulties. But there remains a strong implication in the text that new principles will inaugurate a style of politics quite unlike anything that has preceded it. Power and interest will be replaced by equity and rights. Like so many brave new beginnings, the politics of the French Revolution very soon exposed the shortcomings of pure theory.

The *Declaration*, however, is not a treatise of political theory. It provides a series of rallying cries, rather than closely argued political and constitutional proposals. Yet its basic implications were clear to the established princes of Europe. No state could be regarded as legitimate in light of these criteria. Positions hardened after 1792, as France found herself at war, striving to fend off counter-revolution at home aided and abetted by interested powers. The formal overthrow of the monarchy on 10 August 1792 polarized views throughout Europe. And with the execution of Louis XVI on 21 January 1793, an ideological line was drawn in European politics that left little room for compromise.

A new phenomenon was unleashed in 1793. The *levée en masse* declared on 23 August saw the whole of France set on a war footing. This was a first taste of 'total' war, with all the ideological mobilization and centralized control that later became typical features of European states at war. Indeed, nothing so terrified the elites of *ancien régime* Europe as the spectre of French revolutionary armies demanding 'liberty, equality and fraternity' for all men, everywhere. Such ideological motivation was difficult for established elites to counter, generating enthusiasm and fervour comparable only with earlier wars of religion. It cut across traditional territorial and dynastic claims, leading to a redrawing of the political map of Europe according to new and uncertain standards.

Revolution had been 'internationalized'. The progress of French armies would be met by uprisings of 'patriots', anxious to see the principles of the Revolution established in their own countries. Republics were declared in Milan in 1797 and Naples in 1799, though they lasted no longer than the military hegemony of France. It was clear to all, nevertheless, that peace and stability in Europe would henceforth be decided at continental level. For better or worse, the involvement of the masses was a factor in politics, even if they were exposed to hideous exploitation by elites.

Revolutionary principles thus had dramatic intuitive appeal. Yet, for all that they were presented as self-evident truths, they were always contentious and divisive. The *Declaration of the Rights of Man and of Citizens*, in particular, presupposes elaborate theoretical arguments that are taken for granted in the text. It is best considered a brilliant feat of synthesis. How the grounding principles should be interpreted, however, remains deeply problematic. We can go some way towards unpacking the colossal burden of the text by looking at contemporary defences of some of its leading themes. Defences of revolutionary principles, of course, were far from dispassionate. They were conceived as contributions to dramatic political events, written in haste, and sometimes placed their authors in acute personal danger. But a common pattern of argument emerges. Universal claims are advanced for an understanding of the proper relationship between political institutions and the citizens they are designed to serve. Arguments which had been introduced into political debate by Locke and Rousseau were given a democratic twist that made immediate demands on political institutions. Indeed, it remains a moot point whether any actual institutions could possibly sustain these normative expectations. At any rate, theory and rhetoric were mixed together in an explosive political cocktail. Theory had become subversive as never before.

In terms of immediate impact, Emmanuel Sieyes's *What is the Third Estate?* (1789) was a resounding success.[3] The text is a response to a very specific political crisis. Problems for the French monarchy gathered pace in the 1780s, threatening the capacity of the king and his ministers to perform basic political functions. The crown had become virtually bankrupt, unable to raise credit on financial markets, hemmed in ideologically by radical intellectuals on the one side and a disaffected aristocracy on the other, anxious to maintain fiscal and other privileges. Reform of the monarchy had thus become imperative if it were to survive. A consensus emerged for convening the Estates-General, which had not met since 1614, in order to consider far-reaching financial and institutional reform. In its previous incarnation the Estates-General had been grouped into blocks, representing the 'first estate' (clergy), 'second estate' (nobility) and 'third estate' (representatives of the wider population). As voting had been in blocks, it was easy for the first and second estates to combine to counter radical proposals from the third estate. If the Estates-General were to convene again, even in an advisory capacity, it thus made a huge difference how the estates would be represented, whether they would meet in combination, and who should be authorized to speak for the nation as a whole.

Sieyes addressed the issue directly. Previously the third estate, effectively the working population on whom all functions depended, had been excluded from decision making. In institutional terms it was virtually invisible. And yet all 'private activities and public services' were provided by the third estate (p. 53). It was a 'complete nation' (p. 53). The clergy and nobility, by contrast, were entirely parasitic. Sieyes's argument is stark and simple. The political fate of France should be in the hands of the working population of France. He put the point succinctly: 'Nothing will go well without the Third Estate; everything would go considerably better without the two others' (p. 57).

In terms of basic principles that should underpin any legitimate polity, Sieyes appeals to a version of social contract theory. He simply assumes that 'every nation ought to be free', and that its freedom is made manifest in a form of voluntary association (p. 119). He pictures a 'fairly considerable number of isolated individuals who wish to unite' (p. 121). This is sufficient in itself to form a nation. Once associated together, however, the collective actions of individuals constitute a 'common will' (p. 121). What individuals lack in isolation is the power and resources to achieve their objectives. Crucially, they form a nation precisely because they recognize the necessity of a social union. It would be absurd to identify a set of ends and objectives without the requisite means. Hence individuals must be assumed to authorize the 'common will' that makes a community effective. Sieyes thus sees power as a social product, indispensable for attaining anything like a reasonable life. But wielders of power must remain answerable to the community as a whole.

How this should be achieved is a matter of detailed constitutional design that cannot detain us here. Sieyes (we must remember) was contributing to an urgent debate about constitutional reform. What needs to be stressed for the purposes of this book is the normative argument that warrants partic-ular constitutional schemes. Sieyes accepts that the complexity of social co-operation commits us to 'government by proxy' (p. 122). An institutional body will act on behalf of the community, but cannot replace the will of the nation or community. That will, insists Sieyes, 'is inalienable' (p. 122). Functions can be delegated, but not the will. Agents of government enjoy powers conferred on them by the nation; and those powers may always be withdrawn and placed in other hands.

These are rhetorically powerful arguments, but they gloss over problems that haunted revolutionary France and continued to occupy political theorists and commentators throughout the nineteenth century. Sieyes asserts that 'the nation is prior to everything. It is the source of everything. Its will is always legal; indeed it is the law itself' (p. 124). But having delegated powers to agents of government, the 'nation' is in an ambiguous position. Pronouncements of government are made in the name of the nation, and the authority of the nation is said to be unconditional. How, then, do the people hold governors to account? 'Prior to and above the nation', says Sieyes, 'there is only natural law' (p. 124). Yet natural law may be interpreted in a variety of ways. Sieyes insists that government cannot change constitutional terms of reference, but is unable to address effectively problems of mundane accountability.

Throughout his career Sieyes remained fascinated by the intricacy of constitutional theory, shifting position later to support Napoleon's exercise of power. Yet he never managed to resolve the basic conundrum facing all constitutional theory. Constitutional rules apply in normal political condi-tions. We can recognize their desirability when they are lacking. But political crises create pressures that cannot always be resolved by constitutional means. Normative theory then has to switch to justify extraordinary actions in exceptional circumstances. The best we can hope for in these situations is broad normative guidelines. It should not surprise us that outcomes in revolutionary contexts are deeply uncertain.

Sieyes highlights the contrasting themes of individualism and collectivism in French revolutionary theory. For, while the nation is constituted by the association of individual wills, the nation cannot be constrained in turn by constitutional (or other) rules that assembled representatives might devise. 'A nation must not and cannot identify itself with constitutional forms' (p. 128). This point, for Sieyes, follows from the simple observation that political divisions should not be construed as divisions within the nation. The nation remains a conceptual whole, though it exists only as a form of association. On extraordinary occasions, such as the convening of the Estates-General to address a crisis for the French nation, it is the nation itself that must be supreme, not any preconceived notions about the way in which the nation is represented. Hence the proposed divisions within the Estates-General are conceptually flawed. 'A political society', Sieyes insists, 'cannot be anything but the whole body of associates' (p. 135). And the associates gathered as a nation cannot bind themselves in perpetuity to fixed rules and procedures. The nation specifies appropriate rules, and remains the judge of performance of functions under those rules. The fact that 'the sole elements of the common will are individual wills' does little to mitigate the collective authority of the nation (p. 136).

Attempts to realize the freedom proclaimed in the *Declaration of the Rights of Man and of Citizens* is thus compatible with significant constraints on the discretion of individuals in the name of nation or state. What later liberals saw as a paradox at the heart of democratic theory had yet to be clearly expressed, but contemporaries were nevertheless well aware that the pursuit of liberty in radically unequal societies could generate an oppressive and intrusive governmental apparatus.

The democratic theory advanced in the early revolutionary period barely hinted at problems that lay ahead. Thomas Paine, for example, whose defence of both American and French revolutions made him an international celebrity, based his argument on a doctrine of natural sociability that advocated the lightest touch from government compatible with co-operative efficiency. He is adamant in *Common Sense* (1776) that while 'society in every state is a blessing . . . government even in its best state is but a necessary evil'.[4] He describes government as the 'badge of lost innocence', evoking the possibility of decisions made after due deliberation among people motivated by a clear conscience.[5] It is sufficient that such circumstances are conceivable for us to deplore the heavy hand of actual government.

When Paine turned to the French Revolution in the *Rights of Man* (1791–2) he continued to extol limited government. 'The more perfect civilization is', he urges, 'the less occasion has it for government, because the more does it regulate its own affairs, and govern itself.'[6] Ordinary transactions among human beings who recognized their mutual dependence and vulnerability served as his model of good government, not the inherited privileges and arcane practices of a landed elite. In the text he castigates Burke's refusal even to consider the possibility that political affairs could be radically different. Burke had portrayed precedent and custom as institutionally enshrined wisdom.[7] For Paine it is simply avoidance of clear thinking on the part of interested groups who had a great deal to gain from the perpetuation of manifestly unfair practices. The mystery and ritual of established government, far from lending authority to political decisions, is a massive exercise in obfuscation. A principal task of theory, in Paine's eyes, is to dispel that confusion and open institutions and practices to the scrutiny of untutored common sense.

The course of the Revolution did little to justify Paine's optimism. Indeed, as events unfolded, the idea that reasonable social co-operation could be readily attained sharpened reactions to the ordinary disagreements and compromises that are a feature of any political process. Lofty expectations led to disappointment and recriminations. Political conflict was at its most bloody in 1793–4, as Robespierre and his Jacobin colleagues sought to establish a regime of republican 'virtue'. This was political ambition on a new scale. It was not sufficient that reasonable people should establish acceptable terms of social co-operation in order to facilitate their various projects; they were exhorted to identify with the republican nation as the embodiment of their better selves. A distinction between public and private spheres could be maintained in this scheme of things only if the priority of the public sphere were always acknowledged. Pretexts for the vilification of political opponents multiplied. Stability and predictability, necessary conditions for social co-operation among strangers, were undermined by infighting among revolutionary factions. The revolution threatened to destroy its tangible achievement as the pursuit of 'liberty, equality and fraternity' brought France to the verge of anarchy. This was not an auspicious beginning for mass-based democratic politics. Finally, the Revolution had to be brought to an end. A more conventional style of authoritarian politics was introduced, first under the Directory in 1795, then under Napoleon as First Consul in 1795 and as Emperor in 1804.

The American Revolution, though inspired by the same principles as the French, followed a significantly different path. The detailed story of events cannot be told here. But in *The Federalist Papers* we have a remarkable set of articles revealing the thinking behind the federal constitution. The absence of a hereditary aristocracy, and the fact that American independence had been declared after a successful war against Britain, doubtless helped to make democratic procedures and principles more broadly acceptable than was the case in France. We must remember, however, that the United States under the Articles of Confederation (1781–9) was regarded as a failure by its citizens. The confederal union had not provided stable government. The powers of the constituent states, which were technically regarded as sovereign units under the constitution, left the confederal centre too weak to raise taxes on a consistent basis to pay for debts incurred in the War of

Independence. The confederal union was dependent on the good will of the constituent states for the provision of military forces. It could not control a national political agenda effectively, or sustain a framework for pursuit of a consistent foreign policy, leaving the constituent states a prey to interested powers (Britain, France and Spain) which might be tempted to pursue their rivalries on the American continent. Electoral and legal systems varied in the constituent states. Those that endorsed annual elections were regarded as too 'democratic' to sustain stable government. Legislatures were generally seen as too strong, the state and national executives as too weak, to dispatch the ordinary business of states and union.

In 1787, when a congress to revise the Articles of Confederation was convened in Philadelphia, it was by no means clear that the union would be retained in its current form. Disaggregation into constituent units was a possibility, as was a division into two or three broad groupings. And there were even voices that harked back nostalgically to British imperial rule. Democratic politics itself was cast into question, not least because received wisdom from classical Greek and Roman political history equated democracy with instability and factional strife. Debates in Philadelphia thus touched on themes that would be vital to a form of political order that had yet to establish itself as a viable proposition in a mass-based polity. Had American revolutionary politics followed the pattern of France, we must assume that prospects for democratic politics in the nineteenth and twentieth centuries would have been significantly different.

We note from the outset in *The Federalist Papers* a very different tone from Sieyes and Paine. If the spirit of Rousseau haunted the French Revolution, Montesquieu was a moderating influence in America. Hamilton, Madison and Jay by no means saw matters alike. Hamilton, the organizational driving force behind the project, was anxious to see a consolidated national government in the United States, while Madison placed greater emphasis on the need for constitutional checks and balances to contain the exercise of power. All three were clear, however, that national government had to be strengthened in light of the experience of political life under the Articles of Confederation.

The real question was whether democracy is compatible with good government. We should be wary of attributing a common position to the authors of *The Federalist Papers*. Yet they each discounted a form of politics that reduced government to the whims of fleeting majorities. Democracy thus had to be contained, whatever its wider merits might be. Unlike in French revolutionary rhetoric, there is no suggestion that constitutional change can somehow transform the human condition. The approach of *The Federalist Papers* is pragmatic, not utopian. A strong commitment to rights is evident, but balanced by recognition of the intractability of individuals driven to pursue their interests and happiness in various ways. *The Federalist Papers* do not assume that competition and co-operation between equal citizens will always be benign, but rather set out to fashion institutional structures that make a virtue out of competitive human traits. Constitutional devices are treated as limited devices to channel the ambition of each and every citizen, such that the clashing interests of individuals might serve as means to guard against abuses of power.

Madison goes to the heart of the issue in Paper 10.[8] He focuses directly on the problem of factions and instability. But instead of striving to remove the causes of factions, as Robespierre urged in his quest for republican virtue, Madison accepts that factional disputes are an inescapable feature of any polity that takes liberty seriously. The choice he set before citizens is clear. If Americans value freedom, they must find means to live with the consequences of faction. And since 'the latent causes of faction are . . . sown in the nature of man' (in the variety of opinions, abilities and circumstances that shape human conduct), any attempt to eradicate faction would require a draconian and intrusive politics (p. 41). The remedy would be worse than the disease. The benefits of liberty were obvious to Madison and his contemporaries. Human beings are free to pursue a variety of interests, to associate together as and how they please, to resolve private controversies through formal and informal channels that seem reasonable in particular circumstances, without seeking permission from a distant (and ill-informed) authority. If one faction or another were to dominate in a polity, however, the consequence for other groups and factions could be disastrous. The solution, for Madison, was to ensure that representation of citizens was sufficiently broad that no faction could expect to dominate permanently.

Madison accepted that fallible human beings might always abuse power. The problem would not disappear with the emergence of a democratic politics that professed to respect the rights of citizens. Disputes would arise; interested parties would manoeuvre for position; efforts would be made to keep certain issues off the political agenda. Power and its temptations remain a factor in any polity. But if power were dispersed, the worst consequences for marginal groups would be less likely to materialize. And if the exercise of power required agreements across (shifting) factions, all political agents would have to moderate their ambitions in order to assure themselves sufficient support to pursue (at least some of) their projects.

Majorities are, in any case, fickle and unreliable. To give a passing majority the right to speak for (and bind) a whole community is a recipe for authoritarianism. If we take rights seriously, we necessarily have to contain the options available to governments, in a democratic polity as in any other. Thus democracy in itself should not be treated as a solution to the various ills of bad government. Democracy may be desirable for any number of reasons, but it is not a panacea.

Madison specifically defends a representative system against 'pure democracy' (p. 43). He conceives of democracy operating within the confines of a small-scale society, involving direct citizen participation in government.

In a system of this kind, he says, there can be 'no cure for the mischiefs of faction' (p. 43). Passions will be raised; a majority will speak for the whole of society, with no safeguards in place 'to check the inducements to sacrifice the weaker party, or an obnoxious individual' on the part of government (p. 44). In an extended republic, by contrast, direct citizen involvement in government is impossible. The interests of citizens are in the hands of representatives (who, of course, are electorally accountable to the citizen body). Passions are mediated through institutional channels. Representatives will take a detached view, dependent as they are for electoral support on a variety of factions and interests. Intense citizen identification with the nation is anathema to Madison, who values instead the plethora of interests that effectively check each other as they contend for power and influence. In an extended republic, though 'factious leaders may kindle a flame within their particular states', they will hardly be in a position 'to spread a general conflagration through the other states' (p. 46). Madison pictures 'a variety of sects dispersed over the entire face' of the union (p. 46). Nothing will change the partiality and limited vision and understanding of the ordinary run of citizens. But with an appropriate constitutional and institutional structure, 'a republican remedy' can be applied to 'the diseases most incident to republican government' (p. 46).

Madison gives further detail on how this might be achieved in Paper 51 (pp. 251–5). In a characteristic article, combining foundational argument with detailed constitutional and institutional proposals, Madison defends a principle of separation of powers in both public and private spheres. Where division of functions is possible, he urges that it should be pursued. But in order to make such a system work, we need more than constitutional rules. People in any sphere of authority require 'the necessary constitutional means, and personal motives, to resist encroachments' of other sectors (p. 252). 'Ambition must be made to counteract ambition' (p. 252). Should we deplore this concession to selfishness and partiality? Madison argues that we should not. No good purpose is served by presuming that human beings are other than they are. 'If men were angels, no government would be necessary' (p. 252). Madison is adamant that we must take men as we find them, as we do in pursuit of our private interests. If we expect too much of our fellow human beings, disappointment and frustration may encourage draconian forms of persuasion and enforcement.

We are all aware in our private and business dealings of the need to balance 'opposite and rival interests' (p. 252). Madison suggests that we extend the same caution to our management of public affairs. The United States is thus presented with a unique opportunity. The confederal union had shown that government within the separate states was likely to be unstable, inconsistent, riven by faction. The extended republic, however, could use the combination of confined perspectives for its own purposes. In addition to formal separation between legislative, executive and judicial branches of government, the United States could exploit a 'natural' division between regional and national levels of government. Madison could conclude from experience that 'oppressive combinations of a majority will be facilitated' in more narrowly 'circumscribed confederacies or states' (p. 254). But instead of rejecting democracy as a principle of government, he argues that it can be contained by its very vices in the wider context of an extended republic. The key is that concentrations of power should be avoided, if possible, at all levels of society. Since we would require massive concentrations of power to counter the partiality of citizens in local politics, we should instead use local rivalry and competition to prevent excessive concentration across the continent as a whole. In this way, we can combine the merits of local democracy with the wider benefits of stability and predictability on a continental scale.

Among the authors of *The Federalist Papers*, Madison is the most anxious to constrain the exercise of power through constitutional procedures. But all three are aware of the limitations of any conceivable political system. Hamilton, in particular, is so concerned about the weakness of a politics dominated by strong legislatures that he adopts an almost Hobbesian tone in his discussions of the necessary conditions for peace and stability. He insists (in Paper 9) that 'a firm union will be of the utmost moment to the peace and liberty of the states as a barrier against domestic faction and insurrection' (p. 35). He has no faith in mini-democracies effectively managing their own affairs in the absence of a sufficiently strong central power to guarantee their subordination. Where Madison sees power as a matter of containment, Hamilton focuses rather on the need to wield it effectively if peace is to be secured. 'The hope of impunity', he says in Paper 27, 'is a strong incitement to sedition'; and he happily draws the corollary that power must be adequate to foster a 'dread of punishment' (p. 126). Whatever their differences on power, Hamilton and Madison share a pessimistic view of human capacity for naturally enlightened judgement. Though they champion natural rights, they have no faith in natural sociability. What we are presented with is a novelty for the times – a robust defence of democratic politics built on deeply sceptical assumptions about human nature.

The intriguing dimension here is that commitments to freedom and equality, prominent in both American and French revolutionary rhetoric, should generate such strikingly different politics. The political trajectories in each case, of course, were products of much more than theory. Detailed analysis of why the revolutions diverged so markedly cannot detain us here. We need to focus, however, on the foundational assumptions that began to enjoy widespread political currency. Henceforth claims that human beings (in some sense) are free and equal could not be ignored, though they might well be disputed. The destructive course of the one revolution could not be attributed solely to ideas that had proved to be remarkably benign in the other. Yet we might wonder what commitments to freedom and equality really amount to in the light of contrasting political experience. This raises deeper philosophical questions than the revolutionary texts of the period ever address. But we do have the remarkable philosophical texts of Immanuel Kant to hand to give a more rigorous account of these foundational ideas.

Kant has not always been accorded a standing in political philosophy that matches his eminence in philosophy more broadly. His 'critical' philosophy, built around the *Critique of Pure Reason* (1781), *Critique of Practical Reason* (1788) and *The Critique of Judgement* (1790), marks the beginning of a new era in philosophy, focusing on the criteria human beings use in their active engagement with the world and one another.[9] All these texts make fundamental contributions to the way in which we see ourselves and our minds, though they have little to say directly regarding classic questions in political theory. Yet it was clear to Kant himself and his contemporaries that his philosophical approach left no area of philosophy untouched. He proclaimed that he had launched a 'Copernican revolution' in philosophy; and for once an author's confidence was not misplaced.[10]

Kant's working assumption is that people see the world through structural criteria (forms of intuition and categories) that impose a pattern on experience that would otherwise be unintelligible. These criteria are not arbitrary. For minds constituted such as ours, it is simply the case that we use notions of space and time to order experience. We cannot say what the world would look like if we did not invoke such terms. But we cannot conclude from the way we happen to perceive the world that the world in fact is so structured. In Kant's view, we cannot jump out of our minds to make a judgement from a perspective that is not shaped by the way we order our experience. He thus insists on a distinction between the way in which the world appears to us and the way the world is in itself.

This is not an argument for radical scepticism. Kant presupposes in the *Critique of Pure Reason* that natural science has produced a body of reliable knowledge. Yet, since we cannot understand the world intuitively, it remains a philosophical puzzle how knowledge is attained, and why we should be reasonably confident about (at least some of) the claims we make.

In the moral sphere, matters are significantly different. Here we do not make judgements about a world given in experience that we are trying to grasp. We make judgements which dispose us to behave in certain ways rather than others towards people. The fact that we make these judgements is not in question. Yet we do not regard all the judgements people make as authoritative. People can deceive themselves, act partially towards friends and family, and use extraordinary ingenuity to justify themselves in the pursuit of their interests. We recognize this in our ordinary practical experience. Kant asks himself what we may be presupposing about ourselves to make these judgements at all. We carry on trying to distinguish sense from nonsense, right from wrong, despite the evidence before us that people are very often deeply mistaken. We have no choice but to think hard when we are not sure what we should do next. As a philosopher, Kant asks what precisely may be said to be going on in such cases.

These issues may appear to take us a long way from political theory. But if we think about what we implicitly assume people are capable of when they make moral judgements, we are led to question the kind of politics that would be appropriate for beings with these capacities. Kant's treatment of these matters is highly technical, and it is not possible to pursue the finer points of his moral theory here. Yet close attention to the form of moral judgements committed Kant to strong normative views in politics and ethics. Moral judgement involves reflection. In our ordinary moral language we urge people not to do things for reasons we assume they can grasp. We are also sometimes categorical in urging them to respond in particular ways in given situations. We might say that everyone should tell the truth, simply because it is the right thing to do. For the moment we need to focus on the form of the imperative. It applies to everyone, equally. We presuppose that all normally functioning people are able to make moral judgements. We know that they may not always do the right thing, but we assume that they can. They are free to do the right thing if they are so minded. (It would make very little sense to urge them not to do what they are biologically determined to do in any case. I could not be taken seriously if I instructed someone to stop breathing.) Simply by focusing on our ordinary moral language, we are thus led to a view of people as free and equal, at least in certain respects.

Kant advanced these arguments initially in the *Groundwork of the Metaphysics of Morals* (1785), a preliminary version of the *Critique of Practical Reason* that continues to demand the attention of moral philosophers to this day.[11] The text, though short, is very demanding. For the purposes of political theory, however, it is possible to distil arguments that Kant deployed in his political writings towards the end of his career.

The first (and crucial) point is that if human beings are creatures who can do things for good reasons, then they must be treated as autonomous agents. We implicitly value our own autonomy when we wonder seriously what we should do. It follows that we should also respect the autonomy of others. Kant formulated the point categorically. He insists that 'all rational beings stand under the law that each of them is to treat himself and all others never merely as means but always at the same time as ends in themselves' (p. 83). The implications are profound, and cannot be pursued fully here. We may take it as a fact about human conduct that we can give ourselves goals. Kant asks us to reflect on a logic that could claim this capacity for ourselves but withhold it from others. We would be involved in an internal contradiction. Where Paine or Sieyes would argue that we are the possessors of natural rights, Kant contends that we are logically committed to endorsing a principle of reciprocity in our dealings with people. Kant formulated this commitment as a 'single categorical imperative': 'act only in accordance with that maxim through which you can at the same time will that it become a universal law' (p. 73). Kant's various iterations of this principle in the text need not detain us. The point to stress is that a specific moral law is implicit in our conduct as rational agents. It follows that we should apply it to any conceivable rational agent.

Universality is a key dimension of Kant's 'categorical imperative'. It applies to all human beings, everywhere, no matter what values they may have. He specifically contrasts rational freedom under universal law with what he calls 'heteronomy', a condition in which motivation is dominated by specific interests or passions (p. 83). In the latter case, we adopt an instrumental style of reasoning. If we happen to want A, we should pursue B. But if we do not want A at all, the imperative would have no force for us. In such a situation the imperative to act would always be conditional upon the end to be pursued. (Read Kant carefully if you want to be a philosopher; practise the guitar if you want to be a rock star.) What makes Kant's position distinctive, though, is his claim that conditional imperatives would make no sense unless at least some imperatives were categorical or unconditional. Kant sees this as a logical point, not a comment on our ordinary experience of human motivation. Yet, recognizing its force changes the way we may view moral and political questions.

Kant says very little about specifically political issues in the *Groundwork*, though there are startling implications. He insists, for example, that we should all regard ourselves as legislators 'in a kingdom of ends' (p. 83). The phrase is used metaphorically in the text, but we must assume that Kant intended us to take the political connotations seriously. In a later text, *Toward Perpetual Peace: A Philosophical Project* (1795), he shows how the universal scope of moral reasoning obliges us to take a global view of political affairs.[12] His central point is that the conventional distinction between politics and morality is untenable, just as he had argued in the *Groundwork* that conditional imperatives depend upon the possibility of unconditional (or categorical) imperatives.

Toward Perpetual Peace is especially revealing, because it was written in the aftermath of the French Revolution. Kant was an enthusiast for French and American revolutionary ideals, though he denies that revolution is a legitimate means to attain them. His reasoning here, though contentious, is not obscure. If we are to treat 'autonomy of the will as the supreme principle of morality', as he insists in the *Groundwork*, we must accept that we cannot use violent or manipulative means to achieve our ends. Radicals have never been entirely happy with the passivity of Kant's stance. But it clearly follows from his moral theory.

Kant views the French Revolution as both opportunity and warning. The emergence of republican states had opened up prospects for more stable and peaceful international relations, since governments answerable to their peoples would not be in a position to pursue reckless policies that threatened the basic interests of citizens. Yet the French revolutionary wars had also shown that modern warfare could be desperately destructive and difficult to contain. Kant thus sees political prudence and moral principle tending in the same direction. Peace and stability are desirable in themselves as a background condition for autonomous agents to pursue their many goals. Citizens can also see that the risks attached to warfare far outweigh any possible speculative benefits.

Kant is much less happy with French revolutionary experiments with democracy. He maintains that 'democracy in the strict sense of the word is necessarily a despotism', because there are no constraints on what an executive may do in claiming to represent the democratic will of the people (p. 324). Typically, democratic legitimacy will stem from a majority vote. But if democratic authorization is sufficient warrant for anything a government may decide to do, prospects for minorities look decidedly precarious. Kant's preference, instead, is for a republican constitution, embodying commitments to 'the freedom of the members of society (as individuals) . . . the dependence of all upon a single common legislation (as subjects), and . . . their equality (as citizens of a state)' (p. 322). Only these three commitments taken together are compatible with 'the idea of the original contract', which would guarantee that all citizens are treated as ends in themselves, and not simply as means to the (supposed) greater good of the community (p. 322).

In the text Kant uses the idea of a social contract to justify both the original emergence of civil society and the commitment which republican states should make to ensure that international relations are as law-like as possible. Kant argues for a loose federation of 'free states' rather than a global state, since he regards the diversity of cultures as a limiting condition for the formation of a narrowly political order (p. 325). To reduce a variety of cultures to a single state would inevitably distort the 'natural' development of some cultures. The concentration of power that such a political order would require could not be justified in terms of the requirements of a republican constitution. Yet citizens and leaders of all republican states could appreciate the benefit of making international relations more law-like rather than less, just as individuals can recognize the advantage to be gained from the hypothetical sacrifice of natural freedom for civil freedom under a republican constitution.

Toward Perpetual Peace barely gets beyond the idea of a republican state in terms of constitutional and institutional detail. Kant has much more to say on the matter in *The Metaphysics of Morals* (1797), which is among his final publications.[13] Here again, as with the case of revolution, radicals have often been disappointed with the strictly rule-based model of the state that Kant defends. He accepts that political orders are coercive, but wants to limit the legitimate use of coercion to occasions that all rational agents could accept. Kant adapts the formulation he had developed in the *Groundwork*. 'Any action is right if it can coexist with everyone's freedom in accordance with a universal law, or if on its maxim the freedom of choice of each can coexist with everyone's freedom in accordance with a universal law' (p. 387). Kant's derivation of institutional consequences from this maxim is not as rigorous as we might expect, often reflecting the preferences and prejudices of the period. But we should note that the scope for positive legal action is always limited by the 'innate' and 'original right belonging to every man by virtue of his humanity' to have his freedom and autonomy respected (p. 393). The will of a legislator is, of course, in one sense arbitrary. Hence, whenever we urge a legislative remedy for any dilemma, we have to ensure that the freedom and independence of individuals is not 'being constrained by another's choice' (p. 393). Whether this requirement can be strictly met in any actual polity is a much disputed issue. The point to stress, though, is that procedural rules can be much more readily justified than substantive goals.

A specific politics cannot be deduced from Kant's moral theory, any more than a set of institutions and laws can be deduced from the *Declaration of the Rights of Man and of Citizens*. Controversial issues remain that cannot be decided by appeal to foundational principles or maxims. What we find in Kant, however, is open recognition that human beings, viewed as free and equal, require a certain kind of consideration. We cannot guarantee that we are 'right' in our politics. But we can at least offer reasons to fellow agents who find themselves involved with us in the pursuit of their various projects. In the last resort, it is not policy or institutional detail that is vital for Kant, but respect for the autonomy and dignity of fellow human beings. For Kant this is an unconditional commitment. It does not follow that we should all be fellow citizens, subject to identical laws and professing the same values and beliefs. The point is that we should give due consideration to each other, knowing that our best efforts will not always be satisfactory. We can recognize the need for specific laws, without necessarily agreeing what those laws should be. We can acknowledge the force of laws we would not have chosen, provided those laws are framed in such a way that our freedom and autonomy are respected.

Kant went to the heart of the issue in a short but celebrated essay, 'What is Enlightenment?' (1784).[14] Much as we might have strong reasons to adapt our politics to certain principles, adoption of that politics would not be sufficient to see those principles realized. 'A revolution may well bring about a falling off of personal despotism and of avaricious or tyrannical oppression, but never a true reform in one's way of thinking' (p. 18). Yet, without that reform, 'new prejudices will serve just as well as old ones to harness the great unthinking masses' (p. 18). What was crucial to Kant was that a commitment to 'freedom to make public use of one's reason in all matters' should be assured (p. 18). Though our reasoning on any specific occasion may be flawed, we cannot renounce the use of our reason as various contingencies present themselves. It may be more comfortable for us as individuals to follow designated authorities. But that, says Kant, is the path of 'laziness and cowardice' (p. 17). We owe it to ourselves and others to think hard as problems arise. We cannot allow custom or dogma to do our thinking for us.

'What is Enlightenment?' can be read as an intellectual manifesto. It certainly makes unprecedented demands on the energy and resolve of citizens. Governments of the revolutionary era clearly failed the test demonstrably. It remained an open question at the time, and is a matter of dispute to this day, whether a principled politics could ever replace the politics of custom and precedent. It was clear, however, that public arguments had to be fashioned to defend political positions as never before.

3 Reaction

Political expectations were so high in 1789 that frustration and disappointment were inevitable. Intractable problems of co-ordination and control persist, no matter what style of political management is adopted. Initial attempts to introduce a modest measure of constitutional government in France gave place to the more ambitious pursuit of a democratic regime based upon respect for natural rights. But what emerged instead was a reign of terror in 1793–4 in France and the disruption of war on a continental scale. Quite why the revolutionary project should have gone so badly wrong was much disputed at the time, and continues to excite academic and political controversy. It soon became clear that some of the basic requirements of any political regime, stability and order, had been sacrificed in the quest for more ephemeral political goals. Natural rights could hardly be enjoyed if stability and order were not maintained in the first place. The very thought that rights were somehow a natural birthright was brought into question, along with the idea of fashioning a political order anew from first principles.

In the eyes of some critics it was not simply the case that the revolutionaries had made political mistakes and found themselves embroiled in factional struggles that wiser counsel might have avoided. Root and branch transformation was rejected. Significantly, the reaction against revolution focused almost exclusively on France. The manifest success of the American Revolution was discounted, along with affinities between American and French revolutionary ideals.

Edmund Burke is perhaps the most celebrated critic of revolutionary politics. His *Reflections on the Revolution in France* (1790) set a style in theoretical and ideological argument that continues to influence modern conservatives.[1] Long before the Revolution had skirted with terror, Burke had predicted that contempt for established institutions and practices would generate a cycle of violence that could only be terminated by the imposition of authoritarian rule. The fatal flaw at the heart of the revolutionary project, in his view, was the presumption that political institutions could be devised to meet the requirements of a purely theoretical model. It is not a question of theory being more or less adequate. Theoretical models simplify the political world to the point of distortion. Burke objected to (what was later described as) 'rationalism in politics' in any of its guises.[2] No matter how much we assume we know about politics, Burke contends that our theorizing could never be rich enough to grasp the complex interdependence of institutions and practices.

In Burke's analysis, more was at stake than the straightforward folly of the revolutionaries. He was perfectly aware that institutions require reform and amendment in the light of changing circumstances. When we confront abuses and anomalies, however, it should be in relation to settled habits of conduct and practice. We are able to take stock of the shortcomings of some of our institutions and policies in the context of other aspects of our political experience that are serving us reasonably well. For Burke, effective politics is a matter of managing (unavoidable) change in piecemeal fashion. But if we presume to put (abstract) theory into practice, we will confound our problems. Innovations will lead to unforeseen complications that might well be worse than the original dilemmas that demanded attention. As our predicament deepens, so we will have recourse to further theoretical remedies, thus exacerbating a spiral of confusion and disorder.

Burke is deeply sceptical. Yet, before the French Revolution he was widely regarded as a progressive thinker. He had been particularly vociferous in defence of the cause of the American colonists, arguing that the attempt by British governments to exploit America for economic advantage contravened standing assumptions about good government.[3] That Burke should have been so hostile to the French Revolution from the outset surprised his contemporaries. What he deplored in British policy in America, however, was precisely the transgression of deeply entrenched conventions about the appropriate relationship between rulers and ruled that had become a distinguishing trait of British political culture. Burke thus endorsed not the abstract slogans of the American revolutionaries ('no taxation without representation'), but the reaction of the colonists to Britain's arbitrary departure from established practices.

Burke distinguished sharply between the American and French revolutions in his own mind. He was also anxious to disavow any connection between the French Revolution and the English Revolution of 1688. Radicals in Britain (such as Richard Price, whom Burke seeks to counter specifically in the *Reflections*) interpreted 1789 as the French version of the 'Glorious Revolution' that established the broad terms of limited and constitutional government in Britain. Burke rejects the link categorically. He describes the English Revolution as 'a small and a temporary deviation from the strict order of a regular hereditary succession'.[4] Doubtless this is rhetorical understatement. No one could say in 1688 just how radical the constitutional changes would prove to be. Certainly, in themselves, they were not vastly different from initial French moves to transform an absolute into a constitutional monarchy. But, despite his distortion, it is fruitful to pay careful attention to Burke's language. He treats 'the statute called the Declaration of Right' as a means of 'declaring the rights and liberties of the subject, and for settling the succession of the crown' (pp. 14–15). He rejects any suggestion that this should be construed as the initiation of an elective monarchy. Indeed, he insists that, 'so far is it from being true, that we acquired a right by the Revolution to elect our kings, that if we had possessed it before, the English nation did at that time most solemnly renounce and abdicate it, for themselves, and for all their posterity for ever' (p. 18). He stresses concrete rights already embedded in constitutional practice. And if reform was perceived to be necessary in 1688, it was in terms of established conventions and with a view to creating more stability rather than less.

It is important to stress that Burke recognizes the necessity of change. He has no sympathy for theorists who dream of a supposed golden age which they seek to restore. States are complex bodies, dependent on a whole series of factors that defy complete theoretical elaboration. If they are unable to adapt to shifting circumstances, they will not flourish. 'A state without the means of some change', he insists, 'is without the means of its conservation' (pp. 19–20). Everything depends on the way change is managed. Leading themes for Burke are 'conservation and correction', recognizing the force and utility of established practices, while amending them to meet the demands of new situations (p. 20). Thus, 'when England found itself without a king', efforts were made to preserve the principle of hereditary succession by modifying the line of descent as little as possible, yet ensuring a Protestant succession to the throne (p. 20). Principles that clash in the person of one king are restored to harmony in the person of another. This, argues Burke, is wisdom at work. He is strangely silent about the events of 1649, when England decapitated a king.

At the heart of Burke's argument is a categorical dismissal of the idea of natural rights. Here, as ever with Burke, his language repays close attention. He is a master of rhetorical presentation, capturing whatever of sense his opponents may have to say while ridiculing the form of their arguments. In rejecting natural rights, for example, Burke holds that he is defending and advancing 'the real rights of men' (p. 56). He pictures civil society as a complex network of conventions, all devised to facilitate human engagements, but without anything like a preconceived plan. We enjoy the benefits of civil society, and 'all the advantages for which it is made become [our] right' (p. 56). What might rights so conceived amount to? Burke focuses on the ordinary things we do every day of our lives. We 'have a right to the fruits of [our] industry', a right to 'instruction in life, and to consolation in death', a 'right to the acquisitions of [our] parents', a right to associate together in manifold ways to pursue our interests and advantage, provided we are not thereby 'trespassing upon others' (p. 56). He sees society as a partnership in which we all 'have equal rights, but not to equal things' (p. 56). There is no naturally just way of organizing these various and bewilderingly complex engagements. All our practices are entwined in a rich social fabric. The details, he says, must 'be settled by convention' (p. 57).

Civil society thus supplies the standards against which actions must be judged. We cannot assess the adequacy of these criteria against a notional natural standard, for no such standard exists. What we gain in civil society are regular procedures for managing affairs. Among other things, we acknowledge 'that no man should be judge in his own cause' (p. 57). We cannot both endorse the value of civil society and refuse to be judged by its standards. That, according to Burke, would amount to claiming 'the rights of an uncivil and of a civil state together' (p. 57). We accept that judgements will not always go our way. Expecting more from civil and political life would actually deliver a good deal less. In our ordinary affairs, we do not delude ourselves with images of perfection. If we see the force of not being judges in our own case, it follows that we could not claim to be judges of the legitimacy of our own polity. Civil society enables us to 'secure some liberty', on condition that we make 'a surrender in trust of the whole of it' to the authoritative institutions of our society (p. 57). It is the best that we can reasonably expect.

In human affairs, the notion of 'abstract perfection' ceases to be helpful, even as an ideal (p. 57). Institutions and practices are matters of compromise, trading off certain benefits and advantages against others. Burke describes government as 'a contrivance of human wisdom to provide for human wants' (p. 57). There is no avoiding the messiness here, because we cannot always be sure what we do want. And we may be sure that human beings gathered together with limited understanding and limited benevolence are likely to clash in a world of limited resources. We accept restraints as a means of gaining concrete satisfactions. Burke (again exploiting the language of his opponents) argues that 'the restraints on men, as well as their liberties, are to be reckoned among their rights' (p. 58). But because liberties and restrictions will 'vary with circumstances, and admit of infinite modifications', we cannot specify the appropriate institutions and practices that should be respected in all times and places (p. 58). An 'abstract rule' is neither possible nor desirable (p. 58).

There can be no short cuts to good government. Political judgement depends upon experience, more indeed than any individual can accumulate in a lifetime. No matter how well prepared we may suppose ourselves to be, our wisdom is no match for the variety of circumstances. We have to proceed cautiously. A measure that may initially appear to be 'prejudicial may be excellent in its remoter operation' (p. 58). And the reverse may also be true, as 'very plausible schemes, with very pleasing commencements' may often have 'shameful and lamentable conclusions' (p. 58). Theory will never be sufficiently flexible to grasp the 'obscure and almost latent causes' that determine a pattern of events (p. 58). We have no choice, of course, but to apply our minds to practical problems. We cannot simply carry on exactly as we have in the past. But neither can we disregard the lessons of the past. We have to appeal to 'models and patterns of approved utility' (p. 59). Experience may be fallible; but it cannot be remedied by recourse to abstract theory.

Implicit in Burke's beguilingly effective rhetoric is a powerfully sceptical argument regarding the strict limits of pure theory. We are ingenious creatures. We can contrive metaphysical theories that doubtless capture some aspect of what it might mean to lead a human life. But what we have to deal with in politics is 'the gross and complicated mass of human passions and concerns' (p. 59). If we try to picture these concerns through the prism of our pet theories, we are bound to deceive ourselves about genuine possibilities for improvement. 'The nature of man', says Burke, 'is intricate; the objects of society are of the greatest possible complexity; and therefore no simple disposition or direction of power can be suitable either to man's nature, or to the quality of his affairs' (p. 59). These are limiting conditions for any possible political theory. Simplicity may be a merit in pure theory; in government it is quite the reverse, encouraging us to be fanciful where caution is appropriate, distorting our perception of the very real difficulties which we may well be able to do something about were we not tempted by the theoretical prospect of resolving all our political problems in one revolutionary sweep.

The implications of Burke's stance are far-reaching. Paine and Sieyes had both sought to question the legitimacy of absolute government as a matter of principle. For Burke the question makes no sense. He insists that 'the speculative line of demarcation, where obedience ought to end, and resistance must begin, is faint, obscure, and not easily definable'(p. 28). We cannot even begin to frame the dilemma to ourselves in these terms. Everyone knows that governments sometimes act badly, that there are instances of corruption and abuse of power in any regime. But we confront these cases as they arise, in the context of a host of attendant circumstances. We cannot focus on a 'single act, or a single event' to determine the limits of our obligation to the state (p. 28). Burke has no doubt that (on rare occasions) governments implode catastrophically, undermining the very possibility of an ordered civil life. His point, however, is that precise theoretical lines cannot be drawn. In extreme circumstances, subjects and citizens may be compelled to fend for themselves. This, for Burke, is the real connotation of a state of nature. Government has broken down, leaving us no choice but to devise alternative means of social co-operation. It is not that government has abused the trust placed in it in any conceptual sense. The conduct of political affairs may degenerate to a 'lamentable condition'; but in that dire situation, 'the nature of the disease is to indicate the remedy to those whom nature has qualified to administer in extremities this critical, ambiguous, bitter potion to a distempered state' (p. 28). We are driven into revolution. We cannot reasonably choose it as a means of pursuing our interests.

Allegiance to the state is simply not a theoretical issue for Burke. He assumes that people develop attachments and dispositions in the course of their lives that serve as tangible points of reference for their activities and pursuits. Theory will not help us to understand these attachments. We acquire loyalty to people and places, along with the ordinary habits that get us through from day to day. As a matter of principle, Burke takes human beings as he finds them. He turns Paine's argument in *Common Sense* upside-down. Where Paine had stressed natural reasonableness, Burke highlights the quirks and idiosyncrasies that distinguish individuals and peoples. We delight in our own ways of doing things, not because they are rational, reasonable or exemplary, but because they serve us in socially embedded circumstances. Instead of stressing reason, Burke delights in the prejudices that are characteristically our own. When we wonder what to do next in difficult situations, it is in terms of the 'latent wisdom' implicit in our habits and customs (p. 84). Our sense of what we should do, for Burke, is more reliable than our metaphysical speculations; and it also motivates us in social dealings. 'Prejudice is of ready application in the emergency; it previously engages the mind in a steady course of wisdom and virtue, and does not leave the man hesitating in the moment of decision, sceptical, puzzled, and unresolved' (p. 84). Reflection of the right kind can help us to discriminate among the various habits that constitute our identities. Thinking about what we should do is not qualitatively distinct from our ordinary dispositions and prejudices. 'Prejudice renders a man's virtue his habit', says Burke, 'and not a series of unconnected acts' (p. 84). And in a delightfully paradoxical phrase, he insists that 'through just prejudice', our 'duty becomes a part of [our] nature' (p. 84).

Burke's politics is thus deeply passive. He presupposes a natural hierarchy in a society, with power and influence shared between landed elite and crown. He can envisage adjustments to patterns of land holding and decision making, but not according to the specification of an ideal theory of justice. If this natural order is disrupted by foolish speculation and political enthusiasm, Burke assumes that the ordinary enjoyments of social, economic and civil life will be rendered precarious. He paints a dire picture of the consequences of trying to reduce complex management of practical affairs to rational order. 'This was unnatural. The rest is order. They have found their punishment in their success. Laws overturned; tribunals subverted; industry without vigour; commerce expiring; the revenue unpaid, yet the people impoverished; a church pillaged, and a state not relieved; civil and military anarchy made the constitution of the kingdom' (pp. 36–7). A meddling politics threatens the everyday expectations on which human beings depend. And since human foresight is not sufficient to grasp the complex interdependence of institutions and practices, human efforts to remedy the consequences of human folly are as likely to produce further difficulties as tangible improvements.

Burke's tone is dramatic. His comments (we must remember) are addressed to his contemporaries in England, rather than the citizens of France striving to reduce the chaos of revolution to institutional order. His picture of France is, in any case, deeply distorted, especially as things stood in 1790. He treats order as a seamless web, despite his recognition of the minute adjustments we make to our affairs on a daily basis. Over time, minute adjustments might lead to a qualitatively different regime. But the process will be long, slow and barely perceptible to agents attending to their concrete concerns.

There is clearly a desperate edge to Burke's writing. As an expert in British constitutional history, he is fully aware of the political significance of the Glorious Revolution of 1688. He also knows that the achievement was couched in terms of a natural rights argument drawn from Locke.[5] There are very real affinities between Locke and Paine, as between Locke and the American revolutionaries. Burke sees all this, but doubts the sophistication and self-restraint of his contemporaries. Endorsing the Glorious Revolution with the benefit of a century of hindsight is very different from advocating a radical shift in succession to the crown in the fevered atmosphere of 1688. The implication of Burke's position in the *Reflections* is that Britain had been fortunate not to reap the revolutionary consequences that beset France in the 1790s. He sounds a warning, quite as much as an argument.

There are two quite distinct dimensions to Burke's political theory. On the one side, he endorses a cautious, sceptical approach to politics that should not be identified with any specific regime. On the other side, we have a spirited defence of a balance of institutions in *ancien régime* Europe, focusing on a complex interrelationship between crown, nobility, church and broader landed interests. As the French Revolution progressed, we see a marked polarization of positions. Prospects for any political accommodation between revolutionaries and reactionaries looked especially bleak after the execution of Louis XVI in 1793. Crown, church and nobility were then implacably opposed to regicides. What they deplored was not the theoretical folly of revolutionaries who had failed to grasp the complexity of government, but a wilful and wicked assault on a way of life.

The most formidable theoretical statement of a sharpened royalist position is Joseph de Maistre's *Considerations on France* (1797).[6] Maistre's politics is avowedly theological. He opens the book with a powerful contrast between the perfection of God's order and the obvious imperfections of anything human beings might have created. 'In the works of man, everything is as wretched as their author; views are restricted, means rigid, motives inflexible, movements painful, and results monotonous' (p. 23). The French revolutionaries had inverted the natural relationship between divine and human achievement. If men make themselves the measure of all things, they open themselves to a torrent of abuses. Revolution is not simply a political mistake, but a sin against human nature itself.

Maistre takes the doctrine of original sin very seriously indeed. He sees Christian doctrine as an appropriate response to the prevalence of evil in the world. It constrains us doctrinally, reinforcing the established (yet apparently arbitrary) power of monarchs. Left to ourselves, we would be ruinously self-destructive. Maistre regards war as the 'habitual state of mankind' (p. 51). Striving to set ourselves free politically would only unleash heightened levels of violence. The only hope for us is to embrace political constraints. Yet the intellectual optimism of the Enlightenment had extolled our powers of reasoning and our hopes for radical political improvement. What Maistre sees, instead, is a world in which 'evil has tainted everything, and in a very real sense, all is evil, since nothing is in its place' (p. 62).

In more narrowly political terms Maistre highlights the novelty of the Revolution as a sure indication of its absurdity. He asks rhetorically, 'Can the French Republic last?', clearly suggesting that a political arrangement so unprecedented could not be expected to survive (p. 65). Having dismantled the institutional structure of *ancien régime* France, all the revolutionaries are left with is a principle of representation that is designed to bind the people together, while somehow preserving their collective status as a sovereign authority. Yet all this could amount to, according to Maistre, is a system of republican representation based in Paris dominating the country as a whole. He takes Rousseau as the theorist of republican representation and glosses over American and British experience of indirect representation. In his rather jaundiced view, this leaves France with a scheme of representation that might see each man 'exercise his turn at national sovereignty once in every sixteen thousand years' (p. 71). We need not dwell on the detail of Maistre's discussion of representative government. The point to stress is his contention that a republic on this scale would necessarily be a despotism, reducing the people to 'the most deplorable slavery' (p. 71).

Maistre finds no mitigating features in the Revolution. While Burke had conceded that there could be a case for reform in France, Maistre castigates the Revolution as 'an event unique in history' in 'that it is radically bad' (p. 73). He contrasts republican talk of virtue with a collapse of morals in both public and private spheres. The French manifestly do not love their revolution, yet they fear the consequences of a restoration. How, in these circumstances, can they hope to escape from the nightmare of revolution?

Maistre urges a rather bleak patience. We can no more expect to plan a counter-revolution than a revolution. But, in time, revolution will devour its own children. No parties or groups are exempt from the orgy of destruction initiated by revolution. 'In the French Revolution the people have continually been enslaved, outraged, ruined, and mutilated by all parties, and the parties in their turn, working one against the other, have continually drifted, despite all their efforts, toward breakup at length on the rocks awaiting them' (p. 135). Providence, in Maistre's account, can be guaranteed to lead France back to monarchy through republican anarchy. The best that right-minded thinkers can do is maintain faith in the proper order of things.

In the last resort, it is France's departure from God's order that has upset her affairs so calamitously. Maistre recognizes that people have grown tired of convulsions and fear the consequences of any renewed constitutional conflict. Restitution of property cannot be achieved without disturbing a range of interests. Families, too, may have scores to settle in any new scheme of things. Counter-revolution thus cannot be undertaken without some consideration of likely consequences. Maistre objects, however, to the 'cowardly optimists' who had initially embraced revolution, now recognize their folly, yet lack the courage to 'bring the king back to his throne and restore order in France' (p. 144). Attempts to terrify people into permanent acquiescence in a regime that they plainly see is intolerable are contemptible in Maistre's eyes. Yet, fundamentally, argues Maistre, 'it is a great error to imagine that the people have something to lose in the restoration of the monarchy' (p. 145). Kings work through people and institutions. People's real interests are served when institutions function effectively. And it cannot be in the interest of a king (or within his power if he were so minded) to undermine the smooth functioning of institutions of state that are his vital concern.

For Maistre, in any case, counter-revolution is 'not a contrary revolution, but the contrary of revolution' (p. 169). It is an attempt to exploit the chaos of revolution in order to restore a natural balance to the workings of institutions and practices. 'The return to order will not be painful, because it will be natural and because it will be favoured by a secret force whose action is wholly creative' (p. 169). No lasting achievements can follow from persistent contempt for the grain of human nature. Institutions that respect ordinary human failings are actually indispensable to genuine human flourishing. Revolutionary rhetoric had pandered to human vanity, promising heaven on earth, but delivering turmoil. Events disabuse people. Genuine philosophy can restore faith in institutional certainties, even in a political world rocked by 'enlightened' excesses.

The scope for a discursive politics is deeply limited in Maistre's scheme of things. Elite co-operation constrains the practical options of monarchs to a certain extent, but constitutional boundaries cannot be drawn around spheres of activity. As with Burke, we have a powerful critique of political rationalism, but with even less prospect of the emergence of a moderate consensus. Maistre's terms of political reference encourage oscillation between revolutionary and reactionary extremes.

Reflection on the impact of revolutionary politics in other European contexts, however, sometimes generated a more balanced theoretical response. Vincenzo Cuoco is an intriguing case in point. His life (1770–1823) spanned the period of revolution which was the crucible that formed the character of so much of the political thought of the nineteenth century; yet events viewed from the rather more confined perspective of Naples and southern Italy looked significantly different. The contrast at the heart of his thinking is between positions that judged the adequacy of institutions in terms of the requirements of abstract theory and those that sought to understand the rationale of institutions in terms of their relations with popular attitudes, dispositions, even prejudices. Cuoco's hostility to revolutionary rationalism was influenced by the strictures of Maistre and Burke. But he was a better historian than either of them, and his theoretical reflections are accordingly more subtle. Crucially from the perspective of the history of political ideas, he endorsed the theoretical critique of political rationalism without embracing either conservative or reactionary positions. Cuoco deployed anti-rationalist arguments in defence of liberal constitutionalism; and while he was aware of the gulf that separated elite and popular views, he contended throughout his career that an effective political culture had necessarily to accommodate both perspectives.

Cuoco found the vocation of political theorist forced upon him by circumstances. Working as a young lawyer in Naples, he found himself associating with men whose ideas had been formed in the great reform movements of the eighteenth century. Jacobin ideas were almost irresistible to educated young men confronting the immobility of church and crown. Cuoco himself, though he was acutely aware of the deadening effect of the feudal heritage on the political, economic and social development of the Kingdom of Naples, could never view Jacobinism as other than an excessively abstract and alien ideology. In this he was out of line with his fellow intellectuals. With the advance of the French revolutionary armies through Italy in the later 1790s, hopes were raised of the formation of a republic in Naples on the French model. The eventual achievement of a republic in 1799 owed less to popular initiative than to French military supremacy. When the French army was withdrawn, the 'patriots' (as the Neapolitan republicans styled themselves) were swept aside in a brutal reaction. A generation of intellectuals was either killed, imprisoned or exiled. Cuoco, despite his deep reservations about Jacobin ideas, had participated in the revolution alongside the republicans. Following the reaction, he found himself briefly imprisoned and finally condemned to exile. In these traumatic circumstances, Cuoco set himself the task of distilling the essential political lessons of the abortive revolution. His *Historical Essay on the Neapolitan Revolution of 1799* (1801) served as a theoretical point of reference for a generation of Italian theorists striving to understand Italy's place in wider European political and intellectual developments.[7]

What Cuoco offers is not a sweeping condemnation of the ideas, ambitions and motives of the revolutionaries, but an analysis of the way in which noble ideals are undermined simply because they are formulated with no regard for the constraints which established customs impose on the scope for political change. The mood is that of remorse or regret, rather than contempt; and the intention is to glean such lessons from the disaster as would enable future plans for institutional reform to be set upon a secure foundation.

Cuoco's distance from Burke and Maistre is especially evident in his treatment of the Bourbon regime. He sees ineffective co-ordination and control, competition among ministers for the ear of the king, and high levels of taxation coupled with public debt. The only group to do well out of the situation were lawyers, whom Cuoco describes as 'wasps' living off the honest endeavours of ordinary citizens (p. 56).

Cuoco attributes the French Revolution itself to the failure of the monarchy to adapt to changing circumstances. Radical ideas have a secondary role in

Cuoco's analysis. Indeed, he claims, 'the French themselves had misunderstood the nature of their revolution, and believed that to be an effect of philosophy which was in fact an effect of the political circumstances in which the nation found itself' (p. 37). He treats the abstract nature of revolutionary ideology as a response in kind to the abstraction of royalist ideology. 'The French were compelled to deduce their principles from the most abstruse metaphysics, and fell into the usual error of men who follow excessively abstract ideas, which is to confuse their own ideas with the laws of nature' (p. 39). This is the crux of the argument. By divorcing ideas from the real needs of society, both royalists and revolutionaries had cut themselves off from any prospect of improving (or even understanding) the society they were trying to mould. And while it had become customary to pour scorn on the naïve rationalism of the Jacobins, Cuoco insists that the particular cast of revolutionary ideology was a natural product of the French political tradition.

Cuoco presses his point further. The French Revolution had been understood by only a few; fewer still actually approved of it, and hardly anyone wanted to see it initiated. But even if a revolution on the French model had been deemed desirable in Naples, it would still have been fruitless, 'because a revolution cannot be made without the people, and the people are moved not by reason but by need' (p. 40). The needs of the Neapolitan people, in Cuoco's view, were so different from those of the French that the particular arguments advanced by the revolutionaries seemed abstruse, wild and incomprehensible. Nor were Neapolitan intellectuals sympathetic to French revolutionary theory. The Italian tradition in moral and political thought had followed quite distinct principles. The trend had been to relate consideration of political ideas to close study of historical circumstances. A lead had been given by Machiavelli, Gravina and Vico; and anyone who had profited from their work would find French revolutionary discussions of theory and practice fanciful (see pp. 40–1).

Given the gulf that separated French and Italian political traditions, how could it finally come about that a generation of reformist intellectuals should transform themselves into Jacobin revolutionaries? Cuoco's answer is simple. The first mistake had been to try to suppress ideas rather than to disregard them. The second was to identify the fortune of the Bourbon rulers of Naples too directly with the *ancien régime* in France. The combined effect was that theoretical differences on specific points, or interest in particular practical proposals that had been advanced in France, would be interpreted as evidence of total rejection of Bourbon rule in Naples in the name of Jacobin principles. In truth, according to Cuoco, Neapolitan intellectuals became 'Jacobins' only because they recognized that little could be expected in the way of concrete reform from an obscurantist and timorous monarchy. When intellectuals welcomed the invading French army as the harbinger of political change, they had merely accepted the characterization of events that their own ruling house had foisted upon them.

Cuoco deplored the impact of the new Jacobin principles on the political life of the Kingdom of Naples in terms that echo the analyses of Burke and Maistre. Yet sinister implications did not have time to work themselves out fully. The fledgling republic, hampered as it was by the adoption of an untenable ideology, was further constrained by the alien origin of the newly dominant ideas. Access to French ideas had only ever been open to an intellectual elite. Instead of hailing the overthrow of tyranny, the common people could only deplore the destruction of a distinctive way of life. The 'patriots' had been relatively sanguine about their task: because their innovations had been designed to improve the lot of the common people, they had supposed that they would be greeted with enthusiasm. They found to their cost, however, that 'conceiving a scheme for a republican constitution is not the same as founding a republic' (p. 87). The idea that government should express the public will is itself noble; but in the Neapolitan context, where political life was still identified in the popular mind with royal discretion, the condition of popular culture made talk of a 'public will' purely illusory. As Cuoco put the point, 'one could only establish political liberty if one had first managed to create free men' (p. 87). Popular culture in Naples was an elaborate network of personal relationships, customs and prejudices. From a Jacobin perspective, it could be regarded only as a tissue of errors and superstitions. The Jacobins were effectively cut off from any real contact with the society they were striving to transform. Far from assisting the process of cultural assimilation, their revolutionary strategy had accentuated the gulf that separated them from popular culture.

Here we confront the key strategic dilemma facing the Neapolitan 'Jacobins'. Political leadership in the context of a spontaneous popular revolution might have been relatively straightforward; enthusiasm would need to be harnessed, various initiatives would have to be co-ordinated, but the general objectives of the revolution could be assumed to be shared by both leaders and led. No such cultural harmony existed in Naples. The success of the revolution depended upon the skill and efficiency with which a small elite could impose its will upon a scarcely comprehending populace. But the abstract philosophy that had sustained revolutionary ideology had little to say about purely tactical matters. The principal task in any 'passive revolution' (according to Cuoco) should always be the moulding of 'popular opinion' (p. 90). Yet the differences between the 'patriots' and the populace were so vast – in terms of ideas, customs, even languages – as to vitiate even the most basic communication. The admiration for foreign ideas and customs, which had been such a marked feature of Neapolitan intellectual culture throughout the eighteenth century, could now be seen as 'the greatest obstacle to the establishment of liberty' (p. 90). It was as if the Neapolitan nation were divided into two peoples, separated by two centuries in terms of their levels of cultural development. The cultivated class had nurtured itself upon foreign models. Those who had remained faithful to Neapolitan traditions (the vast mass of the population) were entirely ignorant of modern culture. Thus we find that 'the culture of the few was of no use to the nation as a whole', while the populace 'despised a culture that was of no use to it and which it did not understand' (p. 90).

In Cuoco's interpretation, all the problems of the revolution can be traced back to this basic cultural divide. It was all very well to talk of a revolution in the interest of the people; but the lack of a common political culture meant that individuals interpreted that interest in their own way, leaving the *patria* a prey to ambition, indifference and malice. It was old-fashioned patriotic sentiment that had sustained the French revolutionary armies, not an abstract political ideology. Yet 'the Neapolitan nation, far from enjoying this national unity, can be regarded as a conglomeration of many different nations' (p. 92). The Kingdom had embraced a bewildering variety of cultures; and the feudal system, which had held the balance between anarchy and barbarism for centuries, had merely reflected the diversity of the established communities. The very first task of the revolutionaries should have been to fashion a coherent political culture out of these unlikely materials. Little could be done to make the doctrine of natural rights a political reality until the people themselves had come to associate their concrete interests with the new political creed. Everything should have been done to minimize the formal novelty of the new regime; and this could have been achieved only by attending to the people's needs, not by trying to secure their rights.

What happened, instead, was that the revolutionaries remained faithful to their ideas. If theoretical analysis had shown that established institutions were inadequate, then it behoved them to fashion the social and political world anew. But the commitment to change everything (Cuoco calls it a 'mania') inevitably brought with it the threat of counter-revolution (p. 96). As the revolutionaries sought to root out the abuses of the old regime, so the people would be deprived of the petty advantages that could be enjoyed under a corrupt and inefficient administration. It was the very zeal with which the republicans tried to impose a fair and equal legal system that led the people to complain of the new regime's rigour and severity. Law was evident to the multitude only as a constraint, a wilful denial of the habitual practices of the old way of life. The advantages of a regular system of law would manifest themselves in daily affairs only after a period of peace and stability. Yet time was the one thing that the republic did not have on its side. The deposed Bourbons were waiting in Sicily, intent upon taking advantage of the first signs of popular unrest on the mainland. At the earliest opportunity they would return; and one could be sure that they would not make the mistake of relying on the people's judgement rather than their interests. Despotism (as Cuoco puts it) always depends upon the support of the 'dregs of the people who, without regard for either good or evil, sell themselves to whatever best satisfies their stomachs' (p. 93).

The Neapolitan republic had shown itself to be lamentably lacking in political realism. But the point Cuoco wants to stress is that the abstract nature of republican ideals effectively precluded the kind of balanced appraisal of different courses of action that might have made a success of the revolution. Time and again the analysis comes back to the contrast between a purely theoretical view of politics and one that is attuned to the traditions of a community. The idea is nicely illustrated in discussions of different conceptions of political liberty. The 'patriots' would insist that liberty is a good in itself. Yet, when we ask ourselves why people actually value liberty, we find that a host of other notions have to be introduced. Liberty is seen as a good precisely because it leads to other more tangible goods – such as security, a comfortable way of life, or a flourishing commerce. Indeed, in Cuoco's analysis, it is specifically because people enjoy concrete benefits that they come to love liberty (see pp. 102–8). The first concern of a new republican regime should have been to make some of the concrete advantages of liberty available to the people at large. By concentrating on the moral dimension of liberty, the 'patriots' had effectively surrendered the political initiative to their Bourbon opponents.

The negative side of Cuoco's argument should by now be clear. Scepticism about the role of ideas in politics, combined with an analysis of problems of political leadership, led him to insist that any programme of reform should have roots in a traditional culture. What we find on the positive side (though the point is less fully developed in the *Historical Essay* than elsewhere) is a stress on the importance of sound institutions for sustaining a flourishing political life. Where late eighteenth-century republican thought had set the virtuous individual at the centre of the political stage, Cuoco sounded a warning. In the Neapolitan revolution virtue had been entirely on the side of the 'patriots'; lacking a viable institutional framework, however, their best endeavours had proved to be self-destructive. In Cuoco's view, we can only take people as we find them in politics and hope that individuals will channel their self-interested conduct in directions that benefit the community as a whole. This might have seemed a disappointing conclusion to readers brought up on utopian tracts promising heaven on earth; but theorists of the post-revolutionary generation had grown acutely conscious of the hidden pitfalls that could transform the best-intentioned reforms into sinister instruments of social control.

The wider significance of Cuoco's political thought lies in his refusal to reject liberal constitutional politics in the aftermath of the demonstrable excesses of revolutionary rationalism. It cannot be said that his ideas had an immediate impact on broader currents of European thought beyond Italy. Where Constant and Tocqueville would later deploy similar ideas in defence of a liberalism tempered to suit the requirements of modern states in complex contexts, the more familiar response of Cuoco's contemporaries would equate the critique of political rationalism with an endorsement of traditionalism in politics.

It was easy to discredit democratic and radical ideas in the light of the turmoil and disorder of the revolutionary years. The reactionary assault on revolutionary theory was powerful and persuasive, though wider factors were also at work. Experience of the revolutionary cycle was vivid in traumatized minds – lofty ambitions degenerating through authoritarian terror into dictatorship. Many established interests, tired of convulsion and uncertainty, welcomed the collapse of Napoleonic France as an occasion to turn the clock back. Traditionalism became a dominant cultural *motif*, extending far beyond political thought.

In the domain of law, for example, Savigny argued forcefully against the very idea that constitutions and legal systems could be profitably rationalized to accord with the specifications of a theoretical view of the proper relationship between subjects, citizens and governments. His *On the Vocation of our Age for Legislation and Jurisprudence* (1814) was a polemical contribution to a highly sensitive debate in Germany.[8] Reformers influenced by Enlightenment thinking presupposed that political, social and economic development could be sustained only if self-conscious legislative efforts were brought to bear on the anomalies that get entrenched in any set of practices established over long periods of time. Taking stock and moving on had become an article of faith, even among thinkers who were deeply suspicious of the wilder flights of revolutionary rationalism. Savigny, instead, likened law to a natural language that developed incrementally over centuries, adapting to the vagaries of experience in ways too subtle for legislative modernizers to discern. He contrasted the (apparently) haphazard trajectory of 'natural' development with the distortion that necessarily accompanied the imposition of a legislative code. Savigny defends his view as an 'organic connection of law with the being and character of the nation', manifest with 'the progress of the times'.[9] As an accomplished historian of jurisprudence, Savigny sought in his work to describe complex adjustments of law to circumstance. There could be no ideal model to follow, because cultures and nations deployed different resources to the contingencies that confronted them. Thinking about law in abstract terms could thus destroy the intimate connection between law and culture, making the law seem remote and alien, and individuals strangers in their own land.

The implications of this position are deeply conservative. There is a preference for established practices simply because they are established. And if efforts are made to think theoretically about the variety of practices that have become embedded in cultures, the warning is sounded that neglect of the inscrutable relationship between (apparently) incongruous practices leads inevitably to the horrors of rationalism and revolution. To be sure, this is a highly partial reading of the eighteenth-century reform movement, but its plausibility had become an article of faith in some quarters. Pierre Ballanche, for example, in his *Essays on Social Palingenesis* (1827–9), focused on the organic connection between language and society as a model for political life more broadly.[10] This comes very close to making a historian's working assumptions an ideal form for all normative argument. There is no doubt that the flourishing of historical studies in the early nineteenth century should be seen in this light.[11] The point to stress here, however, is the impact of criteria invoked in the assessment of broader spheres and activities.

Particularity is treated as a value in itself. Whether the issue in question is poetic form, artistic style, fashions in gardens, dress or life-style, the assumption is that no objective or universal standard of value is available to assess the adequacy of practices. The force of the argument is obvious. And its appeal has continued to be felt down to our own day. What it highlights, above all, is the contingency of the positions from which we make any judgements whatsoever.

It is less clear what follows from recognition that we are situated creatures, making judgements in terms of values and preferences that form part of our whole world-view. For while we can readily admit that it is a matter of sheer chance that we have acquired a particular view of the world, we still find ourselves in the position of having to make normative judgements as we confront contingent dilemmas. To embrace tradition as a matter of principle is thus very different from carrying on in the same old way.

In an important sense, the images of 'revolution' and 'reaction' deployed in this book represent ideal types that fix limits to our thinking in modern political thought. We invoke universal normative criteria, while granting that we view the world from a specific cultural and personal perspective. However we are to understand our normative predicament, these two dimensions to our thinking are sure to reassert themselves. If we deny the theoretical validity of universal criteria, we will still find ourselves committed to a moral and political language that has universal connotations. And from a particular perspective, we will have to discriminate between aspects of our practices and institutions as we chart our way through the ordinary dilemmas of practical life.

The tensions we find in modern political thought should not surprise us. It would be too much to expect both 'revolution' and 'reaction' to be accommodated within the terms of a comprehensive or metaphysical view. What we see, instead, is stark confrontation between arguments, but without the possibility of a broad-based or stable consensus. Lasting agreement can thus be ruled out, on both conceptual and sociological grounds. It does not follow, though, that reflection on the course of these arguments cannot furnish normative grounds for excluding certain views as indefensible. We can describe the breadth of arguments available in modern political thought, while sustaining a normative engagement with the terms of reference available. The argument has been managed more or less plausibly in modern political thought. Whether we are theorists, historians or citizens, we are confronted with deeply divisive debates about what it means to be an agent engaged in different styles of social co-operation in uncertain situations.

4 The Constitutional State

Attempts in 1815 to draw a line under the upheaval, instability and turmoil of the revolutionary and Napoleonic years were always deeply problematic. Conservative and reactionary advocates of a return to the dynastic politics of the *ancien régime* had to take account of profound changes that had transformed the economic and political life of Europe since 1789. Two factors, in particular, imposed limits upon the style and character of any viable state. In the first place, there was a need to seek justification for the state beyond the accident of family inheritance. Monarchies which had once been successfully challenged could not simply fall back upon a tacit assumption that hereditary rule was a part of a natural or divinely ordained scheme of things. Order itself, as well as reform or revolution, had to be defended at a theoretical level. The second factor concerned the scale and organization of the state. Technological and economic developments required dynamic political management of society at large. What this involved at the practical level was a mobilization of populations on a larger scale than had been the case before 1789. Such mobilization need not, of course, take overt political form. It was not simply a question of extending the franchise or involving wider groups in decision making. Most people's contact with the state would be through local or national bureaucracies. The point to stress, however, is that the state, in responding to changing circumstances, was impinging on a wider range of interests. And explaining and justifying its procedures would necessarily involve recourse to broad principles. To speak of 'popular' politics in the early nineteenth century would be anachronistic. Yet we can see the beginnings of a process that has continued into recent times, with ideological arguments becoming a crucial factor in the cut and thrust of practical debate.

Attempts to establish a viable political consensus after 1815 thus involved a variety of factors, both practical and ideological, that continued to threaten further revolutionary or reactionary turmoil. Nowhere was this tension more apparent than in France, where the grant of a charter by Louis XVIII in 1814 (which might have been construed as a significant concession to liberal constitutionalism) was qualified by the contention that all authority in France resides in the person of the king. The constitution itself, far from being regarded as the political expression of a people's natural right, was described in the declaration as a gift bestowed by the king upon his people of his own free will. And, of course, what had once been given could always be revoked if circumstances changed and different interests needed to be accommodated.

The 1814 charter was very much a compromise. Just how precarious an achievement it had been became clear in 1824 with the accession of Charles X to the throne. Supporters of the traditional rights of crown, aristocracy and church had never ceased to regard even the semblance of constitutionalism as wholly tainted by the atrocities of the Revolution. The advent of a monarch sympathetic to such views sharply polarized positions, with a seemingly unbridgeable gulf developing between liberals, republicans and anticlericals on the one side and the various species of traditionalist on the other. The tensions and hostilities that had marked the revolutionary years were still as entrenched as ever. What was at issue was not so much the propriety of adopting this or that policy as the character of political life itself. The emergent ideologies were precisely a response to a political situation that had yet to assume a settled form.

Nor were these difficulties unique to France. The experience of revolutionary wars had taught both radicals and reactionaries that international frontiers were no defence against ideologies that challenged the rationale of a state. Rising groups excluded from a political establishment would exploit new arguments in order to justify a measure of political power or influence commensurate with their social and economic significance. France had essentially established terms of political reference that would dominate the thought and practice of the first half of the nineteenth century. A political disturbance on the streets of Paris in 1830 or 1848 would thus be an event that could resonate across the continent of Europe.

The ideological alliances that emerged in Paris in 1830 served as a pattern for wider European conflicts. A reactionary and obstinate monarch had forced opposition groups into the position of supporting revolutionary claims, despite the modest nature of their practical proposals. Liberals, in fact, were anxious to disavow any connection between their own ideas and the principles of 1793. The limit of their ambitions was a return to something like the constitutional principles embodied in the charter of 1814. Through Madame de Stael and Benjamin Constant, they had come to associate popular government with tyranny, despite the lofty ambitions of radicals and reformers. In a seminal lecture delivered in 1819 Constant had specifically contrasted ancient liberty, which stressed direct popular involvement in government, with modern liberty dominated by the idea of the rule of law and representative institutions.[1] He saw the civic republican ideal as peculiarly suited to the small-scale states of antiquity, where a sizeable proportion of the citizen body might plausibly meet to resolve issues in public forums. Citizens had the advantage of a slave class to spare them the burden of maintaining themselves and could be presumed to share strong substantive values. What Rousseau (and more especially his Jacobin followers) had done, in Constant's view, was to lift the ancient view of citizenship out of context, inspired as he was by the example of collective responsibility being assumed for the burdens of public life. In attempting to apply ancient participatory ideals to the modern world, modern republicans had failed to recognize the practical difficulties that made the modern state a different political species from the ancient *polis*. The scale of the modern state, and the diversity of interests it represented, dictated a modification in political and constitutional principles. A cult of virtue, for example, of the kind associated with Robespierre or Saint-Just, might very well be a fitting reflection of the cultural homogeneity of an ancient republic. In a state the size of France in the nineteenth century, however, an insistence on moral or political uniformity would necessarily involve the suppression of a plethora of interests and points of view. Modern citizens prized individual liberty above all else. They gloried in the rich mosaic of their private interests and attachments. They were content for the political authorities to 'confine themselves to being just'; they were perfectly prepared to 'assume the responsibility of being happy' for themselves.[2]

The crucial point at issue in Constant's contrast between ancient and modern liberty is the characterization of the proper relations between individual and state. Rousseau and the Jacobins had insisted that each individual had a right either to participate in government or at least to authorize the actions of a government. What this meant in practice was that a government claiming to derive its authority from the people would be blessed with unlimited theoretical powers. An isolated individual opposed to specific policies would place himself in the position of opposing the collective will of the community. In effect, this would mean that opposition could be construed as an assertion of narrow self-interest. Moreover, since the collective will of the community would simply be a partial interest that had succeeded in presenting itself in the guise of the collective interest, there would be ample scope for a determined minority to dominate the many interests of the different groups within the community.

This was clearly a recipe for tyranny. Constant's solution to the dilemma was to treat the state not as an instrument for the realization of liberty in any abstract sense but rather as guarantor or protector of the very many liberties that might be enshrined in a way of life. In any civilized society people enjoyed a variety of rights (to be subject to the law rather than the whim of individuals, to be free to express opinions, to pursue a profession, to associate with others, to be foolish or frivolous in the quiet of their homes). The principal role of the state in this scheme of things was to preserve a system of constitutional guarantees that would enable individuals to go about their business in their own ways. Vested interests, which had been viewed by the Jacobins as a series of obstacles to the inculcation of public virtue, would have to be respected as a tangible means of containing the state within proper bounds, much as they had been for Madison in *The Federalist Papers*. In general, private life would be regarded as the principal focus of an individual's endeavour and ambition. Political devices served merely to facilitate the private realm, ensuring sufficient stability and security for the pursuit of a multitude of individual ends.[3]

Privacy and pluralism became central themes in the liberal defence of the individual against the creeping encroachment of the potentially tyrannical state. Liberals were less certain about the value of popular participation in political life. Though Constant denied that political participation was an end in itself, he saw a measure of participation as a necessary means of securing the state in its rightful role. But this was far from the standard liberal position. If in 1830 French liberals were obsessed by the threat posed to the principle of constitutionalism by an authoritarian monarch, they had not forgotten that an unholy alliance of radical intellectuals and the Paris mob could lead a movement of political reform to degenerate into revolution. What they feared above all was that political liberty would not survive attempts to put the state at the head of a radical programme of social and economic transformation. They certainly had little sympathy with egalitarian political projects. The limits of their political ambitions were very much set by a concern to preserve the prevailing balance in society.

A political theory that essentially championed private interests was not sufficient for all liberals. Hegel, who was to have a decisive impact on the emergence of various species of historically minded political theory throughout the nineteenth century, could not accept that the modern state was simply an instrumental means to attain satisfaction, security and contentment for individuals. Hegel rejected the abstract view of individuals as entities stripped of social relations and identity. He could grant (with Constant) that modern freedom requires a vast sphere for individual initiative and association, but he dismissed the contention that individuals should be portrayed as straightforward calculators of personal advantage. Hegel's emphasis, instead, is on the community that nurtures individuals, enabling each to flourish in a variety of ways in determinate social roles. The significance of the state in this scheme of things is precisely that it embodies interests which people hold in common, interests that cannot be reduced to a sum of individual satisfactions.

Hegel's portrayal of the individual in the community must be seen in the context of a prevalent response to the theoretical and practical limitations of a certain style of liberalism. The nineteenth century witnessed a plethora of political movements that stressed collective identity and involvement. Nationalism, socialism and conservatism in their various guises highlighted the inadequacy of the conception of the individual dear to the Enlightenment and the activists of the French revolutionary years. Liberalism, too, refashioned its commitments, and emerged in the later nineteenth century with a richer account of social life. To be sure, the celebration of community in nineteenth-century political doctrines was not without its dangers and difficulties. Yet, for better or worse, the terms of political discourse had significantly shifted.

What made Hegel's reiteration of a communitarian ideal distinctive was his insistence that the human world as a whole should be seen in historical perspective. He saw cultures as artefacts rather than 'natural' products, animated by distinctive sets of ideas which gave them each a particular character. In this view, the various facets of a culture – art, poetry, religion, morality, even philosophy itself – should be seen as expressions of a single ethos.

The privileged position of the traditional philosopher, for whom the historical development of ideas was a subordinate (or irrelevant) consideration in the pursuit of truth, had thus been undermined. His standard of judgement had been reduced to the status of contemporary prejudice. Philosophical ideas, as cultural artefacts, could not be compared in the way that a zoologist classifies forms of animal life, because cultures were meaningful only within their own terms of reference.

It should be clear that Hegel's interest in the past was quite different from that of the orthodox historian. What he sought was not a detailed description of remote ways of life, but a developmental thread that could be seen to have informed the progressive unfolding of the modern world. He was concerned throughout his career with the various, contrasting views of the moral significance of the idea of community that had been mooted in different cultures. From his early essay, *The Positivity of the Christian Religion* (1795–6), through the *Phenomenology of Spirit* (1807), to the *Philosophy of Right* (1821), and the posthumously published *Lectures on the Philosophy of World History* and *Lectures on the History of Philosophy*, he had explored the institutional preconditions for well-being and contentment.[4] True fulfilment, he argued, could be achieved only if people saw the institutions and conventions of their society in a proper light. It was an ideal which he supposed had been realized in an unreflective way in pre-Socratic Greece, where there was no awareness of any other life than that prescribed by the customs of the community. But this harmony of morality, religion and society was precarious. It depended upon a naïve acceptance of a given set of customs. Once a spirit of criticism had arisen, such arrangements were bound to collapse. The rise of Socratic philosophy, for Hegel, marked the demise of the substantial unity of Greek society. Thereafter, moral and political discourse would be characterized by the clash of competing principles. The emergence of Christianity denoted a similar transition in its distinction between worldly and heavenly concerns. But while philosophical or religious criticism estranged one from the life of a society, each nevertheless afforded a heightened awareness of possibilities and satisfactions that had previously been foreclosed. Hegel saw the culmination of history as the restoration of the original unity of the ethical community, but with the added dimension of self-consciousness. The task of philosophy was to portray the succession of cultural forms as a necessary chain of development: not a more or less arbitrary set of institutional restrictions, but an expression of the possibilities of human freedom. It was an ambitious scheme, involving a radical reconstruction of both philosophy and history.

It will be evident how much the moral and political dimensions of Hegel's philosophy owed to the reaction of conservative theorists to the excesses of the French Revolution; yet he was anxious that philosophy as a whole should not be identified with the irrationalism or intuitive understanding that became a dominant *motif* in Romantic political thought. Indeed, the complex relationship between Hegel and his predecessors is a central issue in the interpretation of his thought. In his philosophy, error is not simply a negative phenomenon. It is a half-truth that is retained in the succeeding, more mature forms of experience. Hegel held that the adequacy with which a philosophy could include within its compass modes of experience excluded by other systems was a crucial criterion for assessing its merits. Competing philosophies could thus be regarded as partial realizations of truth. It followed that a new philosophy should be seen not simply as a portrayal of present problems of knowledge, but rather as a reinterpretation of the whole of the history of philosophy from its particular perspective. Such knowledge presupposed, beyond a conception of the technical problems of past philosophies informing the philosophical discourse of the present, a view of the cultural forms that sustained these philosophies as necessary stages in a logical development whose meaning and significance could be appreciated from the retrospective vantage of the philosopher.

Hegel's most detailed specification of the successive transformation of cultures was in the *Phenomenology of Spirit*. There, in what is arguably his most singular and exciting text, he treated the development of consciousness as the key to historical change. The details of this extraordinary odyssey cannot detain us here. The point to stress is that, for Hegel, a philosophical analysis of a form of consciousness necessarily involved a re-creation of the way an attitude to the world had emerged from its intellectual and institutional antecedents. Each culture was regarded as the consummation of all its predecessors. The discipline of philosophy was itself seen as a historically specific product. A philosopher tackling the most minute contemporary issue was thus implicitly making a judgement about a whole tradition of enquiry. It followed that philosophical transparency required the adoption of an essentially historical point of view, not as an optional extra but as an integral dimension of philosophical enquiry.

When Hegel came to give a definitive form to his political philosophy in 1821, he thus had behind him an elaborate and comprehensive system. Though the system was cast in a strictly deductive form, he was insistent that what appeared to be purely conceptual relationships should actually be seen as expressions of a developed cultural and institutional life. The two dimensions were held together by the stress on human activity. Hegel pictured human beings as engaged in a ceaseless struggle with a natural world that could never assume any significance in itself. Nature was merely a *datum*, a means for people to satisfy their desires. Whatever identity it had derived from the assumptions people made in the course of their endeavours. In the struggle to subdue nature, however, people found themselves engaged in relationships that involved mutual recognition. Through their activities, they would in time transform both themselves and the world about them. The initial stark opposition between the human and natural worlds would be mediated in the form of institutions and practices. Institutions channel activities and may, at first glance, appear to restrict people's options arbitrarily. But Hegel is adamant that they are, in fact, an expression of the character and identity of agents themselves. It was only in the sphere of institutions, what Hegel called 'Objective Mind', that people's evanescent whims assumed the settled form of tangible intentions and ambitions. By working for their ends through established institutions, people learnt to distinguish between passing fancies and rational pursuits. Their conceptions of themselves were determined by the institutional framework that constituted the context of their lives. Their sense of identity, indeed, was given through awareness of sharing a common life. And by continually refining their institutions in accordance with that (developing) identity, they were fashioning a world which (unlike nature) supplied its own criteria of intelligibility.

Hegel's most detailed specification of the realm of 'Objective Mind' was in the *Philosophy of Right*. His central concern in the text is to grasp the character and significance of the modern state, considered as the culmination of a long tradition of practice and reflection. The approach exemplifies the fusion of logical and historical analysis. He divides the state into its logical constituents, examining legal entitlement ('abstract right'), the domain of individual judgement ('morality'), and the claims of the community ('ethical life'). But these spheres ('moments'), far from being purely logical constructs, are in fact mutually dependent dimensions of the modern state. They can be isolated for purposes of analysis, but are interwoven in daily life in a fashion that distinguishes the modern state from its precursors. Each of these subordinate 'moments' has, moreover, been intimated in the course of political history as the characteristic feature of a dominant polity. What marks the modern state, though, is its capacity to overcome the one-sided currents which sustain it, furnishing an institutional framework sufficiently flexible to absorb the aspects of historic polities that are of permanent value. Thus the naïve unity of the Greek polity (where individuals hardly have an identity outside the community), the formal rule of law in the Roman Empire, the right of individual conscience stressed by Christianity, the abrasive pursuit of self-interest in the modern economy, are each preserved as logical 'moments' that contribute to the fulfilment of the individual in the state.

Hegel saw the state, then, as a product of its history, properly intelligible only as a repository of practical wisdom. This gave his political philosophy a distinctively interpretative thrust. In a polemical preface, in which he comments in uncharacteristically harsh fashion upon various political developments in his own day, he is at pains to distinguish his own approach from currently accepted views of the relationship between philosophy and politics, theory and practice. What he objected to was the conception of political philosophy as a projection of a preferred scheme of things, a recipe for a more or less far-reaching reconstruction of the state. We can all give vent to our frustrations and disappointments by imagining a world in which things are ordered differently. But we would not ordinarily mistake our day-dreaming for philosophy. This, according to Hegel, is precisely what had happened in a Europe which had yet to settle down after the traumas of the French revolutionary and Napoleonic upheavals.

Hegel was adamant that political philosophy should not 'attempt to construct a state as it ought to be'; its task, rather, was to 'show how the state, the ethical universe, is to be understood'.[5] Nor was this limitation specific to political philosophy. Philosophy as a discipline was bent upon exploring the immanent logic of whatever form of experience had been disclosed in the course of historical development. 'To comprehend what is, this is the task of philosophy, because what is, is reason' (p. 11). To attempt to conjure up merely possible worlds, whether political or natural, is idle fancy. Even when philosophers appear to be depicting an ideal state, Hegel insists that they are in fact giving expression to fundamental assumptions which inform their own cultures. Like every other pursuit, philosophy is a product of its past. 'Whatever happens, every individual is a child of his time; so philosophy too is its own time apprehended in thoughts' (p. 11).

Hegel's concern with changing patterns of thought and practice in the past should not be confused with the orthodox historian's insistence upon an exact portrayal of events. As a philosopher, he had little interest in what was haphazard or contingent, the unique form which ideas or institutions might assume in response to particular circumstances. He was intent, rather, on grasping the essential form, or identity, of an idea or practice. Thus in the *Philosophy of Right* his focus was on the character of the modern state, and not the particular characteristics of the Prussian, French or British states. One could not, of course, make sense of the modern state as a phenomenon without studying specific states. But Hegel's point is that one should not lose the conceptual identity of the state in the motley array of practices and procedures which might have emerged to meet the demands of ephemeral exigencies.

In the last resort, Hegel held that the idea, or conceptual identity, of the state was more solidly based in reality than its transitory manifestations in empirical guise. 'What is rational is actual and what is actual is rational' might be a dark and potentially misleading saying; but the thought behind it is neither obscure nor paradoxical (p. 10). When we think about the modern state (rather than this particular state), we call to mind certain universal attributes and functions – a potentially all-embracing and reciprocal relationship between government and governed, a publicly acknowledged legal system applied without discrimination to all ranks and classes in society, administrative provision relating to all matters of public concern. In any specific state these functions will be performed in all manner of ways. The distinction between public and private spheres will differ; law will be variously formulated and enforced; public administration will be more or less extensive. What matters to the philosopher is not how particular functions are performed, but that the community as a whole should be organized into a complex of institutions which reflect a shared responsibility for the public good.

Public responsibilities can, of course, be indifferently or deplorably fulfilled. When Hegel equated 'rationality' with 'actuality', he was not suggesting that whatever institutions happened to exist should be adjudged to be rational and therefore defensible. His point was that the modern state should be identified with a certain general (and, in his day, novel) conception of public life, involving an elaborate series of relationships, rights and duties. Our understanding of ourselves as both individuals and members of communities hinges upon a proper specification of this overall conception, as indeed does our capacity to make intelligent criticisms of the conduct of business in public life. But a political philosophy is not a blueprint for policy; nor can it aspire to more than a provisional understanding of how we happen to see ourselves and our past for the moment.

Hegel makes it clear throughout his argument that he is presupposing the complex institutional adaptations and refinements which have made the modern state what it is. But his attention is fixed on the 'proper immanent development of the thing itself', the rational core which is the truly significant dimension in the long history of political organization (§2). And though the various conceptual stages can often be equated with specific historical innovations, the argument is cast in strictly deductive form. Hegel generates the idea of the modern state, which happens to have emerged historically, from first principles, thus supplying a rational justification for what might otherwise be regarded as merely fortuitous. What he sought was the logical presupposition of institutional life as we know it. And, significantly in the light of his reputation in some quarters as an apologist for the authoritarian state, he found this logical presupposition in the human will.

Hegel saw the whole panoply of institutions, laws, social procedures, practices and relationships as an expression of the human will. He did not mean, of course, that we had each chosen to live in certain ways or had formally endorsed the political and social arrangements of our communities. His point is more fundamental. If we try to think of ourselves as individuals, we find that we cannot but think in terms of social relationships, obligations and duties. Though the specific institutions and relationships we encounter daily may be analytically separable from our identities (we could, after all, have grown up in other cultures), we cannot think of ourselves outside some sort of social framework.

But this is only the beginning of the story. Acknowledging the necessity of some sort of social framework, Hegel invites us to ask ourselves whether we can actually think of our identities other than in terms of (something like) the culture and institutions we have grown up in. His contention is that we should see our political and social institutions as a 'world of mind brought forth out of itself like a second nature', an expression, in other words, of our identities rather than an arbitrary restriction upon our options and possibilities (§4).

Nor does Hegel see his defence of (something like) the prevailing world of institutions as a denial of human freedom. He specifically identifies the will with freedom, not in the sense that we are blessed with an arbitrary capacity to choose the other thing, but because of our nature as thinking beings. Thinking involves evaluating more or less adequate concepts of things, refining our views in certain ways, or embroiling ourselves in error. In each of its operations there is thus an active assertion of ourselves against an initially alien or impenetrable world. Thinking is something we do, not something that simply happens to us. In the light of this active dimension, says Hegel, it is no more possible to conceive of thought without freedom than to imagine bodies without weight (see §4A).

Hegel's account of freedom of the will, though distinctive, is not controversial. Where he leaves his readers uneasy is in his claim that social and political institutions are in fact 'the realm of freedom made actual' (§4). Here we must remind ourselves that he is referring not to institutions which simply happen to exist, but rather to those that reflect the modern state and its potential for the sustenance of human well-being and fulfilment. The crucial point to focus upon is the role of institutions in enabling us to develop our capacities and form conceptions of ourselves. Whether or not we care to admit it, argues Hegel, this is the function that institutions fulfil. We can live and enjoy ourselves in ignorance of this truth; but we would be living a stunted life, oblivious of our natures and tangling our best endeavours in a web of conceptual error.

Will and personality are thus crucial to Hegel's wider account of politics and the state. In the *Philosophy of Right*, however, his discussion of these matters is condensed into a tightly argued introduction. He presupposes that his readers are familiar with the more developed statement of his philosophy of mind in the *Encyclopaedia of the Philosophical Sciences* (1817), and makes few concessions to a more narrowly circumscribed interest.[6] Yet attentive reading provides a sure foundation for later sections of the text dealing with more straightforward ethical and political issues.

Paragraphs 5–7, for example, should be savoured, both for their substantive content and as an illustration of Hegel's characteristic mode of argument. In paragraph 5 he asks us to envisage a perfectly free will, bound by neither external constraints nor physical, social and psychological needs. This he calls 'the pure thought of oneself'.[7] But what exactly do we call to mind? Stripping ourselves of our particular characteristics, roles, obligations, etc., involves setting aside precisely the features that serve to identify us as individuals. We can assume any role in principle; but an actual role cuts us off from the endless options that alone seem to be commensurate with our freedom.

The practical implication of this 'unrestricted possibility of abstraction from every determinate state of mind' is a 'flight from every content as from a restriction' (§5R). In political terms it amounts to a restless dissatisfaction with whatever arrangements happen to prevail. Hegel sees the process at work in the French Revolution, where institutional innovations would always be found wanting when compared with the purity of an ideal, leading revolutionaries to destroy 'once more the institutions which they had made themselves' (§5A). The gulf between an abstract idea of perfection and its realization in practice is so wide that 'giving effect to this idea can only be the fury of destruction' (§5R).

The instability of negative freedom is evident even as we try to characterize it. We might think of ourselves as free to be or do anything; but as soon as we focus upon who we actually are, we find that we have to have recourse to descriptions that seem to commit us to a particular identity and no other. Hegel calls this the 'finitude or particularization of the ego' (§6). It might be regarded as the antithesis of the limitless potential he had portrayed in paragraph 5; yet we cannot avoid limiting descriptions when we speak of willing something.

Paragraphs 5 and 6 each present one-sided pictures of the will. Hegel shows how reflection on the will leads us to see ourselves as both free and bound by circumstances. The apparent contradiction between the two positions is overcome if we modify our views of both freedom and circumstantial constraints. We should see the will, in fact, as 'the unity of both these moments' (§7). When we decide or act we certainly exclude alternative courses of thought or action. But we should think of these commitments not as constraints but as expressions of our identities. Our style of life (career, interests, indulgences, etc.) is not accidentally appended to us, but an embodiment of our individuality. Our friends can say on particular occasions that we have behaved in (or out of) character. In being 'restricted and determinate', we retain our 'self-identity and universality' (§7). We are still free (in principle) to do the other thing, express ourselves in different ways. In pursuing a particular course of conduct, however, we are not denying our freedom, but making a reality of it.

The conception of personal identity advanced in paragraph 7 is purely formal. In arguing that we have necessarily to express our freedom in determinate ways, Hegel has not given grounds for preferring any particular attitudes or patterns of conduct to any other. What he needs in order to sustain his view of the state, though, is precisely a demonstration of the necessity of the institutional framework in which our conceptions of ourselves develop. In other words, he wants us to see the familiar institutions and conventions of our society as no more separable from us than our personal characteristics.

The crucial point, for Hegel, is that institutions should be derivable from the formal properties of the will. He is interested in institutions not as more or less efficient means of advancing human interests (peace, security, well-being or whatever), but as an essential dimension of our identities. We might put the point somewhat differently by asking ourselves what makes individuality possible? To see ourselves as individuals presupposes that we exist in a world of other individuals. At the very least, we must see ourselves as 'persons' – that is, as potential bearers of rights. This is the sphere of what Hegel calls 'abstract right' (see §§34–104). It is a sphere characterized by legal or social recognition, rather than developed relationships. Hegel sums up the 'imperative of right' as: 'Be a person and respect others as persons' (§36). We remain mutually indifferent, but cannot do without one another if we are to have any conception of ourselves at all.

But it is not enough to be simply potential bearers of rights. As Hegel puts the point, 'a person must translate his freedom into an external sphere in order to exist as Idea' (§41). This 'external sphere' is the realm of private property. What we gain through property, however, is not simply the use and enjoyment of things, but an 'embodiment of personality' (§51). The things I own are useful to me; but in a wider sense they give other people some indication of the person I am.

Yet I cannot identify my personality unconditionally with the things I happen to own. Ownership, as an expression of will, presupposes a capacity to sell or transfer possession of a thing when that thing no longer reflects the identity of its owner. Divesting ourselves of things thus involves us in relationships with others. In contracting to buy or sell, for example, we necessarily recognize others as 'persons and property owners' (§71R). Hegel describes 'this relation of will to will' as 'the true and proper ground in which freedom is existent' (§71). In place of the straightforward relation between ourselves and the things we use and enjoy, we now have a complex relationship between agents who have chosen to 'embody' their personalities in particular ways.

With contractual relationships comes the possibility of deception and wrongdoing. Sometimes this will be inadvertent, or 'non-malicious', as when individuals contend over the legitimacy of a title of ownership (see §§84–6). In these cases there is no dispute about the right of ownership, only about the possession of that right. Matters are complicated when one party to a transaction knowingly presents a false claim in the guise of an honest one. Even in cases of fraud, however, the 'principle of rightness' is respected, though the intention is clearly to mislead (§87). Rightness itself is directly challenged in the case of coercion and crime, where an individual seeks to impose his capricious will without regard for propriety. The challenge must be met, since it threatens to undermine the conventional framework that makes the expression of our individuality possible (see §92).

Punishment is justified precisely because it is a reassertion of a necessary condition for the continued flourishing of a community of individuals with varied interests, dispositions, weaknesses and foibles (see §99). A criminal, in trying to impose himself upon others, is implicitly asserting the unconditional right of a particular will to impose itself in whatever way it sees fit. If his conduct were adopted as a universal principle, however, we would be unable either to estimate the consequences of our actions or to anticipate the likely responses of others to our initiatives. Willing of any kind would be problematical. Since the criminal has been asserting the claims of the particular will, his conduct can be regarded as not only wrong, but contradictory. His punishment can thus be seen as a correction in both the legal and conceptual senses, restoring the conditions in which it might be meaningful to deliberate, resolve and act.

Non-malicious wrong, fraud and crime each highlight in their different ways a dilemma which cannot be resolved within the conceptual world of abstract right. Abstract right is best equated in modern terms with formal legal entitlement. The application of that entitlement is largely a procedural matter, ambiguous perhaps in marginal cases (such as minors), but seldom involving a reappraisal of basic principles. But where legal entitlement is wrongly denied, a new situation arises, demanding a response in a particular case which will be unlike any other in detail. What we are concerned with, in the first instance, is a specific crime, not crime as such or even a given class of crimes. A particular problematic situation faces us that *ought* to be remedied. And this 'ought' implies that we have acknowledged the significance of a principle and made it a ground for our own actions. We reassert the value of right in the face of its denial by wrongdoing (see §104).

The crucial dimension which emerges here is self-consciousness. We begin to see ourselves not simply as bearers of rights (and by definition identical with all other bearers of rights), but as subjects with a distinctive identity. In recognizing that a wrong needs to be addressed we have specifically identified ourselves with a principle, adopted a particular course of conduct that fits our view of ourselves. Hegel describes this assumption of responsibility for our characters and actions as the sphere of 'morality' (see §§105–41). It involves a differentiation of ourselves from one another, but, at the same time, a recognition of wider obligations and duties which both facilitate our mutual dealings and enable us to recognize ourselves as individuals.

How can wider responsibilities be generated from reflection upon will and agency? In the first place, we cannot but accept responsibility for our immediate purpose in performing an action without rendering the idea of an action unintelligible. (I am throwing a ball, not simply waving my arms around or enduring involuntary spasms.) But our responsibility initially extends no further than the consequences we actually envisage (see §§117–18). Actions, however, have an external dimension. What we do might spark off a concatenation of reactions that we could reasonably be expected to have anticipated (see §119). (It would make little sense to say that I did not intend to break anything if I were throwing a ball in a china shop.)

Nor would it be realistic to isolate particular actions. We might class various actions together as means towards more general goals ('welfare or happiness') (see §123). And this clearly involves taking stock of our lives and acting with a view to the satisfaction of a certain conception of ourselves. In forming a general view of our fulfilment, however, we necessarily find ourselves taking account of the fulfilment of others, initially as components of our own satisfaction, but later as ends in themselves (see §125). We are thus led to see our actions in ever more complex interrelationship with others, culminating not in a pursuit of particular satisfactions but in an overarching idea of goodness (see §128).

Hegel describes the idea of the good as 'the unity of the concept of the will with the particular will' (§129). The will has now become thoroughly self-determining, choosing to pursue specific goals precisely because they accord with a universal ideal (see §132). But nothing yet has been said about the character of these ideals. Our conception of the good remains formal and self-imposed. We recognize that we should fulfil our duty, but are not told what that duty entails. Indeed, we regard it as essential to our status as free and responsible agents that we should be answerable only to ourselves in the specification of our duties. Duty 'should be done for duty's sake', with appeal neither to tradition nor to authority (§133).

Hegel identifies the formal conception of duty with Kant's moral philosophy. Kant's achievement, according to Hegel, was 'to give prominence to the pure unconditional self-determination of the will as the root of duty' (§135R). But his insistence that duty in particular problematic situations could be determined by universalizing moral judgements ('act only in accordance with that maxim through which you can at the same time will that it become a universal law') was vacuous according to Hegel.[8] If the criterion of good conduct is said to be 'absence of contradiction', then 'no transition is possible to the specification of particular duties'.[9] Without recourse to a 'fixed principle' of some sort, Kant's moral philosophy amounted to an 'empty formalism', opening the way to the justification of any and every 'line of conduct' (§135R). A philosophy that sought to secure moral judgements against contingent considerations had actually made them vulnerable to special pleading.

What makes the Kantian position untenable, in Hegel's view, is its reliance on individual judgement. In the absence of a binding logical resolution of moral disputes, we are left with only conscience to guide us (see §136). But we have no guarantee that our most sincere convictions correspond with a viable system of principles and duties (see §137). We can give or withhold consent to any moral practice (see §138). And our dissatisfaction with some actual practices can readily extend to a rejection of all. With a little ingenuity, we can present our private predilections in the guise of the good, elevating evil itself to the status of a universal principle (see §139). If private conviction is our only criterion, there is nothing to prevent us from defending evil as an end in itself (see §149).

Hegel's analysis highlights a crucial limitation in the 'moral' point of view. That we should act in accordance with principles which fit our conceptions of right conduct is essential to our status as free and responsible agents; but without reference to an actual way of life, our moral reflection can easily prove to be counter-productive, enabling us to distance ourselves from any practices that we might find irksome or restrictive. The dilemma is resolved if we set our moral reflection in proper perspective. Self-conscious deliberation on how we ought to behave necessarily involves abstraction from how we actually behave. Yet it does not follow that we should isolate the moral point of view as (arguably) Kant had done. The things we value are rooted in the complex interrelationships which make up a way of life. Reflection can enable us to find our way around that life, and recognize both its richness and its limitations. But principles alone cannot serve as an adequate foundation for the manifold practices and attitudes that happen to distinguish our conduct of social and political life.

Hegel's point is that our ability to think in principled terms derives from an established moral and institutional framework. He conceives of that framework in the broadest terms, extending from the family, through the various organs of civil society, to the state and the international arena. What institutions supply is precisely the objective point of reference that is so conspicuously lacking in the moral sphere. But they should not be regarded merely as external constraints upon our subjective opinions and caprices. We certainly need institutions in order to function in social and political life; yet at the same time they directly embody our needs, aspirations and awareness of ourselves. We are 'linked to the ethical order by a relation which is more like an identity than even the relation of faith or trust' (§147). When Hegel speaks of institutions being necessary, he has in mind the stronger logical, rather than instrumental, sense.

Nor is the institutional framework which nurtures us morally neutral. Hegel sees institutions as the embodiment of value, furnishing us with a sense of direction and significance which we could not attain through purely conceptual analysis. To identify with our institutional order, whether through 'simple conformity', 'habit' or active endorsement, lends substance to our otherwise ephemeral pursuits, enhancing both our personal dignity and our understanding of the wider importance of familiar patterns of conduct (§§150–3).

Hegel refers to the established institutional order generally as 'ethical life' (see §§142–360). It is something we encounter in the very first moments of our lives, and from which we can never finally detach ourselves. We grow to an initial awareness of ourselves, indeed, not as individuals but as members of a family, where bonds are based upon natural affection rather than reflection (see §158). As lovers, we renounce our individual personalities in union with our partners; as parents or children, we acquire duties and rights that have not been chosen specifically; but we also learn to confront an indifferent or potentially hostile world where affection holds no sway (see §§162, 173–5, 181).

The limitations of the family are both natural and necessary to the development of personality. As children, our identification with the family is unconditional, both in our own eyes and in wider social and legal terms. With adulthood, however, comes an assumption of roles and responsibilities of a quite different kind, involving relations with others based simply on the reciprocal satisfaction of needs and appetites (see §§182–3). This interrelated 'system of needs' is essentially the world of work and consumption (see §§189–208). Hegel understands it broadly in the terms of the classical economists (Smith, Say and Ricardo), though he is more interested in the sociological impact of patterns of work than in mechanisms of production and exchange (see §§189R, 201). He stresses, for example, the varieties of outlook and attitude that are generated as work is divided into narrow specialisms, leaving only a small class of civil servants (the 'universal class') to concern itself with the general interests of the community (see §§202–5). The crucial factor at this stage, though, is that through the system of production and exchange we are mutually dependent upon one another, whether we recognize it or not.

A complex economy, though it might be an integrated system, is not self-regulating. It requires an extensive and comprehensible legal framework to serve as a point of reference for the decisions of individual agents (see §§211–18). And where wrongdoing does occur, individuals must be familiar with the procedures to follow if their particular interests (and, by implication, the interests of the whole community) are to be safeguarded (see §§219–29). What we see in the legal field is explicit recognition of our interdependence in civil society. We become aware, even if only formally, that the pursuit of private satisfactions cannot be isolated from the larger concerns of the community.

Hegel describes the political and legal apparatus characteristic of civil society as 'the external state, the state based on need, the state as the Understanding envisages it' (§183). It is a contrivance for fulfilling limited ends, a more or less useful mechanism enabling us to pursue our private interests, but neither an object of affection nor a dimension in our understanding of ourselves. In theoretical terms, it has become familiar through Hobbes, Locke, Hume, Constant, Humboldt and others, and has enjoyed something of a renaissance in recent times with the resurrection of the 'night-watchman' state in the works of Hayek and Nozick.

For Hegel, however, it is an arrested political form. The exigencies of civil society demand intervention in social and economic life on a scale that makes certain theories of the state obsolete. Civil society is morally significant precisely because it fosters a multiplicity of talents and life-styles; but with variety comes discordance. Interests clash, fortunes are won and lost through chance or misfortune, while at the bottom of the social hierarchy a 'penurious rabble' is created that has neither a stake in society nor any expectation of tangible improvement in its lot (see §§213–45). Anticipating Marx, Hegel had seen that 'despite an excess of wealth civil society is not rich enough' to cater for the needs of the poor (§245). Yet what Marx would see as an incentive for revolution was, for Hegel, an impulse propelling civil society 'beyond its own limits' towards more extensive management of resources, both domestically and internationally (§§246–9).

Nor is social and economic management invariably imposed from above. Within the business class, entrepreneurs begin to accept that their interdependence demands an assumption of responsibility for a whole sector of the economy, and not simply for particular enterprises. Corporations emerge which concern themselves with welfare, education and planning within sectors (see §§250–2). But the affairs of sectors cannot be isolated from the wider interests of society (see §253). Work for the specific interest of a corporation inexorably broadens intellectual horizons, transforming the interdependence that was originally a crude fact of economic life into a guiding principle of policy (see §256).

The organs of civil society never afford more than a partial understanding of the complex relationships that constitute the life of a society. We aspire to an inclusive perspective through the state, where subordinate, and often apparently contradictory, aspects of our lives are set in a wider institutional frame of reference. The conceptions of human nature implicit in family and economic life, for example, might seem at first glance to be irreconcilable. Yet, viewed in a different light, we can accept emotional identification with others and the need for self-assertion as equally necessary to our development. What the state provides is precisely a conceptual and practical focus for our endeavours, enabling us to recognize the larger significance of pursuits that might otherwise seem restrictive and belittling.

Hegel describes the state as 'the actuality of the ethical idea' (§257). His point is not simply that the state embraces the gamut of our moral and practical affairs, but that through the state we are led to identify ourselves with the community which has nurtured and framed our lives. In a purely empirical sense, we might be regarded as the products of long-entrenched customs, practices and habits that are simply handed down from generation to generation. Reflection on the state, however, ensures that we go about our ordinary business with a deeper awareness of social bonds and reciprocal obligations. We may not act differently, but we gain in clear-sightedness.

The point may be clarified in relation to Hegel's concept of freedom. In his view, we are always implicitly free. We cannot conceive of ourselves as agents without invoking notions like deliberation and choice, which presuppose a capacity to do the other thing. But what that freedom amounts to in practice is obscure to us until we gain a proper understanding of the relation between the individual and the community. In the state our rights and duties are embodied in institutions. We wonder what to do not in abstract terms, but in determinate circumstances. Freedom so structured Hegel describes as 'concrete', in contrast to the purely hypothetical capacity to do anything whatever (§260). What the state recognizes is not simply our right under the law to pursue a course of conduct, but our identities and interests as these have emerged in the family and civil society. Our pursuit of private interests becomes, indeed, a contribution to the 'universal end' of the state, cementing bonds within the community and enlarging our social and political understanding (§260).

There is no need to dwell here on the details of Hegel's legal and constitutional proposals. It is important to note, however, that, traditionalist though he was in certain respects, Hegel opposed unthinking adherence to customary practice. He did not share the misgivings of Savigny and the historical school of jurisprudence about the formulation of a systematic legal code. The codification of a system of law in a rational constitution was not, for Hegel, a distortion of a tradition. His contention, rather, was that the ideals which inform a tradition had to be given the status of coherent legal principles before people could fully profit from the educational experience of being members of a political community (see §211R).

The constitution which Hegel recommends is an articulated reflection of the functional interdependence of significant sectors of the community. It is essentially a constitutional monarchy, with a monarch at the head as a symbol of unity and focus of ultimate authority, supported by an executive, in which a dispassionate class of civil servants serves as guardian of the higher interests of the state, and a bicameral Assembly of Estates, representing the particular concerns and dispositions of agricultural and business classes (see §§275–320). We may quibble with Hegel about the proper distribution of roles and responsibilities. The point to stress, however, is that he saw a constitution not simply as a means of channelling the exercise of power, but (more importantly) as a public expression of the character and identity of the community.

Hegel presents political life very much as a voyage of discovery, leading us to a proper appreciation of our relations with the community and the state. The harsh tone of his dismissal of the abstract individualism so characteristic of seventeenth- and eighteenth-century political theory has often alarmed readers accustomed to seeing the state as a vehicle to serve the interests of the individual. He attributes to the state, for example, a 'supreme right against the individual, whose duty is to be a member of the state' (§258). And in the international arena, where conflicts between states can sometimes be resolved only by war, he sees the sacrifice of the individual for the good of the state as a 'universal duty' (§325). But we should be clear that, though the state encompasses our lives, it nevertheless preserves ample scope for the expression of our personal interests. We identify with the state as the public embodiment of our culture; but the state does not assume the detailed direction of all our affairs.

We have come a long way from Hegel's initial characterization of will and agency. He sought to explain the structure of modern political institutions as a corollary of the properties of the human will, linking our inner life inextricably with a wider social and political context. It was an audacious undertaking. Whether his argument is ultimately successful remains a hotly contested issue. Few philosophers today would follow the form of his argument, presenting as it does a variety of more or less plausible transitions in deductive guise. Nor is the metaphysical view which underpins his system widely held to be compelling. More narrowly conceived, however, his political philosophy advances an analysis of the modern state as penetrating as any that has come down to us. He has shown how modern political and economic life demands at once ample freedom for the pursuit of private interests and intense identification with the community. Precisely how the institutional balance between these conflicting demands should be struck is still a vexed question. In one sense, of course, this is a perennial dilemma, going back to Plato and beyond. Hegel's *Philosophy of Right* is a sustained philosophical analysis of the issue as it emerged in the aftermath of the French Revolution. Much has changed in our day to make the state both more pervasive and more alarming. But Hegel's terms of reference continue to be indispensable for an understanding of the philosophical significance of institutions, focusing our pursuit of self-knowledge on the mutual involvement of public and private worlds.

5 The Nation-State

Constitutional theory in the nineteenth century was much more concerned with containing the state than involving people in public life. Yet a principle of popular legitimacy could hardly be avoided, as political functionaries found themselves directing, regulating and educating populations on an ever-increasing scale. Liberal fear of popular enthusiasm gave the doctrine an elitist, class-based ethos. Nationalism, by contrast, which also had roots in the French revolutionary identification of the people as a sovereign body, was cast in broader terms. Though, like liberalism, it was very closely associated with the newly emerging professional and business classes, nationalism as an ideology was never simply a political guise for their social and economic interests. Nationalists could defend a seemingly endless range of (often contradictory) constitutional and policy positions. Where they came together was in their insistence that the identity of the nation confers value and legitimacy on the state. The capacity of this notion for popular mobilization was unprecedented.

The roots of nationalism, however, should be sought beyond the sphere of politics. It emerged initially in the eighteenth century as a reaction against the hegemony of French culture in the world of European literature. In the minds of most intellectuals, France and the Enlightenment had been identified as the height of civilization and refinement. Yet to critics such as Herder, especially in his early writings (1769–74), French cultural supremacy was intellectually and morally ruinous. Herder contended that Enlightenment thinkers had tended to adopt an abstract, generalizing vocabulary, blind to the subtle distinctions and nuances embedded in local cultural traditions. What made matters worse was that German or Italian or Czech writers were being encouraged to couch their work in an idiom and style modelled essentially on French work. Peoples were being alienated from their roots.

The only way to halt the decline was to foster local cultures. Herder himself spent a great deal of time seeking to restore national traditions through collections of folktales and songs. He loathed the 'good taste' and 'decorum' of high (French) culture, and admired instead the 'natural' products of unsophisticated cultures. Homer and Ossian were his favoured poets, not Pope and Racine. In his travel diary of 1769 he gives a bitter account of the artificial education to which he and his contemporaries had been subjected, an education calculated to stifle any spontaneity or original thought.[1]

> O you great masters of all time, you Moses and Homers! You sang from
> inspiration! You planted what you sang in eternal metre, in which it was held
> fast; and thus it could be sung again for as long as men wanted to sing it. We
> in our dull, uncertain prose, at the mercy of ourselves and of every passing
> moment, repeat ourselves and drone prosaically on until at last we say
> nothing any more.[2]

Herder's is a panegyric to the creative possibilities of primitive cultures,
rather than the measured rationalism of the French Enlightenment.

Herder's distance from the Enlightenment is best gauged from a consideration of *Yet Another Philosophy of History* (1774). The aim of this work is
openly polemical. It is a response to an age that acknowledged 'only one
authentic voice'.[3] The attempt to classify phenomena as types of occurrence,
particular examples of universal laws, was anathema to Herder. He considered the comparison of things essentially unique to be blindness to a realm
of experience. 'In order to feel the whole nature of the soul which reigns
in everything, which models after itself all other tendencies and all other
spiritual faculties, and colours even the most trivial actions, do not limit your
response to a word, but penetrate deeply into this century, this region, this
entire history, plunge yourself into it all and feel it all within yourself – then
only will you be in a position to understand; then only will you give up the idea
of comparing everything, in general or in particular, with yourself.'[4] The only
way to make sense of history or culture, on this view, is to immerse yourself in
it; impose an alien classification, and you are lost before you have begun.

The comparative method, moreover, according to Herder, is based on
a misunderstanding of the nature of society. He saw life as an intimate relationship of struggle between nature and tradition. A particular climate and
natural environment encourages particular occupations; a tradition emerges
which is the heritage of a particular struggle, the acquired wisdom that
enables decisions to be made without recourse to the drawing board;
a language sums up the spirit of a society in its unique struggle for existence.
The criteria by which we judge a particular society should not be the
(purportedly) universal maxims of the philosopher; they emerge in a particular situation and are valid only in that situation. 'Each form of human
perfection then, is, in a sense, national and time-bound and, considered
most specifically, individual' (p. 184). For Montesquieu, on this question of
the comparative method, Herder reserves the full force of his sardonic pen.

> Words torn from their context and heaped up in three or four market-places
> under the banner of three wretched generalizations – mere words, empty,
> useless, imprecise and all-confusing words, however spirited. The work is a
> frenzy of all times, nations and languages like the Tower of Babel, so that
> everyone hangs his goods and chattels on three weak nails. The history of all
> times and peoples, whose succession forms the great, living work of God, is
> reduced to ruins divided neatly into three heaps, to a mere collection even
> though it does not lack noble and worthy material. O, Montesquieu! (p. 217)

Herder's specific focus is on the value of particularity. Not only is he antag-onistic to the tendency to reduce history to order under the head of certain arbitrary generalizations, he is also opposed to the habit, dominant in the Enlightenment, of judging historical periods from the standpoint of the pre-sent. He is not content, for example, to dismiss the ignorance and super-stition of the medieval period, the so-called dark ages; rather, his concern is to understand each period or culture on its own terms, as a unique contribution of the human spirit. He stresses empathy as a necessary condition of cultural understanding, enabling observers to grasp the organic nature of societies.

> All the books of our Voltaires, Humes, Robertsons and Iselins are, to the delight of their contemporaries, full of beautiful accounts of how enlighten-ment and improvement of the world, philosophy and order, emerged from the bleaker epochs of theism and spiritual despotism. All this is both true and untrue. It is true if, like a child, one holds one colour against another, if one wishes to contrive a bright, contrasty little picture – there is, alas, so much light in our century! It is untrue, if one considers the earlier epoch according to its intrinsic nature and aims, its pastimes and mores, and espe-cially as the instrument of the historical process. (pp. 191–2)

Herder considers all periods and cultures to be intrinsically valuable. 'I cannot persuade myself that anything in the kingdom of God is only a means – everything is both a means and an end simultaneously, now no less than in the centuries of the past' (p. 194).

On this view, the unique perspective of each culture should always be accorded normative priority. Above all, for Herder, it was language that distinguished natural cultural units. Individuals identified with their language at the most basic level. They acquired not only a means of commu-nication, but a broader perspective that made the world intelligible to them. A view of culture that countenanced neglect of so much that was important to people ran the risk of moral and intellectual atrophy.

A concern with roots and identity became a leading theme in later nation-alist writings. So, too, did Herder's rejection of the idea of progress. Where Enlightenment thinkers had tended to see the past as a succession of types of society culminating in the present, Herder, instead, saw a society as a unique focus of a particular way of life. His nationalism, indeed, was of a deeply apolitical kind. He thought in terms of cultural diversity, language, shared myths and traditions, rather than in specifically political categories. He had a profound suspicion of the modern state as a vast bureaucratic machine that would tend either to ignore or to trample upon the distinctive customs of local communities.

What transformed nationalism into a political movement was the reaction against the attempt to return to a system of dynastic politics in 1815 following the defeat of Napoleon. Peoples had grown accustomed to new styles of polit-ical thought and practice, and new loyalties had emerged. Problems were most acute in the sprawling Austrian Empire. Educated Slavs, Hungarians or Italians simply could not identify with rule from Vienna. Within these suppressed nations (for that is how they began to regard themselves) movements arose with a very clear political objective – to rid the nation of foreign rule. The ideal of national self-government was thrust to the forefront of political debate, with the question of the kind of constitutional arrangement that might be appropriate for a community being treated as a secondary issue.

The most striking representative of this new style of nationalism was Giuseppe Mazzini (1805–72). His bent was much more for propaganda than systematic social or political theory. In 1831 he created the organization *Young Italy*, geared to the formation of a united Italian republic through popular insurrections. And indeed, throughout his career, much of it spent in exile in England after 1837, he was indefatigable in keeping the idea of a united Italy before the educated public in a stream of impassioned publications. Despite a deep personal commitment to republican principles, he always stressed that he would support any movement devoted to the liberation of Italy from foreign rule. He insisted, however, that liberation should be the work of Italians themselves, and not the product of a fortunate concatenation of diplomatic circumstances. The manner in which Italian unity was finally achieved in 1861 thus deeply disappointed him.[5] And he remained an embittered and isolated man until his death in 1872.

Mazzini's nationalism had a specifically political focus. Yet he shared many of the assumptions that had informed Herder's view. He rejected, for example, abstract 'scientific' analysis of history and society, focusing instead on identification with the non-reflective attitudes and dispositions that he saw as the foundation of a way of life. He also opposed the narrow individualism that the Enlightenment had bequeathed (in his view) to liberal thought. What mattered to him was not so much that individuals should be enabled to pursue their particular interests, but that they should be aware of the ties which bound them to their communities. Harmony and co-operation were his watchwords. The stress on competition and conflict in contemporary liberal and socialist doctrines was for him a principal obstacle to the well-being of communities. Instead, he contended that individuals would grow in moral stature only by co-operating in a common enterprise. Hence it was crucial for him that a people's sense of identity (formed through the medium of language, education, cultural traditions and so forth) should be reflected in their political institutions.

Mazzini's early writings addressed literary themes, almost exclusively, yet he was clear in his own mind that the literary controversies of his day were implicitly political. The great debate between romantics and classicists directly raised the question of the relation between literature and its social and political context. Mazzini's sympathies were entirely with the romantics. In an essay of 1828 he claimed that the romantics 'want to give Italy an original, national literature, a literature that is not simply pleasing to the ear . . . but which interprets the events, the needs, the ideas of the social movement'.[6] And in another essay of the same year he endorsed the view of Herder, Schlegel and others that 'the intellectual life of peoples should not be separated from their civil and political life'.[7]

Mazzini's commitment to the politics of national liberation thus had broad cultural roots, and was by no means focused narrowly on Italian cultural experience. His most significant early essay, published in the influential journal *Antologia* in 1829 and significantly entitled 'On European Literature', linked developments within particular nations to the wider sweep of a civilizing process that would embrace Europe as a whole.[8] He insists, in the first place, on the need for literature to adapt to the requirements of a changing social and political climate. He describes 'literature which is not involved with the civil and political life of the nations' as 'trifling and debilitating to the mind' (p. 178). His point is not that literature should simply reflect changing fashions, but rather, that it is an integral part of a wider network of institutions that will determine the development and fortune of a community for better or worse. Political argument could not ignore a wider cultural context.

Developments towards national unification in Italy, for Mazzini, were but an aspect of a wider process that would be evident throughout Europe. Everywhere the trend was away from the radical individualism that had been characteristic of the Enlightenment and the French Revolution, and towards a deeper awareness of the ties that bound communities together. These sentiments were more basic than a straightforward recognition of mutual interests, embracing unspoken assumptions embedded in a way of life. A national literature was perhaps uniquely fitted to give expression to a bedrock of shared feeling. But Mazzini insists that a vigorous national literature should be neither narrow nor insular. Awareness of national identity necessarily involved recognition of the identity and autonomy of other nations. Nationalism, in Mazzini's formulation, can thus be seen as a European phenomenon that reinforces the bonds between separate peoples. The lesson for Italy was clear: 'the specific history of nations is ending; European history is beginning; and Italy cannot allow herself to be isolated in the midst of a common movement' (p. 218).

A great future thus beckoned both Italy and Europe. But it would come to fruition only if the separate nations were able to establish themselves on a proper foundation. They required both 'political independence and moral unity', not in order to assert claims against each other, but rather as a means of making their distinctive contributions to an evolving European culture (p. 219). Mazzini, at this stage of his career, had yet to work out the political dimension of his argument in detail. But he had a developed view of the dynamics of historical change and institutional interaction that would serve as the basis for the elaboration of more narrowly political strategies in the 1830s.

In 1831 Mazzini's thinking focused almost exclusively on analysis of the underlying shortcomings of revolutionary tactics in Italy since 1815. Whatever the next steps forward might be, it was clear to him that little would be achieved until the lessons of revolutionary failure had been thoroughly assimilated. Mazzini was convinced that the political transformation of Italy required (at least) the acquiescence of broad sections of the population. Yet such acquiescence would not be forthcoming if insurrectionary activity were left in the hands of small sects whose ultimate objectives might well be obscure even to some of their active members. A necessary backdrop to a successful and co-ordinated insurrectionary campaign should be an elaborate propaganda exercise.

A more broadly based revolutionary strategy was thus a crucial requirement for Mazzini. To this end, while exiled in Marseilles in 1831, he focused his energy on the mobilization of a new movement, *Young Italy*, which would combine the dual aims of educating the people politically and organizing popular insurrections. Immediate political goals would be set in the widest ideological context. Mazzini explained the rationale of the movement in his 'Manifesto of *Young Italy*' (1831). He felt himself to be engaged in a battle of ideas that would encourage groups untouched by sectarian activity to flock to the standard of a free, independent and united Italy. 'The truth', he claimed, 'is indivisible', and for the most part already received.[9] The point of the movement was to explore the implications of this central moral insight in such a way that each and every individual would be in a position to further the Italian cause. The tone was thus didactic and exhortatory. Mazzini had grasped the significance of ideology as a political weapon. He was aware that a political message had to be projected and reiterated incessantly in a readily assimilable form. His initial statement of the principles of *Young Italy* might be taken as a model of ideological propaganda. Italians are brought together by geography and language, but political commitment gives them identity. 'The nation', he declares, 'is the universality of Italians, united by agreement and living under a common law.'[10] Nature can provide only the circumstances in which nations might arise. It is for people to embrace that possibility for themselves, growing in moral stature as they strive to bring that political identity to fulfilment.

Mazzini was intent upon rallying Italians to the national cause. But he was adamant that the cause would not be advanced simply by appealing to a lowest common denominator of political support. 'The strength of an association', he insists, 'is to be found not in the numbers' of its followers so much as in the 'homogeneity' and 'harmony' of its support (p. 46). Given the urgency of the political task, it was thus essential that ideological goals be formulated with crystal clarity. Members of *Young Italy* should be in no doubt about the political complexion of the Italy they were struggling to attain. The movement 'is republican and unitary' (p. 47). Mazzini's more narrowly political thought was built around these two principles. He could envisage temporary tactical alliances with monarchical groups in particular circum-stances; but he would not countenance any deviation from the commitment to a unitary state.

Of the two principles, republicanism was the more straightforward to defend in the 1830s. In the 'General Instructions for Associates in *Young Italy'* Mazzini could do little more than hint at a barrage of arguments that had enjoyed wide currency in radical circles since the French Revolution. He saw republicanism as the only political principle which recognized the 'liberty, equality and fraternity' of all men, with 'sovereignty' residing 'essentially in the nation' (p. 47). Hereditary monarchy he saw simply as the embodiment of despotism, while elective monarchy tended always 'to generate anarchy' (p. 48). Nor could he accept the monarchical principle as a natural product of modern Italian history. Neither a national monarchy nor a national aristoc-racy had emerged; and any attempt to exalt the position of one of the estab-lished Italian monarchies would either weaken the commitment of the other Italian states or undermine the national movement by attempting to balance too many regional interests. The lessons of history pointed unambiguously in a republican direction. Echoing Sismondi, Mazzini insisted that 'the Italian tradition is entirely republican' (p. 48). Despite the apparent absence of republican institutions in Italy in the 1830s, popular attitudes and dispos-itions were wholly in accord with the republican principle. If one had once decided that a united Italy would emerge only in the wake of a popular revo-lution, it followed that a revolutionary movement could only be republican in tone, since 'to arouse a whole people it is necessary to have a goal that directly and intelligibly reflects their rights and advantages' (p. 49).

Unitarism presented far more problems. The reality of French power and policy in the revolutionary and Napoleonic periods, coupled with suspicions of the efficacy of French revolutionary leadership since 1815, had led radicals to look beyond the Jacobin model of a unitary state.[11] Mazzini was clearly concerned. Though anxious to distance himself from the francophile current in the revolutionary movement, he was deeply suspicious of the federal proposals that had surfaced in the 1820s. He had always regarded federalism as a mantle for the assertion of the privileges of local elites. All it would achieve in the Italian situation was the reinforcement of the municipalism that had been a principal obstacle to the emergence of national conscious-ness. In later writings the theme became something of a preoccupation, especially as the federal movement gathered momentum in Italy.[12] All he could do in the 'General Instructions', however, was to reiterate the unitarist position in the most emphatic terms.

Mazzini declares roundly that 'without unity there is not truly a nation', stressing the need for Italy to defend herself against potentially hostile powers.[13] In internal affairs, federalism would foster the rivalry of local groups, pushing Italy 'back towards the middle ages' (p. 50). Regional aris-tocracies would emerge which would quickly erode the efforts that past generations had made to sustain genuinely national sentiment. In the wider international sphere, federalism ran counter to the trend towards large unitary states throughout Europe, thus threatening to undermine Italy's special mission for humanity.

What objections to unitarism amounted to was a fear that centralization inevitably entailed despotism. In Mazzini's view, however, this was to confuse political centralization with administrative centralization. He championed the 'inherent life of localities', and sought to set 'administrative organization' on the widest possible foundation. Yet there could be no alternative to centralization in relation to the political representation of the 'nation in Europe' (p. 50). Mazzini focused specifically on 'unity of belief and a social consensus', with a corresponding 'unity in education and representation' and a homogeneous system of 'political, civil and penal legislation' (p. 50). The nation was not simply there as a fact of national life, but had to be nurtured, cultivated, brought to fruition. The significance of politics was that it focused attention on common bonds which nature, history and culture had forged over centuries. Political arrangements badly conceived, on the other hand, could stunt the nation's growth and development, forestalling the flowering of a people's potential. The problem with federalism, for Mazzini, was precisely that it reflected the weakest and most backward aspects of Italian social and political practice. An Italian state cast in its image would amount to little more than a political rearrangement, setting back the social and cultural rebirth which nationalists anticipated in a new scheme of things.

Throughout his career Mazzini was haunted by the prospect of a sectional interest usurping the position of the nation as a whole. But his discussions of precisely how the national interest might be expressed are far from clear. Following Rousseau, he held that sovereignty was indivisible and was derived not from a set of authoritative procedures but from a substantive moral truth. In *On the Duties of Man*, for example, written in 1859, he identified the moral law with God's providential design. But he was no more successful than Rousseau in pinning down the moral law to any specific authoritative pronouncements. It would be revealed to men, he claims, through the 'inspiration of men of genius and the tendencies of humanity in the diverse epochs' of its history.[14] He denies, crucially, that sovereignty can ever reside in either the individual or society 'except insofar as the one and the other are in line with that design, with that law, and direct themselves to its end' (p. 910). Legitimate government should be distinguished from tyranny only in terms of adherence to the moral law. Mazzini's dismissal of constitutional mechanisms is scathing. 'The straightforward vote of a majority does not constitute sovereignty if it evidently contravenes the supreme moral law or deliberately obstructs the path to future progress. Social good, liberty, progress: outside of these three terms sovereignty cannot exist' (p. 910). Moderate constitutionalists who looked askance at Mazzini certainly knew their man.

Mazzini's view of the state was never fully worked out. In 1831 he had been sensitive to the threat posed to his conception of the national movement by the growing popularity of federalism. He was aware of the appeal of federalism to those who sought a purely political solution to the Italian question. A loose institutional arrangement could be devised that would harmonize procedures in certain spheres without undermining the basic autonomy of the constituent states. Local interests would remain secure, and cultural and linguistic identity need not be threatened. In short, things could carry on very much as before. This was precisely Mazzini's objection. His advocacy of unification stemmed not from political or geographical neatness, but from a passionate desire to see a general regeneration in Italian life, embracing moral and spiritual as well as social and economic affairs. Ambition on this scale would necessarily challenge established interests. Hence Mazzini was insistent that an Italian state required a central political focus in order to shake local elites out of their complacency.

Mazzini's most sustained treatment of these issues was in an essay which he began in 1833 and did not finally complete until 1861.[15] 'On Italian Unity' is more closely argued than his overtly propagandist articles and pamphlets. He takes the federalist case seriously, seeking to rebut both the historical account which had tended to underpin federalist positions and the prospective impact that federalist proposals were likely to have on subsequent Italian development.

Not the least interesting aspect of 'On Italian Unity' is that Mazzini should choose to return to it after twenty-eight years marked by bitter arguments for and against federalism that had divided the national movement.[16] The perspective cannot have afforded him much comfort. The unitary principle had certainly triumphed, but in a form which involved the sacrifice of much that he held dear. The elitism of the Italy 'reborn' in 1861 was a severe disappointment to him. Cavour and the Piedmontese moderates had exploited popular enthusiasm for their own ends, ensuring that power and influence remained in their hands, trusting more to diplomatic intrigue than to popular initiative. But it was men and methods that Mazzini questioned, not the unitary state itself.

What, then, were Mazzini's objections to federalism? He was concerned, in the first place, to strike at the root of a view that had begun to erode support for unitarism even among republicans. The conventional wisdom regarding the Jacobin-inspired experiments of the 1790s attributed their failure to the abstract and unrealistic character of their proposals.[17] The language of rights, citizenship and sovereignty had been deployed (so the argument went) with little awareness of the problems that might be encountered when attempts were made to put such notions into practice. Radical reform had been mooted in the name of the people; but very often the people would respond, as at Naples in 1799, by rallying to the defence of local practices and institutions. Schemes which could be regarded as unrealistic in the years of French hegemony had begun to seem dangerously utopian after the settlement of 1815. With experience of revolutionary failure in the 1820s came a yearning for a political doctrine more closely attuned to the conditions and traditions of the Italian regions. Federalism, at least to some observers, appeared to fit the bill.

Mazzini's tactic was to turn the federalist analysis on its head. Federalists might claim that their proposals reflected the polycentric nature of Italian society; that polycentrism, however, far from being a product of indigenous patterns of development, was itself a consequence of the internal dismemberment of Italy by foreign powers. Mazzini insists that 'the states into which Italy has been divided for more than three hundred years did not emerge spontaneously from popular sentiments or trends, but were created by diplomacy, by foreign usurpation and by force of arms'.[18] The much-vaunted realism of the federalists was, in fact, based upon a misreading of Italian history. The natural tendency of Italian history had been entirely in a unitary direction. Federalist proposals, if adopted, would simply serve to reinforce extraneous institutions and practices, perpetuating the divisive trends that had so weakened Italy in past centuries.[19]

Mazzini's sketch of the roots of unitarism is unlikely to impress modern historians. His appeal to the political aspirations of Dante and Machiavelli is convincing enough, but he is on shakier ground when he hints at the institutional developments that are alleged to have sustained the unitary idea.[20] The extensive development of communes from the ninth to the thirteenth century is read as evidence of a 'progressive rapprochement of customs and habits' (p. 300). Even the conflict between the papacy and the empire, which might more naturally be taken to be indicative of a basic political and cultural rift, is seen by Mazzini as an integral step on the road to unity, with 'Italians feeling the need to align themselves' behind one or the other standard (p. 300). Whatever the merits of Mazzini's detailed argument (and he was aware of its limitations, writing as he was 'wandering from house to house, fleeing the persecutions of the French and Italian police'), he is adamant that 'whoever looks at our history with the eye of a philosopher will discover in the trend to unity a generative idea, the life and soul of our affairs' (pp. 300–1).

Mazzini relied on historical analysis, too, in his dismissal of specific federalist claims. Federalists had begun to justify their Italian proposals by appealing to the example of established federal states. Switzerland and the United States of America were often cited as viable alternatives to the unitary state, securing both civil liberty and a cohesive foreign policy. Mazzini, however, insists that the federal state, by its very nature, is bound to be weak in relation to bordering unitary states; and that the liberty which federal states enjoy is necessarily narrowly based, perpetuating the interests of aristocracies threatened by political, economic and social changes.

He ranges widely in his argument. The ancient Greek confederacies are treated simply as responses to difficult international situations, with the separate polities recognizing their mutual vulnerability. But confederal institutions were never strong enough to counter domestic ambitions and rivalries, or to prevent the domination of either foreign powers or one of the constituent polities. In the last resort, the Greek federations proved to be impotent in the face of Roman expansion, emphasizing the weakness of 'all federations confronted by a unitary power' (p. 280).

Modern examples, however, were clearly more germane to the political task in hand. Switzerland, in particular, was very much in vogue in federalist circles, 'particularly among those who proclaim against the utopianism of republican defenders of the unitary state' (p. 282). Switzerland's neutrality, the skill with which she had exploited a European balance of power which had kept her free from foreign invasion, the heterogeneous elements that composed her population, with their diverse beliefs, institutions and practices, seemed to single Switzerland out as a model for Italians to follow. Indeed, there was a clear tendency to idealize Switzerland. Her people were seen to be 'happy and peace loving', sustaining the 'innocence and purity of their customs and habits', free from the 'ambitions, quarrels and corruption' of the wider European world (p. 282). Swiss reality was for Mazzini quite otherwise, however. Whatever simplicity and innocence she might enjoy should be attributed rather to 'education and natural poverty' than to her federal institutions (p. 282). A deeper examination of Swiss history, in fact, revealed anything but innocence. Swiss development had been marked by 'wars and internal massacres prompted by religious intolerance', insidious conflict between competing aristocracies, with the destabilizing influence of foreign powers upsetting the policies of the cantons (p. 282). Far from guaranteeing liberty under the law, federalism had actually secured a balance of regional and class enmities. 'The only consequence that could be attributed to Switzerland from the federation was the inequality of civil development in the various cantons, an inequality which perpetuated seeds of discord that are now more than ever evident in the country' (p. 284).

What made the adoption of Switzerland as a model all the more absurd was the specific circumstances that had nurtured federal institutions in the first place. The association of cantons that constituted the Swiss polity had developed gradually over centuries, as local elites sought to secure their interests in difficult circumstances. Italians, on the other hand, were striving to make a nation for themselves, inspired by shared convictions and a common conception of the future. It would be folly, accordingly, to follow a path that had been forced on Switzerland only by circumstances. 'Events created the Swiss federation; among us it would be nothing but a capricious act of will' (p. 285).

The United States posed rather different problems for Mazzini. Certain of the drawbacks that he had identified as endemic to federal systems had yet to manifest themselves in the United States. Federalism could hardly be seen as a buttress for a declining aristocracy, since an identifiable aristocracy had not emerged. Nor would a federal constitution seriously handicap the United States in its external relations, because significant competitors were simply not at hand. A financial aristocracy would doubtless establish itself in due course; but in a new country with immense possibilities for expansion, it might very well take a radically different form from the aristocracies of the Old World.

The United States had clearly developed in unusual circumstances. Mazzini does not deny its strength, resilience or potential power. But what sorts of lessons could Europeans draw from an experience so remote from their own? Mazzini is emphatic. 'Whoever tries to apply the example of the United States specifically to Italy violates every law of analogy, sees uniform conditions where there are none, forgets history and topography' (p. 289).

It was easy enough to understand the attraction of the United States to Europeans weary of their own intractable problems. But if serious efforts are made to identify the precise contribution of the federal constitution to the well-being of the country as a whole, the balance of advantage is by no means entirely positive. A confederal or federal arrangement might originally have been seen as a fitting reflection of the diverse origins, customs and experience of settlers, living and working in isolated and strikingly different circumstances from one another; but a federal system also served to perpetuate differences and to sow seeds of discord. Writing in 1833, Mazzini noted that a state's notional right to secede from the union was very likely to issue in serious civil strife sooner or later. In a footnote added in 1861, with civil war raging in the United States, he felt able to congratulate himself on his prescience (see p. 291).

What finally counted against federalism, for Mazzini, was its growing irrelevance in an age dominated by the interrelationship of larger social groups. He saw federal theory in its developed form as a typical product of the waning age of individualism, when primary emphasis had been placed on the defence of individual rights against potentially tyrannical government (see pp. 266–7). Constitutional procedures which had been devised to forestall the depredations of absolute monarchs made little sense, however, in an age of popular politics. As Rousseau had previously observed, it would be futile to try to defend the people against themselves.[21] Mazzini's concern was to mobilize the people in a common cause, not to institute procedural impediments which would set different groups apart from one another. The divisions which were all too obvious in Italy to the superficial observer would (in his view) only be reinforced by federalism.

Mazzini urged Italians to look to the future rather than the past. Federalism had served a purpose in other contexts. The principal need now was to embrace the national principle whole-heartedly, focusing on the ties that bound Italians together rather than the conflicts of interest that divided them. The identity of the nation was implicit in Italian history. But without political expression, it would only ever enjoy a stunted life, overlaid by regional and economic rivalries. But the regeneration of the nation depended crucially on the form of the state. Italians could either seek to accommodate the established balance of regional power in a federal state or pursue a brighter future in a world destined to revolve increasingly around the national principle. On both moral and historical grounds, Mazzini could see no alternative to the unitary state.

It would be misleading to suggest that Mazzini was original either in his portrayal of the state or in his wider nationalism. He shared many of the assumptions of earlier 'cultural' nationalists. His conception of a nation's unique mission is very much in accord with the views expressed in Herder's early writings, where universal criteria of judgement are rejected in favour of a panoply of perspectives, each uniquely valuable in itself. To be sure, Mazzini did not match Herder's breadth of sympathy. His preoccupation with the larger sweep of historical development, rather, left smaller nations out of account. The French had fulfilled their mission by bringing the age of individualism to a close with the Revolution; the Italians were destined to inaugurate a new age of national harmony; but smaller nations could well find themselves swallowed up in wider regional groupings. Writing in 1857, Mazzini could find no place on the political map of Europe for Austria, the various Slav nations, Holland, Belgium or Ireland.[22] But, of course, such narrowness of vision was not uncommon among nationalists. Even Michelet, whose radical credentials were impeccable, sought to mobilize the French people around a very specific image of their civilizing mission.[23] Mazzini differed from Michelet only over which nation's hour had struck.

Mazzini had absorbed, too, the communitarian assumptions that were a common property in Romantic historical and political thought.[24] Thinkers across the political spectrum had come to regard Enlightenment individualism as narrow and restrictive, reducing human beings to calculators of material advantage. Mazzini's language, indeed, with its stress on duty to the community, self-sacrifice, harmony and co-operation, might well, in other circumstances, have marked him out as a man of conservative inclinations. The emphasis on competition and conflict in contemporary liberal and socialist doctrines seemed to him a major obstacle to the well-being of communities; and though he did not go so far as to subordinate the individual to the state, he never wavered in his belief in the superior moral value of co-operation in a common enterprise.

What made Mazzini a radical was his insistence that community values could not flourish if artificial constraints were placed upon development. Foreign rule or dominance had distorted the natural pattern of institutional relationships throughout Italy, leading to the emergence of local elites whose positions of authority depended upon foreign political patronage, setting groups and individuals against one another within regions, and region against region in the wider context. Mazzini's ambition was to restore the functional harmony which should have obtained naturally, enabling Italians to perform particular roles in full awareness of their obligations to, and dependence upon, their fellow citizens. Not only would future economic, social and cultural progress thereby be guaranteed, but consciousness of national identity would be sharpened by being brought into political focus.

But Mazzini's nationalism was never narrowly Italian in scope. His early essays in literary criticism had stressed the need for Italian writers to assimilate and respond to European themes, without thereby undervaluing the distinctive contributions which Italians had made to European culture.[25] In the 1830s he adopted an analogous stance in the political field. He had always been aware of the wider European implications of the Italian national revolution. Indeed, the Italian campaign was, for him, but the first step on the road to the liberation of other European nations whose development had been stunted by dynastic and imperial rivalries.

Mazzini felt himself to be engaged in a struggle not only against oppressive foreign rule in Italy, but also against mistaken conceptions of revolution and liberation. Older-style revolutionaries still thought essentially in the cosmopolitan categories that the French Enlightenment had bequeathed to European thought. Yet this cast of mind, according to Mazzini, had reached its apogee in the French revolutionary period, and had proved to be incapable of responding to the demands of the new century. What Mazzini sought was a revolutionary movement which would set collective goals rather than individual rights at its centre. Popular nationalism was the perfect vehicle for his ideas, destined, as he saw it, to give 'its name to the century'.[26]

Mazzini's first organizational venture into wider European nationalism occurred with the formation of *Young Europe* in 1834. He had conceived of *Young Europe* specifically as a sister movement to *Young Italy*. Yet, from the outset, he was under no illusions about its practical effectiveness. It was formed very much in response to the failure of insurrectionary initiatives in Savoy and Lyon. There was no serious prospect in 1834 of orchestrating revolutionary activity on a European scale. Mazzini saw *Young Europe*, instead, as an alternative focus for the revolutionary movement. Even as a forum for the propagation of ideas, however, *Young Europe* only ever enjoyed a most exiguous existence. It was identified so closely with Mazzini himself that his revolutionary rivals could only look upon it with the deepest suspicion. In itself it might be said to have been stillborn. But it remains important as an indication of the distinctive character of Mazzini's nationalism.

Young Europe underlined the international dimension in Mazzini's thinking. He envisaged in a distant future a federal republic of European nations. Each nation would have rid itself of foreign rule, and would henceforth be able to co-operate with its neighbours in peace. Once a nation had acquired its own political institutions, it would have no further need to assert itself. Internal security and war, the preoccupations of the politics of the *ancien régime*, would have faded from the scene along with kings. What Mazzini pictures is a delightful harmony in which each nation makes its distinctive contribution. A nation, like an individual, has 'a particular mission to fulfil'; and in fulfilling that mission, it 'necessarily makes a contribution to the general mission of humanity'.[27] Italy thus found herself crucially placed in the developing international situation. Her challenge to Austria would mark the first breach in the outmoded imperial edifice, enabling other nations to emerge on the European political stage.

Mazzini's practical achievements were limited. Insurrections planned for Savoy and Naples in 1833–4 were abortive; and various uprisings in the Kingdom of Naples after 1837, culminating in the failure of the Bandiera brothers in 1844, were easily suppressed.[28] To many sceptical observers it seemed that Mazzini had simply encouraged idealistic young men to embark upon foolhardy expeditions that would almost certainly cost them their lives. But even failure has propaganda value. Mazzini had become the *bête noire* of the authorities. Though the insurrections he inspired might look pathetic in retrospect, they could not be disregarded. Governments had been momentarily overturned in Milan and Naples in 1820–1, and no government could be sure that a local spark would not ignite a wider conflagration. Events came to a head in the colossal events of 1848, when civil order was threatened throughout Europe. More important from a long-term political point of view, though, Mazzini had forced Italian activists to think in terms of national political categories. Traditional loyalties to city or region had begun to seem anachronistic in the brave new world he evoked. Mazzini's tactics might have done little to shake the *status quo*. His propaganda, however, made a lasting impression across the political spectrum.

Mazzini was far from creating an ideological consensus. Even in radical circles, there was widespread disquiet about his aims and methods. What most isolated him from colleagues who shared his contempt for imperialism was his conception of political independence for Italy as an end in itself. Where federalists and moderate constitutionalists saw ridding Italy of foreign rule as a means of securing other values (liberty, justice, economic and cultural regeneration), Mazzini focused on the achievement of an Italian state as the decisive factor in a process of renewal that left a host of issues unresolved. He had said little in detail about the generation of economic growth, or about the vexed question of the relationship between local, regional and national power. Mazzini had proposed a purely political 'solution' to Italy's problems, with little or no awareness of the difficulties that might be encountered as a unitary scheme was imposed upon variegated economic, social and cultural practices. The point to stress, though, is that radicals who shared Mazzini's suspicions of the limited class interests of moderate constitutionalists nevertheless saw national independence as a problematic means, which had to be assessed in relation to wider economic and social considerations. Just how far national independence might constitute an advance for Italians would depend upon the terms on which it was attained. Mazzini's democratic credentials are not in doubt. What is in question is his assumption that power exercised through the people need not be treated with suspicion. It may be less likely that power will be abused in a democracy, but it would surely be over-sanguine to assume that it could not be abused. Human flourishing is not guaranteed by the removal of specific (imperial) constraints; nor is its continued enjoyment in any context exempt from intractable difficulties that might finally have to be resolved by force. The crucial issue is the appropriate exercise of power. There is no substitute for constitutional procedure.

The ambivalence at the heart of Mazzini's political thought highlights a dilemma in the theory of nationalism. When national self-determination is defended, it is generally with a view to consequences of one kind or another that might be expected to follow. Very many nineteenth-century liberals saw imperialism as a principal obstacle to the realization of rights. When they argued against imperial government, it was because they took rights seriously. A liberal could hardly argue that self-determination was an end in itself, no matter what the community might desire. But this is precisely the dilemma that Mazzini evades in his writings. Far from defending a liberal nationalism, Mazzini simply assumes that a democratic nation would not overreach itself. The sorry history of twentieth-century political populism illustrates how dangerous that assumption might prove to be.

Nationalism had assumed the guise of a liberation movement in response to the challenge of imperial rule. As a political movement, however, it embraced a variety of positions, ranging from radical claims for direct democracy to defence of the most extreme forms of authoritarianism. This flexibility, of course, was essential to the appeal of the movement. Nationalists could set their ideological or constitutional differences aside in a common commitment to the contention that communities with a sense of their own linguistic or cultural identity should have a political voice. Here were tantalizing possibilities for established authorities. Through identification with the state as a symbol of the nation, a sense of political participation could be attained without any real extension of popular involvement in government. Nationalism could thus generate from within its own resources a remarkable transfiguration from an ideology of liberation to the official doctrine of a repressive state.

There had, indeed, always been a darker side to the history of nationalism. Fichte, for example, writing at the very beginning of the nineteenth century, saw the nation in such exclusive terms that a national state would be justified in pressing its claims not only against other states but against its own people. The bond between people who spoke a common language was seen to be so crucial to their fulfilment that nothing could be allowed to distract them from their common purpose. In *The Closed Commercial State* (1800) Fichte argued that an individual's noblest qualities would flourish only in a state that controlled all aspects of a way of life, while in his *Addresses to the German Nation* (1807–8) he fiercely rejected any accommodation of one language-based community to another.[29] These were ideas which, with the leaven of social darwinism later in the century, could warrant the most aggressive policies. Nations could be pictured maximizing their moral and political energies in competition with one another, with individuals subordinating their interests, and sometimes their lives, to the pursuit of a common good. Once the interests of the state had been identified with the needs of the nation, it was but a small step from a view of a world of diverse nations, each finding a political outlet for its energies, to that of a world in which a nation is justified in asserting itself against other nations. What Mazzini had conceived as a recipe for international harmony and co-operation could be transformed into a pretext for imperial adventures and war.

6 Liberty

Nationalism was only one among a number of factors threatening liberal political ideas and practice in mid-nineteenth-century Europe. Continental liberals, in particular, though they were profoundly aware of the threat posed to the principle of constitutionalism by an authoritarian state, had not forgotten that an unholy alliance of radical intellectuals and the Paris mob could lead a movement of political reform to degenerate into revolution. What they feared above all was that political liberty would not survive attempts to put the state at the head of a radical programme of social and economic transformation. The limits of their political ambitions were very much set by a concern to preserve the prevailing balance in society.

The over-mighty state was an obvious menace to liberty by the 1830s. Subtler forces were also at work in economy and society which, by degrees, threatened to undermine an individualist culture at its source. Liberals feared that the adaptation of industry and commerce to the demands of an emerging mass society would lead to a levelling of standards, stifling energy and initiative and encouraging a dull, bureaucratic mentality. Constitutional guarantees had clearly only limited value in dealing with dilemmas of this order. Part of the problem was that people had begun to look to the state for a solution to all their difficulties. Yet it was precisely reliance on the state and its cumbersome apparatus that seemed to many to compromise political liberty in the longer term.

The prognosis for liberalism was far from encouraging. Alexis de Tocqueville, for example, surveying the course of recent history in his seminal *Democracy in America* (1835–40), saw an inexorable advance of the principle of equality at the expense of liberty.[1] Political liberty in the past, in his view, had been secured by a balance of powers within society, with vested interests (aristocracy, church, municipalities, etc.) constituting bulwarks against the encroachments of central authority. Doubtless Tocqueville had an excessively sanguine view of the actual power relationships at work in modern societies. He pictures the 'power of a few subjects' erecting 'insurmountable barriers against the tyranny of the king', while kings themselves, 'endowed with an almost divine character in the eyes of the populace', felt so secure in status and authority that they felt no temptation 'to abuse their power' (p. 17). However matters may once have stood, Tocqueville was clear that in modern times a whole series of factors had served to erode hierarchy, rank and privilege. In the wider European context, the Protestant Reformation had given a religious sanction to egalitarianism. And the transformation of industry and trade since the late eighteenth century had made the egalitarian ethos of the bourgeoisie the dominant influence in society.

Tocqueville's view of these developments was always ambivalent. As the product of an aristocratic family, he felt acutely the erosion of respect and security that had shattered a comfortable and complacent social world. Yet he had no sympathy for attempts to restore the institutions, practices and values of the *ancien régime*. He regarded egalitarianism as an irresistible social and cultural force in modern conditions. He describes 'the gradual unfurling of equality in social conditions [as] a providential fact', destined to be 'universal' in scope and beyond any possibility of 'human interference' (p. 15). What disturbed him was not so much egalitarian values as the political implications of those values. A democratic revolution in France in 1789 had swept away institutions which, while no doubt open to abuse, had nevertheless managed to contain central authority to some degree. Once the equal right of all citizens had been proclaimed, however, what moral, political or constitutional principle could counter the collective force of a majority? If the people collectively are regarded as a sovereign body, how could they be effectively opposed? If the people collectively possess the power of both decision and implementation, there is nothing to check the vagaries of popular enthusiasm. This is precisely the issue that had so disturbed Hegel in the *Philosophy of Right* (see above, pp. 45–60). Tocqueville describes it as democracy 'abandoned to its primitive instincts', like children who 'are left to fend for themselves in the streets of our towns and who come to learn only the vices and wretchedness of our society' (p. 16). This, in effect, amounted to 'democracy minus anything to lessen its defects or to promote its natural advantages' (p. 17). The reactionary response to this dilemma was simply to reject the democratic revolution, as if the modern world could somehow be effectively opposed. Tocqueville's stance was much more sophisticated. Theorists and the emerging political class had to learn the lessons of experience, tempering the impact of democratic politics without undermining democratic principles. In short, 'a new political science' was required 'for a totally new world' (p. 16).

Tocqueville's *Democracy in America*, though it has attained classic status, is unlike most of the texts in the canon of political philosophy. It eschews formal political argument, developing instead through close political, social and cultural observation. Indeed, hasty abstraction or generalization is presented throughout the text as a temptation to avoid at all costs. Yet it is driven by a political agenda. If a levelling of social conditions is inevitable, how are European political cultures to sustain their commitment to political liberty in the face of the administrative and political centralization that had been such a marked feature of the political forms that had emerged in the aftermath of the French Revolution? Tocqueville's interest in the United States was precisely that its revolution had given rise to a regime that enabled both liberty and equality to flourish. How had the United States managed to reconcile political values that Europeans had come to regard as mutually incompatible? Tocqueville was clear that theory alone would not resolve the conundrum. Democracy in practice had to be observed at close hand before any sensible political conclusions could be drawn.

Tocqueville used an official visit to the United States to study the prison system in 1831–2 as an occasion to chart the detailed vagaries and development of a democratic culture that had manifestly succeeded where European political cultures had failed. Nothing could stop the social revolution that was everywhere tending towards acceptance of the principle of equality. Europeans, therefore, had to ask themselves how its benefits could be attained without the political tyranny that had disfigured democratic experiments in Europe. Tocqueville was clear that Europeans could not simply borrow from American political experience. The impact of political ideas and innovations is framed and shaped by cultures in complex ways that only detailed observation can discern. Europeans would not be able to avoid the democratic revolution that awaited them. But they could at least understand how democracy had worked effectively in the particular circumstances of the United States. Tocqueville had no faith in the 'absolute perfection' of any actual 'system of laws' (p. 23). If Europeans were to save themselves from a future oscillating between 'democratic' tyranny and blatant authoritarianism, and Tocqueville himself was deeply pessimistic about what could be achieved practically, then they had at least to grasp the complex interdependence of customs, laws and circumstances in a flourishing democracy. What they made of that knowledge in political terms would depend upon the resources of their own political cultures. A necessary condition of any constructive reflection was thus an appreciation of the possibilities of a different political perspective.

Tocqueville's concerns were deep-rooted. His stress on background political culture ruled out the possibility of short-term solutions to endemic problems. Yet he was also clear that it would be futile for liberals to deplore the modern world and all its works. He set himself the task of distilling the political lessons of American experience, despite his scepticism about the direct applicability of institutional and policy initiatives from one context to another. Some of the cardinal assumptions of liberals of his generation had been challenged by the obvious political success of the United States. It could no longer be assumed that a commitment to equality would necessarily involve the sacrifice of liberty. The citizens of the United States had clearly contrived an egalitarian society without the slightest trace of political tyranny. At the very least, this was food for thought. Tocqueville explained much of this success by reference to the origins of the United States. Distant colonial status had obliged settlers to rely on their own resources in the day-to-day management of their affairs. Without an established class structure or 'natural' aristocracy, they had to fashion schemes of social co-operation among strangers if they were to survive at all. In these circumstances, necessity really did prove to be the mother of invention – grass-roots democracy was perfectly adapted to survival and flourishing in a new world.

The Puritan origins of settlers also fostered a culture of self-reliance tempered by reciprocity. Tocqueville was especially struck by the culture of the New England townships, where it would be assumed that 'each man is the best judge of his own interests and best able to provide for his own private needs' (p. 97). Administration was thus massively decentralized; but the corollary was that a vast majority of citizens recognized that such decentralized procedures would work effectively only if there were scrupulous respect for the rule of law. A culture of legality was thus not only seen to be desirable, but was vigorously endorsed in everyday dealings among citizens.

Appreciating the strength of the political culture of the United States involved much more than formal political analysis. Tocqueville had a wonderful eye for detail, highlighting (among many other things) the moral and intellectual equality of women as a basic building block for a 'true concept of democratic progress', a respect for work as an 'honourable necessity for the human race', and a pragmatic approach to matters of judgement that amounted to an 'American philosophic method' (pp. 700, 640, 493). Ready amendment of matters of this order was clearly beyond even the most ambitious legislation. But, in Tocqueville's analysis, there remained lessons from which Europeans could profit. His portrayal of the federal constitution, in particular, gave his contemporaries an unprecedented insight into the workings of the political institutions of the United States (pp. 130–200). At a time when Europeans were beginning to question the appropriate political form of newly emerging states, they had before them for the first time a detailed account of federal theory in practice. Where European liberals still tended to be suspicious of popular involvement in government, Tocqueville insisted that broad-based participation at national, state and local levels had given political life a massive solidity that kept extremist adventurers at bay. Administration itself was so thoroughly decentralized that there was little risk of a single focus of power and influence emerging. And the establishment of clear distinctions between legislative, executive and judicial roles obliged citizens to pursue consensual means of co-operation in (necessarily) complex circumstances.

Tocqueville recognized that it would not be possible to resuscitate European liberalism simply by selectively applying the best features of American political culture in the vastly different situation that prevailed in Europe. Necessity had taught European states to regard their neighbours as potential enemies. War (or the threat of war) had typically driven political and administrative agendas, irrespective of the ideology or values of particular states. In these (necessarily) precarious circumstances, efficiency demanded that powers be centralized, and that executive authorities be granted broad discretion to respond to crises. And resistance to centralization had been signally weakened by the emergence of the doctrine of natural rights, stressing the equality of all and the irrelevance of inherited status or prerogative. If the people as a whole should regard themselves as the collective embodiment of the sovereignty of the state, it was very difficult to orchestrate opposition to political demands on any other basis. Citizens could argue about the appropriate expression of the will of the people, but not about its normative warrant. In practice, argues Tocqueville, 'this naturally gives men of democratic times a very elevated opinion of society's privileges and a very low opinion of an individual's rights' (p. 778). To oppose the pronouncements of 'democratic' governments could easily be construed as opposition to the principle of democracy itself. Individual rights could be rendered very fragile indeed, precisely because they were notionally shared by all citizens indifferently.

For all his fears, Tocqueville could see no alternative to the final triumph of democracy. Europe had endured its worst excesses in the turmoil of the French Revolution. Europeans had to learn either to temper democracy or to live with the consequences. Exposure to the political culture of the United States had shown Tocqueville that liberty and equality were not incompatible conceptually, but there was little chance of enjoying them together in a polity that was driven by circumstances to focus the exercise of power in a few central hands. Europeans could take heart that all was not lost, despite the deep intractability of their circumstances. At the very least, they had to recognize that the demands of democratic politics required a hugely sophisticated citizenry. Tocqueville is emphatic on the point.

> The first of the duties currently imposed upon the rulers of our society is to educate democracy, to reawaken, if possible, its beliefs, to purify its morals, to control its actions, gradually to substitute statecraft for its inexperience and awareness of its true interests for its blind instincts, to adapt its government to times and places, and to mold it according to circumstances and people. (p. 16)

This, to be sure, was a very tall order indeed. Citizens were being asked to acquire the sophistication and self-restraint that were essential to a flourishing democracy without being exposed to the rigours of democracy in practice. Europeans had also seen how devastating the political consequences of democratic failure could be. Tocqueville had no illusions about the enormity of the challenge. Yet he was also aware that a failure of political nerve would be catastrophic. It was important simply to recognize the possibility of a mundane politics, where individuals 'would realize that, in order to benefit from the advantages of society, they would have to bow to its requirements' (p. 18). Nothing could guarantee success. Citizens associating freely together had only their wits to rely upon. It would be certain, however, that if they failed to recognize the fragility of the liberties they enjoyed, they would condemn themselves to the torment of political tyranny.

There was little in Tocqueville's analysis to encourage optimism. To the traditional liberal suspicion of the state had been added the more insidious threat of a tyranny of the majority. While practical exigencies gave every opportunity for further centralization, liberals found themselves unable to reverse the trend. From Wilhelm von Humboldt to John Stuart Mill and beyond, freedom was treated as a precious commodity, more likely to be lost through inadvertence than to be brought down by direct political action. Tocqueville himself, in the face of the revolutions of 1848, was filled with foreboding. A shift was evident in people's attitudes and expectations. Where once the defence of political liberty had been the first concern of the articulate classes, attention was now given to substantive social and economic questions. It became clear to him that the principles of classical liberalism had begun to appear quaintly old-fashioned. If the choice were between basic freedoms and a redistribution of property, too many people (so he feared) would have little hesitation in opting for the latter.

What was at stake in these discussions was not simply the kind of state that might be deemed compatible with political freedom, but the character of the individuals who might emerge under its tutelage. Individuals making choices, bearing responsibility, representing themselves in the various arenas of social life, had always been central to liberal claims about the appropriate limits of political power and authority. To picture, by contrast, 'individuals' shaped, nurtured and moulded by an all-encompassing state, assuming broad economic, social and cultural functions, was to conjure up a very different prospect. Political authorities would be in a position to fashion the 'individuals' they regarded as most effective or desirable, with education and other public goods being considered as instrumental means to the attainment of human 'products'.

In a seminal essay written as early as 1791–2 but not finally published until 1854, Wilhelm von Humboldt focused on the scope for individual development and growth in a context in which options are prescribed by a central authority.[2] Ordinarily we may assess our lives in terms of the commitments we make to projects and people as we encounter new situations and reflect on what we have achieved. This is how we learn from experience and make that experience our own. What can we say, however, if our choices are made for us by various authorities, or we are fitted for careers or relationships to suit the convenience and interests of others? In a literal sense, our lives would not be our own. And in the process, our capacity for fulfilling whatever personal potential we had would be stifled. Not only would our lives be stunted, but the good we could render each other would be diminished.

Humboldt's *The Limits of State Action* was specifically addressed to the dilemmas facing citizens as French revolutionary turmoil unfolded. Yet he had identified the problem of centralized authority in terms that strikingly anticipated Tocqueville. The point was not that an ideal state should assume a specific constitutional form, but rather that centralization itself constituted a threat to liberty. And without liberty, possibilities for human flourishing would be massively reduced. In terms that would be echoed later by John Stuart Mill in *On Liberty*, Humboldt argued that 'freedom heightens energy', while coercion stifles it; that 'political arrangement' should be designed 'to bring a variety of widely discordant interests into unity and harmony', rather than to suppress diversity; and that the state should 'wholly refrain from every attempt to operate directly or indirectly on the morals and character of the nation, except in so far as such a policy may become inevitable as a natural consequence of its other absolutely necessary measures' (pp. 80–1). These 'absolutely necessary measures' amounted to the maintenance of 'the external or internal security of its citizens', leaving them 'in the full enjoyment of their due rights of person and property' (pp. 82–3). Humboldt was aware, of course, that he had laid down a rule of thumb that in practice would have to be interpreted in the light of circumstances. But he took it for granted that 'actions which immediately affect others' might warrant regulation, whereas moral, cultural or religious matters should be resolved by individuals in the pursuit of their diverse and shifting concerns (p. 93).

Humboldt was essentially addressing issues in a society that had yet to develop either a mass-based market or large-scale industrial structures. Problems of economic and social organization were rendered more complex as employment patterns shifted from rural to industrial occupations, with densely populated cities emerging that posed unprecedented health and co-ordination problems. In these circumstances, it was to be expected that states would have to assume broader functions, since individuals and groups were seldom in a position to provide the range of public goods on which their welfare depended. And as wider classes pressed for political recognition, priorities in public debate shifted significantly. Social questions had an urgency and immediacy that was entirely lacking in arcane constitutional discussions of the necessary conditions for the attainment of political freedom. Here were issues that demanded a response from governments, yet effective government response could well change the relationship between citizens and their governments irrevocably.

Conventional liberal constitutional theory was clearly ill-equipped to deal with problems of this order. Arguments that had served effectively to delimit the control that kings could exert over their subjects looked distinctly fragile if the people themselves demanded intervention from governments that claimed to represent the interests of the people. Tocqueville had been despondent as he pictured the prospects for political freedom in an industrial future. John Stuart Mill, however, tried to meet the challenge directly. He recognized (with Tocqueville) that pragmatic adjustment to co-ordination problems as they arose would lead to a structural shift towards centralization of powers and responsibilities. If freedom were to be defended as a value, it had to be restated in relation to dramatically changed circumstances. People had to be persuaded that their long-term interests and potential would not be fulfilled if they sought solutions from government for all the ills that might beset them. It could not be assumed that the prerogatives and values of an earlier political order would be sufficient to contain government in a broadly representative political context. A principle was required to focus the thinking of government and governed alike.

This was precisely the task that Mill set himself in *On Liberty*.[3] First published in 1859, the text has often been regarded as a defence of a libertarian style of government. Yet this is a significant misreading of a deceptively complex text. Mill does not adopt the categorical tone characteristic of Humboldt. His point is not that government intervention cannot be justified, but rather that intervention is intrinsically problematic. If there is a standing temptation for governments to do more rather than less, then it follows that all concerned should be clear about the proper role of government. In *On Liberty* Mill sought to defend what he describes as a 'very simple principle', designed to clarify the complex relationships between government, governed and wider society (pp. 13–14). He contends that 'the sole end for which mankind are warranted, individually or collectively, in interfering with the liberty of action of any of their number, is self-protection' (p. 14). In this scheme of things, it can be no business of either the government or public opinion what individuals do in pursuit of their private interests. They may be misguided, foolhardy or absurd in their conduct, threatening their personal chances of happiness according to any 'reasonable' criterion. They may shock or alarm family, friends, colleagues and associates. And, of course, witnesses to their folly may feel inclined to offer all manner of well-intended advice. If they are adults of sound mind, however, able to bear responsibility for their actions, no one may use or threaten compulsion (either legal or moral) in order to save them from the consequences of their own actions. Compulsion may be used, according to Mill, only if an individual's conduct can be shown 'to produce evil to some one else' (p. 14). He insists that 'the only part of the conduct of any one, for which he is amenable to society, is that which concerns others' (p. 14). Legislation or 'moral' intervention of any kind would have to satisfy this requirement before it could be countenanced. Rules of thumb that had governed conduct in the past would have to be examined afresh in the light of this criterion, as would any remedy for any conceivable difficulty that might confront us in the future. We would all know where we stood and what (in principle) we could expect of one another.

Or would we? Mill's 'simple' principle, on closer inspection, is far from clear in its implications. Early critics pointed out that the distinction between 'self-regarding' and 'other-regarding' actions is difficult to maintain, even in theory. We are social creatures, confronting the options available to us from a background of received understandings and complex involvement with other people. Even our most trivial actions may have implications for others that affect their well-being and interests. Conduct that might once have been regarded as entirely private (such as in the domain of personal hygiene) may later be seen as an important matter affecting public health. Mill is clear that his principle will not enable him to distinguish precisely between public and private spheres. Our conceptions of what is public or private will shift over time in response to changing perceptions of risk. But conceptions of the person will also change, along with what it might mean to engage in any activity.

Mill's 'simple' principle, then, is inherently contentious, but may still be a useful means of distinguishing between spheres of responsibility. Mill needs to show, in addition, that something like his principle is actually in the wider interest of the members of a society, all things considered. Here he produces powerful arguments for 'liberty of thought and discussion' that have remained influential to this day (pp. 20–61). If we assume from the outset that certain courses of action are better than others, but are unsure which option to pursue, we will ordinarily try things out, ask around, and in general endeavour to learn directly or indirectly from experience. Dogmatic views about what should be done in any context will inevitably narrow the range of possible courses of conduct available to us. Certain things would simply be ruled out, irrespective of any assessment of their consequences. Mill's view is that if we want to do the best we can for ourselves, then we have to retain an open mind. And we should extend the same thought to anyone we may encounter in our society.

Mill explores the implications of this idea in relation to both science and morality. As scientists, we may all have an interest in the truth, though we cannot be sure that the theories we currently favour should be regarded as definitive. In these circumstances, we have to insist that enquiry remains open, even if only to increase confidence in the positions we currently hold. To suppress absurdity, rather than to expose it, actually weakens our ability to pursue the truth. Similar considerations apply in the moral sphere. Our conviction that we should do the right thing is not strengthened by a refusal even to imagine other possible values. We are all aware, of course, that moral arguments are notoriously difficult to resolve, even among groups that share fundamental ideas. Christians may disagree about the practical implications of their interpretations of the Bible. Differences of view will always arise. Our primary consideration must be that we pursue the course of conduct that is likely to make our lives go better; and they are unlikely to go better if we deny ourselves the possibility of thinking hard and imaginatively about the choices we have to make. We have to keep the scope for discussion as broad as possible, all other things remaining equal. None of us can be entirely sure of our own rectitude, either in science or in morality. An eccentric question may mark the tentative early stages of an important discovery. We will not help ourselves if we suppress views that we regard as inconvenient or disagreeable.

Mill's argument hinges on an assessment of the likely benefits that may accrue to individuals and the wider society from a clear conception of appropriate limits to the role of government. He was developing a utilitarian line of argument that had become familiar to his contemporaries from his father (James Mill) and Bentham (see below, pp. 94–5). Yet John Stuart Mill did not endorse utilitarianism in the narrow terms to which he had been exposed in the course of a very unusual education.[4] While he continued to treat arguments drawn from abstract or natural right with suspicion, his view of utility was much broader than Bentham's. Instead of a sum of benefits and costs ('pleasures' and 'pains') aggregated across society as a whole, Mill insisted that qualitative criteria had necessarily to be invoked. Unlike Bentham, Mill accepted a conventional distinction between higher and lower pleasures. He continued to view 'utility as the ultimate appeal on all ethical questions', but sought to assess the impact on policy in relation to 'the permanent interests of man as a progressive being'.[5] This was 'utility in the largest sense', and its precise connotation has confounded critics and commentators alike (p. 15). The original attraction of utilitarianism was that it avoided contentious (and potentially futile) arguments about values. Human beings were treated simply as pleasure-seekers and pain-avoiders. Nothing could be gained from trying to assess the relative merits of different kinds of pleasure. Long before 1859, through his reading of Tocqueville, Coleridge and Humboldt, Mill had become deeply dissatisfied with the crass egalitarianism that underpinned Bentham's view. What emerges, however, looks perilously like a juxtaposition of arguments, rather than a constructive synthesis.

The 'higher' interests that Mill champions revolve around broadening the scope for individuality to flourish. We can envisage any number of possible goods for human beings, but (in Mill's view) they can be discounted if they do not enhance the capacity of individuals to respond to an unpredictable future. He has no regard for soporific satisfactions or idle contentment. He sees human beings as actors in an uncertain world, making choices for themselves, bearing responsibility, revising their views in the light of failure or disappointment. Goods may be various, but they must all enhance the human capacity for action, discrimination and choice. The distinctively human faculties, he says, 'perception, judgement, discriminative feeling, mental activity, and even moral preference, are exercised only in making a choice' (p. 65). There is no scope for an idea of an intrinsic good in his scheme of things. Indeed, to be presented with life's delights on a plate would run the risk of undermining practical talents that can be nurtured only in active engagement. An 'enlightened' government that sought to care for the interests of citizens from the cradle to the grave would thus be contributing to their corruption and decline. Mill urges government to encourage 'experiments of living', even if these experiments shock and offend conventional opinion (p. 63). And, of course, in the nature of an experiment, success cannot be guaranteed. Individuals will try things out and sometimes fail abysmally. Provided they are risking only their own interests, however, Mill sees no grounds for intervention. Freedom to fail is a necessary condition for the development of energy and initiative. Such conditions will foster better individuals. They will also maximize prospects for what Mill loosely describes as 'social progress' (p. 63). Mill is emphatic on this point. 'Mankind are greater gainers', he insists, 'by suffering each other to live as seems good to themselves, than by compelling each to live as seems good to the rest' (p. 17).

Mill's central contention has remained at the heart of liberal political cultures throughout the modern period. Yet, for all the sophistication he brought to its discussion, application of the principle to concrete cases has proved to be deeply complex. The prevention of harm to others as a criterion for political intervention looks relatively straightforward. On closer inspection, though, it is by no means evident what should count as 'harm'. Mill is clear that offence or outrage to opinion is not a sufficient warrant. But even if we narrow the notion of 'harm' to focus on fundamental interests, there remains a measure of ambiguity about how those interests should be characterized. In some policy areas it is actually essential that some people's interests are harmed for a policy to be effective. Mill cites the case of competition for jobs in an 'overcrowded profession' (p. 105). We cannot both appoint the best person for a job and protect the interests of all the applicants. They all want the job, and may indeed be reasonably qualified to do it. Yet there is only one job available. Mill simply assumes (quite reasonably) that it is 'better for the general interest of mankind' to select the best candidate, no matter how devastating the disappointment may be to the life chances of the other applicants (p. 105). In this context, harm to others simply cannot be avoided.

Similar considerations apply in relation to competitive markets. Consumers and producers have contrasting interests, just as the success of one producer may be ruinous for another. To use legislation to ameliorate the impact of economic failure may remove incentives to produce quality goods efficiently. Mill accepts this principle in general terms. But he is also aware that 'public control is admissible for the prevention of fraud by adulteration' or 'to protect workpeople employed in dangerous occupations' (pp. 105–6). In these cases judgements have to be made, balancing costs to efficiency against harm to individuals. We can assume that people may be prepared to take some risks for economic gain, though they may not be in a position to assess risks adequately. We cannot specify what should count as a reasonable risk in abstract terms. In working contexts, we rely on received understandings, values, etc., and modify our practices only when we encounter glaring anomalies. Mill is aware that this is how things work in practice, yet he is reluctant to appeal to anything as imprecise as conventional wisdom. In difficult cases, however, there is little else available. Mill's discussion of these issues highlights how inherently problematic it is to put theory into practice.

Mill's suspicion of conventional wisdom is well founded. Where he is on shakier ground is in his insistence that a theoretical criterion will always help us to balance competing considerations. Mill's efforts to apply his principle are actually sensitive to context, sometimes at the expense of theoretical consistency. What emerges from his discussion is a strong commitment to personal autonomy and measures that might be construed as agency enhancing. His treatment of alcohol, drugs and idleness, for example, is far from permissive. While he admits that drunkenness is not ordinarily 'a fit subject for legislative interference', he is nevertheless prepared to place legal restraints on the conduct of individuals who may be suspected of constituting a possible threat to public order (p. 108). And though idleness may be supposed to be open to legal remedy only in the most tyrannical of states, Mill does not hesitate to recommend legal punishment if 'a man fails to perform his legal duties to others' (p. 108). Parents who fail to support their children, in Mill's view, might reasonably be expected to undertake 'compulsory labour' (p. 108).

Mill's views on parenthood more broadly will surprise readers expecting to encounter a social libertarian. Sexual relations are normally considered to be among the most private matters, even in states that are authoritarian in other respects. Yet Mill describes the choice that adults make about having children as a public concern. He sees 'the fact itself, of causing the existence of a human being, [as] among the most responsible actions in the range of human life' (p. 120). What most of us regard as a matter of personal discretion, Mill contends is an onerous public responsibility. Indeed, he treats the birth of a child that cannot expect 'at least the ordinary chances of a desirable existence [as] a crime against that being' on the part of parents (p. 120). And it is not only the child's interest that is threatened, according to Mill. Any increase in population is likely to put downward pressure on wages, thus constituting 'a serious offence against all who live by the remuneration of their labour' (p. 120). This will strike modern readers as a disturbing and surprising view in a professed liberal, though Malthusian conceptions of over-population were widely shared in mid-nineteenth-century Britain. The point to stress here is that the only consideration that prevents Mill from advancing more draconian measures is the misplaced public outcry that he anticipates would follow. Mill is adamant that restrictions on the right to procreate 'are not objectionable as violations of liberty' in themselves (p. 120). Public opinion, in this as in other domains, is a poor guide for policymakers.

Mill's argument in *On Liberty* thus cannot be regarded as entirely satisfactory. He demonstrated through his treatment of examples, however, that tendencies for the state to expand its activities in industrial societies are not easily resisted. The pragmatist will tend to drift towards incremental extensions of state power, running the risk of transforming the relationship between state and citizens through inadvertence rather than design. Mill's concern in the text is to offer a test that must be satisfied before any extension of powers can be justified, rather than a definitive list of powers and responsibilities. His fear is that without a theoretical statement of some kind, centralization would be an irresistible temptation for citizens and government alike.

The 'simple principle' is not self-evident, though. In its defence Mill slips from utilitarian argument (the truth would not emerge without free discussion, the individual is the best judge of her own best interests) to defence of individualism and diversity as goods in themselves. What finally emerges is a preference for the state to do less rather than more, with due allowance made for the overwhelmingly complex co-ordination problems that beset any mass-based industrial society. Mill presumes, for example, that a thing 'is likely to be better done by individuals than by the government', without ruling out cases in which only government intervention will be effective (p. 121). He also assumes that even in cases where individuals do not act effectively, much is to be gained in educational terms from leaving them to assume wide areas of responsibility for themselves. It is hugely important to him that an active citizenry should emerge, rather than a passive but contented populace. And the continual increase in government functions may in time create a beast that is impossible to control. These were articles of faith for advocates of limited government in mid-nineteenth-century Britain that could be defended in a variety of ways. Mill helped himself from a range of plausible theories, without quite achieving the theoretical synthesis he sought. In political terms, however, he had effectively challenged the assumption that the state knows best.

Mill's defence of individual liberty was vigorous. In the economic sphere it reinforced the strong tendency in mid-century capitalism to see the choices of individuals as the basic source of energy and initiative throughout the system. In the classical view of *laissez-faire* economics, it was held that prosperity would be maximized if trade were freed from political, moral and social constraints. Non-economic considerations were treated as external costs which distorted the decision making of individuals striving to maximize their marginal utility. And of the many 'external' impediments to economic growth, political interference (in the form of taxation and regulation) was held to be the most serious and the easiest to mitigate through legislation.

We should be clear here. No one supposed that everyone would benefit equally from an unfettered capitalism. But it was held that the society as a whole would be better off in absolute terms. It is the kind of doctrine that can look very impressive at times of significant economic growth. But any interruption of that growth can lead to questioning of the basis of distribution within a society. Questions of 'justice' or 'fairness' begin to seem more pressing than productivity and growth.

Britain in the second half of the nineteenth century was very much a test case for the impact of industrialization on a liberal political order. What we see, in fact, is a loss of faith in some of the more facile assumptions that had informed the development of social and economic life. In broad terms, governments had to deal with vast shifts of population. The agricultural labourers who flocked to the new industrial towns can be construed as exercising their freedom of choice. Yet they were hardly in the position of the classic characters depicted in liberal theory, rationally plotting a course of life for themselves after examining the various alternatives. In a literal sense, they could not be said to know what they were letting themselves in for. Their haphazard entry into the emerging industrial towns in hordes created unprecedented social and health problems. Issues on this scale had not been envisaged in the pure theory of capitalism. To many observers, it seemed as if the unfettered market, left to itself, would simply exacerbate the problem.

Liberals, then, were faced with a dilemma. By inclination, they were in favour of leaving matters to be resolved by individual initiative. But they were perplexed as to how to respond if the upshot of individuals pursuing their own ends was a deterioration of a situation in which individual interests and well-being were already adversely affected.

There were more direct theoretical and political concerns. The rise of socialism and the trade union movement gave a new currency to demands for political participation and reform. What many people wanted was control over their own lives. Liberalism had set them free in a legal sense; but that freedom would be rendered worthless if the conditions of their lives made them absolutely dependent upon an employer or a landlord.

How could liberals respond to problems of this order? It became clear to many that their traditional concern for the individual had to be extended from the purely formal legal sphere to include substantive questions of individual well-being. John Stuart Mill had already taken significant steps in this direction. The conception of individuality he championed presupposed certain moral, cultural and political values. When he argued that we should all be free to do as we like in areas where our conduct does not adversely affect the interests of others, it was not so that we could creep back to our homes each evening to idle our time away. He was hostile to political and social controls, because he feared that they might lead to the emergence of a stagnant, apathetic society. He defended a very specific conception of vigorous individuality. And he was aware that in certain circumstances the state should intervene in order to encourage (perhaps even to compel) individuals to pursue a progressive course. He had no reservations whatever about obliging children to attend school.

What we see emerging among liberals in the 1870s and 1880s is a much more positive conception of the role of the state. The position of T. H. Green, the Oxford philosopher, is typical. In his *Lectures on the Principles of Political Obligation*, posthumously published in 1882, he distanced himself specifically from the atomistic individualism of Locke, Bentham and Mill.[6] Drawing extensively from the philosophies of Kant and Hegel, he was fiercely critical of both the language of natural right and utilitarianism. But though he objected to the way in which Mill had defended his case, he nevertheless continued to stress a positive view of the individual. Green emphasized the need for individuals to find positive fulfilment in life and work. And he was clear that this could be achieved only if a society were sufficiently attuned to their needs. It would not do, according to Green, for the state simply to provide benefits for individuals. He shared Mill's fears about the emergence of a passive and dependent population. Yet, in his view, there was ample scope for positive action from the state to facilitate the participation of individuals in social, economic and political life.

State intervention could take a variety of forms without undermining individual initiative and freedom. Consider the case of freedom of contract. The classical liberal view pictured society as an aggregation of individuals, each free under the law to make binding agreements among themselves – to buy and sell various items, to render services to one another in return for payment. At first glance this might sound like a fair arrangement, until we consider that a contract drawn up between (say) an individual employer and a hundred individual workers would leave each of the workers (as individuals) vulnerable to the economic power of the employer. A proper balance between the two sides might be struck if the law recognized the collective legal identity of a workforce. Individuals could join together (in a trade union or other such association) in order to press for certain minimal conditions (level of wages, conditions of service or whatever). The point of the amendment to the law of contract is not that the state should confer benefits directly on workers, but rather that the legal framework could be adjusted in order to enable workers to organize in defence of their own interests.

Other liberal thinkers active towards the end of the nineteenth century and beyond were much more directly influenced by socialism than Green. L. T. Hobhouse, for example, sought to distance himself from the German idealist philosophy that had informed the work of Green, Bosanquet and others in the British idealist school. Hobhouse shared the British idealist rejection of narrow individualism, but was deeply suspicious of any suggestion that the state could have any interest distinct from the concrete concerns of citizens.[7] Unlike earlier liberals such as Tocqueville, he saw no necessary opposition between liberalism and socialism. It may be that socialists expressed their political demands in a rather different idiom. But reformist socialists, according to Hobhouse, were essentially intent on extending the advantages of the liberal state to broader sections of the population. Hobhouse, in his widely read *Liberalism* (1911), openly defended what he styled as a liberal socialism, championing democratic involvement in political decision making, redistribution of income through taxation, and close control of the right to own property. Arguments such as these provided the inspiration for the great wave of liberal welfare legislation in Britain in the years immediately preceding the First World War. The theoretical building blocks were in place for the later liberal endorsement of the idea of a welfare state.

An uneasy consensus thus emerged supporting a broader role for government, though policy implications were deeply contentious. Liberals found themselves polarized on opposite sides of a series of vital debates. It was accepted that government could intervene to enlarge options for individuals, without necessarily directing individuals in the choice of personal goals. But there was a fine line between leaving individuals to decide their fate and actively encouraging a certain kind of individual, able to bear personal responsibility in a challenging world. Universal provision of education, for example, presupposed sensitive decisions about what should be taught and to whom. Education directed by the state to the poor might have a very different content from that which the rich could buy for their children. Different kinds of education fashioned citizens for different public and private roles. Questions of active and passive citizenship were raised here that liberal theory was barely able to address. Class attitudes, which had once been seen simply as a natural corollary of a functional division of society, were now being reinforced by state policies. Citizens who had benefited from a rudimentary education were quick to recognize the anomalies of liberal theory. Pressing social and economic problems began to make the principles of classical liberalism appear quaintly old-fashioned. And as new groups began to assert claims to political involvement, the political agenda shifted decisively towards substantive welfare issues.

7 Welfare

A strand in liberal thought had always accorded priority to substantive interests, rather than constitutional or legal entitlements. Jeremy Bentham famously argued in 1789 that basic human desires could be the only legitimate criteria in the justification of coercive measures by the state. In his view, we have no choice but to pursue pleasure and avoid pain. 'Nature has placed mankind under the governance of two sovereign masters, *pain* and *pleasure*.'[1] For Bentham this is a simple statement of fact, but it had far-reaching implications for the way we should regard moral and political questions. Bentham's concern was to expose the illusions at the heart of traditional debates about values, rights, obligations and so forth. He treated the perennial issues in moral and political philosophy as mere verbiage, a misleading gloss on the real sources of human motivation. In Bentham's view, standard discussions of what we ought to do were simply misplaced. We are programmed to assess our actions in terms of pleasure and pain, 'fastened', as he put it, to the 'chain of causes and effects'.[2] It is no more possible for us to urge ourselves not to pursue pleasure than to stop breathing. It is axiomatic for Bentham that we pursue pleasure, no matter what justification we may put to ourselves for our actions. Given that this is the case, it followed (for Bentham) that policy should be assessed in terms of its aggregate impact on the happiness of the community. In his celebrated formulation, 'the greatest happiness of the greatest number' should be 'the measure of right and wrong'.[3] A utilitarian calculation of consequences should replace the qualitative evaluation of moral and political issues. How happiness should be conceived and measured, who should make authoritative judgements about its pursuit, how long- and short-term considerations should be balanced, were, for Bentham and his utilitarian followers, technical issues that could (in principle) be resolved. The crucial point was that traditional questions in political philosophy (What is the ideal form of polity? Do we have any natural rights?) had all obscured what was really going on when we make judgements. Elaborate moral and political principles disguised the beguilingly simple fact of human motivation. Human beings pursue pleasure and avoid pain. They may describe their pleasures and pains in complex ways, but the responsibility of legislators is to cut through false distinctions and ensure that everyone's pleasure and pain should count in policy deliberations.

Counting each individual as one, and none as more than one, as Bentham insisted, did a great deal to change the character and scope of government policy. Governments could not distinguish between the 'higher' and 'lower' interests of citizens. Elite preferences enjoyed no special standing. If people gained more pleasure from football than from opera, then it follows that governments should promote the former rather than the latter. But it also remains possible that after a calculation of costs and benefits, governments might decide to promote neither. Individuals might be left to their own devices to wallow in whatever fancies grabbed their attention. Individuals should simply do what they are programmed to do – maximize marginal utility. Governments had to look to the aggregate utility of the society as a whole, viewed as the sum of the satisfactions of individuals. If it could be shown that the sum of the marginal improvement in the welfare of the vast majority greatly exceeded the pain that might follow from a marginal increase in taxation for the rich, then Benthamite theory insists that governments should pursue redistributive policies.

Utility as an objective criterion always remained more an aspiration than a tangible achievement. It was one thing to identify hypothetical units of 'pleasure', and quite another to compare either the 'pleasure' or marginal importance of different activities. Health and education may both be regarded as public goods, requiring support from the state. Yet, despite the apparent 'objectivity' of Bentham's theory, it is quite impossible to avoid invoking qualitative criteria when considering the allocation of scarce resources to various projects. John Stuart Mill addressed this issue directly, though not entirely satisfactorily, in *Utilitarianism* (1861). Despite an early indoctrination in Benthamite ideas, Mill recognized the force of the objection to the essential comparability of all pleasures. He insisted that 'it is quite compatible with the principle of utility to recognize the fact, that some *kinds* of pleasure are more desirable and more valuable than others'.[4] What he had in mind was not intensity of pleasure, but a qualitative distinction between 'higher' and 'lower' pleasures, pleasures of the mind contrasted with pleasures of the body, pleasures that contribute to the long-term good of human beings rather than ephemeral satisfactions. That we actually make distinctions of this kind when we prioritize our preferences is clear. Whether what we are doing can be characterized in utilitarian terms, however, is quite another matter.

Mill's defence of the 'higher faculties' is categorical (p. 139). He simply could not equate the satisfaction derived from resolving a difficult problem with the pleasure of drinking oneself into a stupor. In his view, 'it is better to be a human being dissatisfied than a pig satisfied; better to be Socrates dissatisfied than a fool satisfied' (p. 140). And if this distinction could make sense only from the perspective of Socrates, so much the worse for the fool. In the text he distinguishes between the 'moral attributes' and 'consequences' of actions, without explaining precisely how these different considerations should be brought together in any particular decision (p. 141). Nor does he stress, though he is perfectly aware of, the damage done to the crude Benthamite version of utilitarianism by his move.

Mill's innovation effectively undermined the determinist dimension in Bentham's theory. Far from treating pleasure and pain as 'sovereign masters' over individual actions, Mill denied that 'the agent's own greatest happiness' should be the relevant standard in the appraisal of actions (p. 142). What mattered was not that an individual should maximize her happiness, but rather that policy should strive to attain 'the greatest amount of happiness altogether' (p. 142). Indeed, Mill rejected a narrow hedonistic criterion at the level of policy. Individuals prepared to devote themselves (say) to the provision of sanitary living conditions in industrial cities were in an obvious sense denying themselves the opportunity of playing golf every afternoon. Yet it was perfectly clear to Mill that their discipline and self-denial contributed massively to public welfare. Far from maximizing the general welfare of a community, Bentham's criterion as a rule of thumb for individual conduct would detract significantly from the provision of public goods. Mill argued, instead, that utilitarianism 'could only attain its end by the general cultivation of nobleness of character', effectively encouraging individuals to put the public good before their private satisfactions (p. 142). In this scheme of things, utilitarianism became an optional theory available to assess the merits of various policy proposals, but clearly could not claim definitive status as a 'scientific' solution to the problem of explaining or justifying actions. It took its place along with a range of contending theories in the public domain, open to various interpretations, applicable to certain spheres of activity more obviously than others, one feature in a complex background of argument and discussion.

Utilitarianism, in fact, contributed signally to the emergence of a reformist ethos in nineteenth-century Britain. This was not so much a matter of putting theory into practice (policy implications were much too contentious for that) as a recognition that the interests of a whole population had to be taken into account. Even those who discounted the crude egalitarianism of the Benthamite creed nevertheless accepted that decisions about public welfare had to be inclusive rather than exclusive. Not everyone counted equally, of course. An elite could portray sectional interests *as if* they were in the wider interest of the community, often in good faith. And the interests of the poor would usually be portrayed as if there were no basic clash between them and the interests of the rich. All this was very comforting to elites. The poor, indeed, were not in a position to represent their own interests to decision-making elites, and were thus vulnerable to portrayals that fitted best with elite interests. By 1830, however, 'right-thinking' people could not simply ignore the poor. There would be more or less ill-informed discussion about the plight of the poor. Would public provision make them apathetic and dependent? Should the education of the poor be geared to the manual jobs they might be expected to fill in the future? Would political order be compromised if the poor were to be directly involved in decision making at various levels? These were vexed questions. At the very least, the poor began to count in public debate, even if they were not heard in their own voice.

The suspicion remained, however, that liberal theory was constrained ineradicably by individualist terms of reference. The supposition that individuals might flourish if opportunities were provided for them disguised wider structural problems that handicapped the well-being and life chances of disadvantaged groups in society. An ideology focused on the individual was perfectly adapted to the interests of an independent and resourceful entrepreneurial class. Yet, while the 'poor' might be described in collective terms, liberals saw themselves as individuals fashioning new modes of production and association for an open future. Complex problems of integration and control had already obliged liberals to take social questions seriously. To many observers, though, it seemed that the individualist assumptions of liberal theory effectively foreclosed discussion of the structural problems that shape prospects for individuals. A genuine concern for individual opportunities seemed barely adequate in relation to the living conditions of the urban poor. Enhancing the life prospects of specific individuals – through education or charitable assistance, for example – would not necessarily have a measurable impact on the poverty of the masses. Facilitating social mobility could actually have a neutral (or even negative) effect on the poorest sections of a community. A calculation of marginal utility, in these circumstances, could justify a restriction of freedom through coercive intervention from the state. If a significant redistribution of resources is seen as a key to greater equality and aggregate well-being, then the limited state advocated by liberal theory could be portrayed as a grossly inadequate instrument.

It is easy to appreciate how ideas of this kind would appeal to an emerging industrial working class. The theoretical attractions of liberalism were superficially obvious. Equality of all before the law could not be construed as a good only for the well-to-do. Yet the reality of that freedom in disadvantaged structural circumstances could well be a life of misery. Industrial workers could see themselves as essential to capitalism, but felt excluded from the manifest productive benefits of industry. Before they could assert themselves politically, workers needed a political language that reflected their circumstances and aspirations. It was obvious to many at least that the rich promise of liberal theory was illusory. Political freedom left them constrained by the logic of capitalism. Liberalism and capitalism thus assumed the guise of Janus-faced villains, effectively perpetuating their subordination while holding out the theoretical prospect of a richer and more varied life.

In the early decades of the nineteenth century, arguments had been mooted urging a high degree of central planning in the organization of an economy. Robert Owen and Saint-Simon, for example, contended that scientific and technical progress had created alternatives to capitalist production which were both more efficient and more humane.[5] Problems that in the past had been treated as the 'natural' concomitants of human life – poverty, exploitation, crime – were, on this view, attributable to an outmoded social and economic system. Owen, in particular, saw the 'moral' shortcomings of workers as a direct consequence of the brutal and insecure conditions they would have experienced in factories. Replace anarchic competition with rational planning, coercion in the factory with co-operation, and not only would productive capacity increase, but there would be no further need for the state to assume a repressive role. Owen tried to put his ideas into practice in the factory he operated in New Lanark (1800–25). His workers were provided with education, good living conditions and co-operative working practices, in the expectation that their personal potential and sense of responsibility would be enhanced, equipping them for wider social and political roles. Meanwhile, Saint-Simon urged that an elite corps of social scientists should directly manage questions of production, distribution and exchange, thus freeing economic life from the vagaries of market conditions. Here at least were proposals that might make the fruits of industrial society available to wider sections of the population, with the tantalizing possibility that a new technology might mark a decisive break with previous modes of political co-ordination and control.

Ideas of this kind were growing in popularity in the 1840s, especially among educated workers in London and Paris. They constituted a frame of reference in which substantive political, social and economic demands could be advanced – for universal male suffrage and annual parliaments among the Chartists of Britain, for a radical redistribution of property among the Paris workers. But, far-reaching though the practical implications of these demands might be, they were thoroughly reformist in tone. They would not change the basic structure of society. The contention was that by amending specific institutions and practices, wholesale benefits would accrue to working people.

What transformed socialism into a deadly threat to the liberal order was the supposition that meaningful change could not be achieved within the confines of a capitalist system. Tinkering with this or that abuse might, indeed, strengthen the *status quo* by distracting working people from their revolutionary opportunities. Where reformists had sought to convince a ruling elite of the justice of their cause, revolutionary socialists vested their hopes for the future in the working class. Capitalism had created, along with unparalleled wealth, an impoverished and brutalized proletariat. With dawning awareness of the logic of their class position, however, the proletariat would undergo a metamorphosis. The passive victims of capitalist exploitation could assume the direction of a new era.

Karl Marx was the principal architect of a class-based socialism. In his early writings he targeted his criticism on the view, central to liberal theory, that moral and political principles have universal scope and validity. The conception of rights embodied in the *Declaration of the Rights of Man and the Citizen* of 1789, for example, which purported to be a statement of the necessary conditions for the rounded political and social development of human beings everywhere, was seen by Marx as a defence of the sorts of conventions that might best advance the interests of the emergent bourgeoisie. Champions of the *Declaration* would not, of course, recognize the narrowness of their perspective. In arguing for certain rights, they meant what they said. What they had not grasped, however, was that the view which individuals form of their predicament (expressed in moral, political, philosophical, religious, aesthetic or whatever terms) is a product of their place in a complex of social and economic roles.

Marx, at this stage of his career, was engaged in the kind of unmasking exercise that had occupied his slightly older contemporaries, Strauss and Feuerbach, in their analyses of religion.[6] Religion had always been taken as a statement of perennial truth. Yet, according to Strauss and Feuerbach, it should be treated as an idealization of a conception of human nature prevalent in a particular historical culture. Strauss interpreted the New Testament in terms of the poetic consciousness of the Jewish and early Christian communities, utilizing a principle of 'mythical interpretation' in order to render intelligible the contradictory and confused stories that had been collected in the Bible. Feuerbach, by contrast, was more radically reconstructive, self-consciously inverting religious argument. His thesis was simple. Religion was not a transcendental realm of truth, but a deification of human characteristics which, if people only saw matters aright, were potentially the attributes of each and every one. Thus he treated the idea of God's perfection as a mirror image of the lack of love, harmony and fellow-feeling that disfigured society. Once this truth had been grasped, all mystification could be set aside. 'Temples in honour of religion' could be appropriately seen as 'temples in honour of architecture'.[7] Interpreted literally, Christianity was meaningless in Feuerbach's view. But when it was recognized 'that the secret of theology is anthropology . . . that the consciousness of God is nothing else than the consciousness of the species', then the way was clear for a realization of the potential that had always been latent in human beings (p. 270).

The implications of Feuerbach's approach extended beyond religion. He construed any doctrine that ignored human striving and feeling as an obstacle to happiness. Ideas that could not be translated into the language of human needs were nugatory. The simple recognition of the material foundation of concepts was (for Feuerbach) the key to a future of unprecedented peace and prosperity, a 'necessary turning-point of history' (p. 270). Henceforth people would recognize that the abstractions of religion and philosophy were but an inadequate means of describing the possibilities of their own nature. And, secure in this theoretical insight, they would fashion institutions and practices appropriate to their needs as a matter of course.

Marx extended this analysis to the political realm. The dominant political philosophy of his youth, that of Hegel, had portrayed the state as the concrete expression of the universal good of the community. Marx, instead, saw it as the protector of the economic and social interests of a dominant class. Faced with any statement of formal principles, Marx would always look to the class interest that had generated it. The whole of the ideological realm was (for Marx) but a reflection of more fundamental conflicts in economy and society.

Marx developed his position through painstaking analysis of Hegel's philosophy.[8] He came to see that it was not enough to apply a Hegelian method to various aspects of the ideology of modern society. The method itself had to be exposed as yet another example of ideological mystification. Hegel had claimed that his philosophy afforded a perspective which enabled the history of philosophy to be portrayed as both a historical and a logical progression; and as his own thought represented the final category of a logical system, Hegel could present his philosophy as the consummation of the Western philosophical tradition. But while Marx could accept that Hegel had brought traditional philosophy to a close, and that a rational process could be discerned within the apparently contingent phases of world history, he rejected the basic premiss of Hegel's system. The rationality of history was not a product of the 'spirit' or 'idea' working out its logical implications in the empirical world; and a phenomenology could not be conceived as an odyssey of consciousness culminating in self-knowledge. The categories of Hegelian philosophy were certainly to be found in history; but they were not the root cause of historical change. The logical 'moments' of Hegel's political philosophy, for example, had nothing to do with the requirements of the 'idea' of the state. They were, rather, products of the striving of individuals to satisfy mundane needs. Hegel had inverted the true order of things, interpreting ideological manifestations of empirical phenomena as the reality which events existed to disclose. Hegel, in other words, had attributed an autonomous existence to concepts, just as traditional theology had attributed an autonomous existence to God. In Marx's view, Hegel's seminal conception of the rationality of history would be turned to human advantage only when attention was once more focused on the empirical events that concepts had disguised.

Marx's shift of perspective involved a quite different conception of political argument. The ingenuity which past philosophers had devoted to the justification of abstract principles was clearly misplaced. What was required was not a titanic confrontation of concepts – divine right against natural right, liberty against equality – but an explanation of the economic changes that had brought forth particular ways of speaking about political life. Marx's focus was on the way in which material conditions impinge on people in the course of their efforts to sustain themselves. Unlike Feuerbach, however, he saw this as a dynamic process. He stressed the predicament of 'real individuals, their activity and the material conditions of their life, both those which they find already existing and those produced by their activity'.[9] The stress throughout is on the logic of subsistence and survival. People must work to satisfy their needs; and by doing so they transform the conditions of human life itself. Work is necessarily a social engagement. But the social relationships that people form in the course of their economic activity will not simply reflect their economic needs. The struggle for subsistence against nature is conducted by means of a technology that demands a certain division of labour. And, since 'the various stages of development in the division of labour are just so many different forms of property', the advantages that accrue to particular groups within a society will depend upon their access to and control of 'the material, instrument and product of labour' (p. 32). The characteristic features of the successive types of society – tribal, ancient urban, feudal, capitalist – are political reflections of the relationships of domination and subordination that arise from the distribution of property in each. The state, though purporting to represent the general interest of society, is in fact an instrument of oppression designed to secure the economic interest of the ruling class. In earlier epochs this economic dominance was tempered by the lingering natural obligations engendered by personal relationships within the family, tribe or manor; but with the development of capitalism, bonds of personal dependence give place to a notional freedom that allows unbridled accumulation of property. The practical corollary (according to Marx) is a progressive concentration of property in ever fewer hands, coupled with the creation of a proletariat utterly dependent on the vagaries of the labour market. Henceforth all relationships are seen in terms of the cash nexus; and (paradoxically) the preconditions are established for the emergence of a theory that, by focusing on the economic basis of society, at the same time offers the prospect of a future in which technological advance might mark the end of such economic dependence.

Nor is the dominance of the ruling class limited to the maintenance of the rule of law and existing economic arrangements. The class that wields economic power within a society is also able to 'regulate the production and distribution of the ideas of their age'; and hence 'the ideas of the ruling class are in every epoch the ruling ideas' (p. 59). This is not a deliberate ploy, but an illusion generally shared by rulers and ruled alike. The coherence of an age, which German historians in particular tended to attribute to the prevailing current of ideas, should in fact be explained as the product of predominant economic interests. A historical theory that 'takes every epoch at its word and believes that everything it says and imagines about itself is true' merely perpetuates a myth of the autonomy of ideas which had first arisen with the fateful distinction between mental and material labour (p. 62). Conflicts in the realm of ideas should be explained in terms of the conditions of production and the conflict of classes. Marx thus rejected the treatment of the French Revolution as a clash between honour and equality. The real battle, in Marx's view, was between an aristocracy clinging to the remnants of feudal society and a bourgeoisie seeking legal and political recognition for economic powers that were already established.

Marx, writing in collaboration with Friedrich Engels, drew these ideas together in a pamphlet, *The Communist Manifesto*, that became a model for a new style of political argument.[10] Conceived as a contribution to the turmoil of 1848, as revolutionary uprisings swept through Europe, the *Manifesto* sought to raise the consciousness of the industrial proletariat by explaining the economic basis of their new-found political strength. Marx's initial premiss was that all conflicts in society could be traced back to class divisions. 'The history of all hitherto existing society', he asserts without qualification, 'is the history of class struggles' (p. 67). These divisions could be complex in pre-capitalist societies, with subtle distinctions of status and rank changing slowly in relation to the distribution of economic power. With the advent of mature capitalism, however, a new phenomenon occurred. The interrelationships of earlier societies were tending to be replaced by a basic division into two broad classes, the bourgeoisie and the proletariat, with implacably opposed interests. The bourgeoisie, as owners of the means of production, would be intent upon maximizing their profits in order to survive the rigours of competition. The proletariat, on the other hand, who were propertyless, would be forced to sell their labour for subsistence wages. Since, according to Marx, the exploitation of the workers was the only source of profit in a capitalist system, it followed that the inexorable logic of competition would compel the bourgeoisie to squeeze ever more production out of workers in return for the lowest possible wages.

But here we see problems looming. Economies of scale dictated that production be concentrated in ever larger factories. Yet the discipline of factory life would accustom the proletariat to working together as a body. And it was but a small step from recognition of the interdependence of the system of production to recognition of the proletariat's collective interest as a class. As competition among producers became more intense, so extra pressure would be put upon the workers. The workers would be forced by their poverty to resist that pressure, first in the factory and subsequently (as political awareness grew) at national and international levels. Capitalists, in their restless pursuit of profit, would have created the conditions for their own undoing.

Marx's crucial point was that these problems were systemic rather than matters of policy. It was not open to enlightened entrepreneurs to modify their management practices in the light of Marx's analysis. Capitalists and workers alike are locked in structural conflict. Their actions can affect the timing of events, but not the long-term course of development. The revolutionary possibilities Marx highlighted in *The Communist Manifesto* depended upon the fullest development of capitalism. Marx was deeply suspicious of efforts by so-called 'utopian socialists' (such as Owen and Saint-Simon) to ameliorate the prospects of workers under industrial capitalism (pp. 94–7). Reform was a kind of prevarication, a failure to recognize that political development was actually driven by structural economic crises.

Through manipulation of propaganda, it might even be possible to persuade workers for a time that in the long term they could expect to enjoy a reasonable share of the fruits of capitalism. These promises, however, in Marx's view, were illusory. Capitalists were involved in deadly competition with one another, and this committed them to ruthless exploitation of workers. The bourgeoisie were thus driven by necessity to create '[their] own grave-diggers', a class (the proletariat) that was indispensable to the success of capitalism yet incompatible with its future survival (p. 79).

Marx's was an avowed determinist argument. Yet, running alongside his predictions for the inevitable triumph of the proletariat are 'moral' arguments that cannot always be reconciled with his theory. He values a form of association 'in which the free development of each is the condition for the free development of all' (p. 87). The implication is that this state of affairs is desirable, not simply that it will inevitably come to pass in due course. And for all that he defends capitalism as a necessary phase in the development of an ideal Communist society, his language regarding the exploitation and degradation of workers under capitalism is highly charged. What does freedom amount to 'under the present bourgeois conditions of production [but] free trade, free selling and buying'? (p. 81). In this situation individuals are free to sell themselves, but not to develop their rounded talents and personalities. Marx's response to the charge that communism involves the abolition of the family is scathing. Family life, he insists, is a disguised system of 'public prostitution', with women treated as 'mere instruments of production' (pp. 83–4). The position of children is no better. Economic desperation drives poor families to maximize the productivity of their children, exposing them to danger, disease and a generally brutalizing culture. Moralizing will not change this situation. Poor parents cannot enjoy the luxury of treating children as ends in themselves. The abolition of the family, in Marx's view, is a necessary condition for preventing 'the exploitation of children by their parents' (p. 83). If this is regarded as a crime, Marx is happy to 'plead guilty' (p. 83).

The *Manifesto* was no more than a schematic account of the economic context in which modern political battles were being fought out. Marx had focused on the need for the proletariat to base its political strategies on a realistic appraisal of the shifting balance of economic power. Capitalism had created a technology with vast economic potential; but that potential could not be fulfilled within the established legal and political order. The task of the revolutionary intellectual, and the specific point of the *Manifesto*, was to bolster the proletariat by showing precisely why capitalism would collapse under its own weight.

Marx's treatment of the detailed mechanics of revolutionary transformation is highly complex. His most succinct statement of the process of systemic change is in the preface to *A Contribution to the Critique of Political Economy* (1859). Here the mainspring of social and political change is located in the uneven development of the 'forces of production' and 'relations of production'. While 'relations of production' correspond to 'material productive forces', they do not adapt automatically to technological innovations. 'At a certain stage of their development, the material productive forces of society come in conflict with the existing relations of production, or – what is but a legal expression for the same thing – with the property relations within which they have been at work hitherto.'[11] Thus, though the definition of property rights will be tied to a particular phase in the development of the forces of production, the forces of production will change in ways incompatible with the established relations of production as these are embodied in legal and moral assumptions. Property rights that had fostered the advance of a particular technology (the unlimited accumulation of the bourgeois epoch was a necessary condition for the development of large-scale industry) finally ossify and are unable to meet the requirements of a new situation (the pursuit of profit, necessary for survival in a market economy, exacerbates the crises of overproduction which are said to plague the later stages of capitalism). 'From forms of development of the productive forces these relations turn into their fetters. Then begins an epoch of social revolution. With the change of the economic foundation the entire immense superstructure is more or less rapidly transformed.'[12]

The relationship between economic base and ideological superstructure has always been a vexed issue in Marxian studies. The tone of the 1859 preface suggests a strong determinism that contrasts sharply with the emphasis on 'praxis' in Marx's early writings. Indeed, it was precisely a passive determinism that Marx objected to in Feuerbach. Even in Marx's later writings, however, in which he self-consciously cast his work in the style of a science of society, a commitment to facilitate revolutionary transformation was always evident. His point was simply that the complexity of the social world obliges anyone who takes change seriously to focus in detail on the structures, practices and institutions that shape a political order. Marx rejected the method of the utopian socialists, but not necessarily their goals. From the outset he had taken Hegel's dictum to heart. Philosophy should certainly be construed as 'its own time apprehended in thoughts'.[13] It was just that, for Marx, philosophy could not be conceived as an independent and autonomous activity. Conceptual clarity can help to change the world, but only if the burden of the world is taken into account.

The only economic system that Marx studied in detail, both because statistics were more readily available and because urgent political questions hinged upon economic analysis, was capitalism. The fortunes of the English economy during the industrial revolution and after served as his model of capitalism as a system. And the point of his enquiries was to show, not that certain economic arrangements were undesirable or reprehensible, but that an economic system had emerged from its predecessor and would succumb to its successor despite (rather than because of) the choices of individuals.

Individuals (to be sure) could hasten the demise of an economic system; but in the last resort all would be obliged to move in the direction determined by the forces of production.

In the first volume of *Capital* (1867) – volumes 2 and 3 only appeared after Marx's death, thanks to devoted editorial work by Engels – Marx demonstrated how the logic of capitalist production created the conditions for the emergence of a new order.[14] A bald summary can barely do justice to the subtlety of the argument. In Marx's account, profit accrues to the capitalist because the subsistence wages he pays to his employees fail to match the value of the goods they produce. This is the so-called theory of surplus-value (see pp. 258–69). With the advance of technology and the threat of competition, however, only large-scale, highly capital-intensive enterprises would flourish. This would make production more efficient, but only by increasing the ratio of fixed to variable costs. Yet fixed costs (investments in land, plant and technology) do not themselves generate profits, at least in Marx's view. As the proportion of variable capital diminishes, so too would the source of the capitalist's profit in the surplus value produced by his employees. This is the root of the vicious circle that creates the periodic crises of capitalism. Each crisis obliges the capitalist to squeeze ever more profit out of the workers; and at the same time competition leads to the extension of automated machinery that puts ever more workers (the only source of profit) out of work. A paradox has arisen: technology has created unprecedented material plenty, but the situation of the worker is such that he can neither enjoy a reasonable share in those riches nor provide a market that would ensure their continuance.

In *Capital* Marx fleshed out in detail the schematic account of revolution he had presented in the *Manifesto*. He showed through minute analysis of capital accumulation and factory organization how the logic of capitalist production engendered implacable hostility between the bourgeoisie and the proletariat. Yet modes of social organization dictated by class conflict would finally resolve the crisis. The discipline and structure of the modern factory would lead workers to recognize that they had interests in common as a class (see pp. 492–639). The discipline of the factory would be a preparation for the political struggle that the workers would wage against the bourgeoisie, while the degradation and uncertainty of factory life would remind them of how little they had to lose. Capitalism, devoted to the production of 'exchange value', would collapse, because it could no longer satisfy economic needs (see pp. 126–8). The poverty of the proletariat would ruin the home market; imperialist adventures in search of markets and resources overseas would offer only a temporary palliative; and developing technology would undermine the traditional source of profit by reducing the man-hours involved in a particular productive process. As economic conditions deteriorated and class conflict intensified, workers would focus more precisely on crucial political goals. The property relations associated with capitalism would be recognized as obstacles to the satisfaction of needs that technological development had brought within reach. In Marx's view, the social organization of the factory should find its proper complement in the public ownership of the economy. With the abolition of private property, production for 'exchange value' would give place to production for 'use value'. Capitalist technology was thus a necessary condition for the achievement of socialism. But once material need had been abolished, the necessity for antagonistic relations of production (and hence the state as a means of maintaining order) would be a thing of the past.

Marx developed his argument with a wealth of economic detail, which it is scarcely necessary to reproduce here. Nor are the niceties of his economic theory of primary concern. The point to stress is that he saw the development of the productive forces of capitalism as the root cause determining second-ary changes in the political and legal superstructure; and saw that the ideo-logical conflict between bourgeoisie and proletariat was but a reflection of the more fundamental contradiction between the forces of production and the relations of production.

Marx is much less precise on what a Communist future would look like. His treatment of the state as a coercive apparatus in the hands of a ruling class to contain class conflict has profound implications for a prospective future in which the fundamental causes of conflict have been removed. Co-ordination problems would remain in any conceivable future. But Marx saw these as essentially technical matters. Efficient administrative decisions need not involve the panoply of instruments of coercion and control presupposed in state-centred theory. Indeed, there are passages in Marx's early writings in which he waxes lyrical about prospects for personal fulfilment in a purely consensual social order. In *The German Ideology* (1846) he pictures a scheme of social organization based upon individual disposition and choice, rather than the division of labour. We would no longer be confined to 'one exclusive sphere of activity', but would each be able 'to hunt in the morning, fish in the afternoon, rear cattle in the evening, criticise after dinner, just as [we] have a mind, without ever becoming hunter, fisherman, shepherd or critic'.[15] But in the same text he also accepts that the proletariat would initially have to 'conquer political power in order to represent its interest in turn as the general interest'.[16] And this, of course, could not be accomplished without the systematic use of force. How long force would be required would depend on the tenacity and resilience of the displaced orders of society, striving desper-ately to maintain their privileges.

Marx was far from mechanistic in the application of his theory to concrete cases. The theory emphasized factors that mistaken philosophical assump-tions had formerly concealed from political analysts whose judgement had been overwhelmed by details. Indeed, Marx was adept at amending the theory of historical materialism to explain political events. His most instruc-tive essays in this vein are *The Class Struggles in France: 1848–1850* (1850) and *The Eighteenth Brumaire of Louis Bonaparte* (1852).[17] In both, Marx is concerned to account for the apparent failure of the European revolutions of 1848 in terms of an alignment of classes that made revolutionary expectations premature. The polarization of classes announced in *The Communist Manifesto* had failed to materialize. But the fragmentation of classes, the principal obstacle to the revolution in France, could be explained by recourse to the same materialist assumptions that had informed the *Manifesto*. The political divisions in the French ruling class before 1848, in Marx's view, reflected fundamental divisions in the economy. The lack of common interest between great landowners, the financial aristocracy and the industrial bourgeoisie was evident in the political sphere in the conflict between Legitimists and Orleanists. Only in the face of a threat from the democratic socialists would such disparate interests find common ground in the need for order to secure their property. Hence (paradoxically) the most appropriate political form for contending royalist aspirations was a bourgeois republic sustained by nothing more substantial than fear of the Paris proletariat.

The mass of the French people did not come into these political calculations. The peasants remained outside the range of class interests represented by the bourgeois republic. For though the peasants 'form a class' in the sense that they 'live under economic conditions of existence that separate their mode of life, their interests and their cultural formation from those of the other classes and bring them into conflict with those classes', yet because they 'are merely connected on a local basis, and the identity of their interests fails to produce a feeling of community, national links, or a political organization, they do not form a class' (p. 239). Unaware of their common interests and unable to represent themselves, the peasants nevertheless constituted a vast latent force which could be exploited by a demagogue. This was the basis of Louis Bonaparte's *coup d'état* of 1851. Despite the opposition of both Legitimists and Orleanists, Bonaparte was finally able to count on the support of the bourgeoisie simply because he seemed to promise an end to the political chaos and uncertainty that threatened the economy. In the last resort, only a class analysis could explain the rise of such a mediocrity.

Nor was Marx's faith in the inevitability of proletarian revolution shaken by the evident success of the reaction. Revolutionary failure was itself an educational experience which helped to dispel the myths and illusions that had informed political conduct in the past. Bonaparte's success had resulted in a simplification of class relationships. Henceforth it would be clear that differences within the party of order disguised a common class interest. Faced with 'a powerful and united counter-revolution', the peasants and the petty bourgeoisie would fall in behind the proletariat to form 'a real party of revolution' (p. 35).

Marx was thus able to refine the schematic account of class consciousness drawn from his theoretical writings in his interpretations of contemporary political events in France. He treated historical materialism, not as an a priori theory of social change, but as an interpretative device that enabled the fundamental factors of a complex situation to be distinguished. Marx did not question the determining role of the forces of production in these essays; but he was clear that their ideological reflection in political struggles would be dependent upon circumstances. The gap between a model of capitalism and its development in practice could be filled only by empirical enquiry.

Marx's writings have always been notoriously contentious, not least because he addressed a variety of audiences in the course of a prolific career. Theoretical treatises, political pamphlets and newspaper articles could not be expected to share a common form. And once a text becomes an authoritative source in political debate, it is likely to be used and abused for any number of strategic reasons. Considered in the round, however, Marx's writings reveal a striking degree of consistency. His specific political predictions, of course, were not to be realized. The revolution which he had confidently expected in 1848 receded in his later writings to a more distant prospect. Nor can it be said that the states which proclaimed themselves to be 'Marxist' in the twentieth century emerged in quite the way Marx had anticipated. But the fact remains that Marxism has signally enriched political debate. As an analytical tool, it has enabled historians and political theorists to set the conventional terms of political discourse in a novel and perhaps more critical context. More important, at the practical level, it has furnished a theoretical framework that lends political significance to ordinary events in the lives of working people. Grinding experience of home and work had never been more than a background condition in liberal theory, an incentive to individuals to try to better themselves, but without positive value. In a broader context, however, the lessons of life's daily round could assume a national or international relevance, extending the horizons of the working class without detaching them from their immediate concerns. By the 1860s the impact of an organized labour movement was beginning to be felt. Groups which liberalism had largely disregarded were now demanding both a concrete improvement in their working conditions and a more active role in political life. And while there was nothing in liberal doctrine that denied the validity of the widest possible participation in politics, the substantive claims being advanced by working-class organizations were scarcely translatable into the formal language of classical liberal theory.

The success of Marxism is best measured in terms of the breadth of its impact. Groups which would not describe themselves as Marxist could profit from the new emphasis on the politics of labour. Nor was Marx's direct legacy uniformly revolutionary. Soon after his death in 1883, leading intellectuals (Labriola and Croce in Italy, Sorel in France, Bernstein in Germany) were debating the practical implications of Marx's theories. Bernstein's *Evolutionary Socialism* (1899), for example, defended the compatibility of socialist goals with the constitutional framework of a liberal state.[18] In his view, social legislation could transform the position of the working class, opening up possibilities for political involvement without necessarily changing the structure of the state. Legislation could ease the passage from capitalism to socialism, without the unpredictable trauma of revolutionary violence. Skilled workers, in particular, were offered much to encourage them in Bernstein's vision of the future. They were already far removed from the plight of the proletariat depicted in *The Communist Manifesto*, with 'nothing to lose but their chains'.[19] Labriola and Croce, by contrast, focused on the claims of Marxism to be regarded as a science.[20] Sorel stressed the role of Marxism as a political myth, effective as a means of mobilizing the working class but self-defeating as a predictive theory.[21] Marxism clearly could not be regarded as an orthodoxy, even when it was taken seriously. Marx himself had shown some awareness of these difficulties, though he always felt torn between the demands of theoretical controversy and effective political propaganda. It became evident, though, that when due attention was given to particular political contexts, Marxism could be used to justify an evolutionary as well as a revolutionary road to socialism. What had originally been presented as the doctrine of a small revolutionary sect could by the 1890s function as the theoretical foundation for a broad-based ideology, embracing a multitude of diverse groups and associations.

Positions within the socialist tradition thus split in a bewildering variety of ways. What they all shared, however, was a preoccupation with the substantive welfare of the working and excluded classes. In time, parliamentary democracies recognized that they would not be regarded as legitimate if they failed to provide for the basic needs of their peoples. An effective political response to Marxism had accordingly to be practical as well as theoretical. It remained to be seen whether liberal constitutional principles would be retained as states sought to maximize their effective capacities.

8 Totalitarianism

Domestic and international insecurity heightened the demands on states, leading elites to take more prominent roles in the direction and regulation of all aspects of their societies. Welfare commitments were massively expanded before 1914 in Europe, significantly eroding the distinction between public and private spheres. Liberal governments in Britain endorsed the more interventionist role for the state that had been advocated by T. H. Green and his school, presenting the state as a driving force for economic and social progress. On health and welfare issues, for example, it was accepted that the state should restrict the freedom of some groups in order to enhance the welfare of the most vulnerable. Lloyd George could picture the state as a substantive provider, caring for citizens 'from the cradle to the grave'. And in 1911 ground-breaking (and highly contentious) constitutional reform asserted the priority of electoral representatives over the inherited political privileges of an aristocracy.

A similar pattern emerged in other European states. In Italy after 1876 the ruling liberals rejected the idea of a night-watchman state in favour of direct governmental sponsorship of industry and commerce. The *Kulturkampf* in Germany, too, saw liberal opinion supporting a role for the state in the spheres of morality and culture that would have been anathema in the days of Wilhelm von Humboldt's influence. And throughout Europe in the 1880s we see states pursuing aggressive foreign policies, especially in Africa, designed both to promote economic interests and to sustain a certain conception of what went with 'great power' status. Perceived weakness was seen as a recipe for political disaster. Hence states had to show expansionist intent, even if their economic, technological and institutional positions made expansion a decidedly problematic option. International politics was a 'social darwinist' game. Only strength could guarantee survival, but the logic of competition meant that all states had to gear their domestic politics to the demands of a perception of ever-increasing military risk. This really was a 'war of all against all', with no prospect of a *Leviathan* in sight to ensure peaceful coexistence.[1]

Experience of war in 1914–18 forced elites to mobilize their populations in unprecedented fashion. Total war called for wholly new modes of organization and control. The effort, in fact, was beyond the capacity of some states. Russia found herself engulfed in revolution in 1917. And revolutionary crises threatened Germany and Italy.

Peace in 1918 brought its own problems. The collapse of the Austro–Hungarian Empire left a potentially unstable power vacuum. National identity and democracy were seen as the twin principles that might guarantee lasting peace. Yet in practice it was by no means easy to reconcile the two in contexts in which population movements over centuries had created deep cultural divisions. The majority principle, in particular, was threatening to minorities throughout Europe. Linking the idea of the 'nation' with the idea of the 'state' created problems for domestic and international order that have remained to this day.

Attempts to establish parliamentary politics proved to be precarious. Minorities in certain states would watch with envy as their fellow nationals fashioned adjacent states to fit the requirements of their culture and interests. Political elites would be under pressure from electorates and wider popular movements to respond to the indignities inflicted on 'kith and kin' across newly significant frontiers. Neither nationalism nor democracy provided obvious resources to deal with these issues consensually.

Economic crisis after 1929 brought matters to a head. The combination of financial collapse globally and international insecurity swept parliamentary regimes away in central and eastern Europe. And even Britain and France continued to enjoy parliamentary politics only in truncated forms in the 1930s. Opinions were being polarized, leaving diminishing scope for the consensual resolution of deep differences.

The stakes in ideological controversy had been raised, and accordingly we find a sharpening of polemical tone. Parliamentary politics was effectively under threat from both left and right. Lenin's *What is to be Done?* (1902) was typical of a style of argument that subordinated theoretical balance to practical efficacy. The point of political debate was to mobilize a constituency. Argument was a political weapon alongside others, depending upon particular circumstances. There was no place, in this scheme of things, for balanced consideration of the views of opponents.

What is to be Done? is best read as Lenin's contribution to the controversies surrounding the (so-called) crisis of Marxism. He discounted the possibility of a parliamentary road to socialism, urging instead the need to form a vanguard party of the proletariat to assume the direction of affairs, in order to raise the political consciousness of workers and peasants. Lenin objected, in particular, to the various species of reformism inspired by Bernstein's defence of an evolutionary transition to socialism. If workers were encouraged to play the bourgeois parliamentary game, they would merely find their interests subordinated to the bourgeoisie. Skilled workers might profit as individuals, but that would necessarily be at the expense of the masses. There is no middle ground here, no scope for a discursive settlement of apparently opposed perspectives. Lenin saw himself as an orthodox Marxist, while recognizing that effective politics depended upon tactical flexibility. He took the materialist analysis of the generation of ideas very seriously indeed.

In Lenin's view, 'there can be no talk of an independent ideology' that miraculously reconciles antithetical class interests.[2] He asserts categorically that 'in a society torn by class antagonisms' a 'non-class or above-class ideology' is conceptually inconceivable: workers will support either 'bourgeois or socialist ideology' (pp. 121–2). The point of polemic is precisely to rid them of self-deception.

Lenin steered a tortuous path between what he styled 'economism' on the one hand and 'terrorism' on the other (pp. 149–52). 'Economism' offered passive explanation of the way in which ideological perspectives were shaped by class interest. As a political strategy, however, it was seriously limited, since (as a matter of fact) workers had shown a remarkable capacity to endorse 'false' ideological positions. The attractions of 'bourgeois' reformism or various species of nationalism had effectively split the working-class movement, with catastrophic consequences for the political mobilization of the interests of workers. Workers had been duped into supporting the political positions of their class enemies, as should have been clear to close readers of Marx's writings.

Disenchantment with 'passive' class analysis could lead workers to embrace 'terrorism' as a political tactic. Violent confrontation might shake both workers and authorities out of their complacency, sharpening the real class divisions that would shape political conflict in the future. Violence as a symbolic and mobilizing strategy had been defended by Georges Sorel in *Reflections on Violence* (1908), and would resonate across the political spectrum in Europe in the 1920s. In Lenin's view, however, the impact of 'terrorism' as a strategy on the working-class movement would be disastrous. Detached from sustained theoretical analysis, political energies would be dissipated, effectively fragmenting the political organization of the working class and leaving them an easy target for their enemies.

Lenin championed working-class interests in a broader context of classes, whose emancipation from the constraints of a bourgeois state would be achieved only with the overthrow of capitalism. Crucially, however, awareness of the need for a vanguard party would not be a spontaneous product of experience of class conflict under capitalism. The working class required a certain kind of political leadership before they could be expected to grasp the revolutionary potential of their class position. Working-class experience itself would not be sufficient. Lenin is adamant on this point. 'Class political consciousness' (he says) 'can be brought to the workers *only from without,* that is, only from outside the economic struggle, from outside the sphere of relations between workers and employers' (p. 152). This was a strong plea for the priority of theory over practice, with fateful consequences for prospects for political freedom under Communist party leadership. An elite would be authorized to lead in the name of the working class, but not through the perspective of working-class values and culture. Propaganda would be required to mould attitudes. And given the urgency of the political situation, and the need to take full advantage of revolutionary opportunities, quiet persuasion and measured argument would be ineffective. Marxist theory could justify ruthless manipulation.

In Lenin's view, then, the very idea of a parliamentary road to socialism is a contradiction in terms. Class conflict could be expected to become more intense as capitalism neared its final crisis. In order to be an effective political force, a Communist party in these circumstances had to be geared to the demands of insurrection, manipulation and control. Democratic politics was a luxury that a revolutionary party could not afford. In *The State and Revolution*, a polemical text written in haste shortly before the revolution in Russia in 1917, Lenin scathingly dismissed democracy as a bourgeois obsession. All it amounted to in a capitalist context was 'democracy for an insignificant minority, democracy for the rich'.[3] Capitalist democracy 'is inevitably narrow and stealthily shoves aside the poor' (p. 79). Given that it is predicated upon political exclusion, it is 'pervasively hypocritical and false' (p. 79). Nor can it be assumed that there will be a 'progressive development . . . towards ever greater democracy', as Bernstein and others had argued (p. 79). The structures of capitalism will not disappear overnight. An initially successful political revolution will need to be followed by ruthless elimination of the remnants of capitalism. Lenin is emphatic on this issue. A temporary 'dictatorship of the proletariat' will be required to break 'the resistance of the exploiter-capitalists' (p. 79). There is no ambiguity in Lenin's language, any more than there can be any temporizing in a revolutionary situation. The previous oppressors of the poor cannot be persuaded to endorse the perspective of the proletariat. They will resist revolution, and 'their resistance must be crushed by force' (p. 80). Just as revolution imposes its own organizational demands, so institutional reconstruction after revolution must be focused on the pressing problems to hand. If resistance is to be suppressed and coercion is necessary, Lenin is clear that there can be 'no freedom and no democracy' (p. 80).

It is a vexed question in Leninist theory precisely how long the dictatorship of the proletariat will be necessary. Lenin assumes that the state will 'wither away' in an unspecified future (p. 80). But he insists that this will be a gradual process, finally coming to fruition once 'habit' has accustomed people 'to observing the necessary rules of social intercourse' (p. 80). A great deal hinges, of course, on what the 'necessary rules of social intercourse' might amount to, and (more importantly perhaps) who will be authorized to declare what they should be. Lenin envisages a utopian future in which 'there is nothing that rouses indignation, nothing that calls forth protest and revolt and creates the need for suppression' (p. 80). But we cannot read these passages with any confidence if we harbour the suspicion that human needs might be controversial. Lenin does not allow his utopianism about the (more or less distant) future to distract him from the more immediate task of consolidating the 'transition from capitalism to communism' (p. 81).

Institutional mechanisms will continue to be required to suppress exploiters and free riders. He simply presupposes that breaches of the 'necessary rules of social intercourse' are caused by poverty and deprivation. This is not an empirical proposition for Lenin. It follows from his analysis of the generation of conflict. It is similarly axiomatic that the state will 'wither away' simply because it is (by definition) an organ of class oppression. State-like functions will need to be fulfilled only so long as the remnants of class oppression persist. And they cannot persist indefinitely. There is no need to specify a time-scale.

Lenin was always much more specifically focused on the strategic demands of revolution than Marx. Two of his most widely read works, *The State and Revolution* and *Imperialism, the Highest Stage of Capitalism* (1917), were attempts to analyse the contemporary situation with a view to maximizing the revolutionary potential of a manifest crisis in Europe.[4] It would be a mistake, however, to treat either work as mere propaganda. The latter, in particular, is a sophisticated attempt to apply Marxian economic analysis to the international political context, effectively extending and revising Marx's discussion of imperialism in the posthumously published third volume of *Capital.*[5] Few years in modern European history have been quite so dramatic as 1917. Europe was embroiled in a war which, within two years, would precipitate revolutionary transformation in Russia and a chaotic dismemberment of the Austro–Hungarian Empire. Two of the principal pillars of European geo-political order would have been swept away. And for the first time, the United States would emerge as a major player in the international politics of Europe.

Lenin continued to insist that Europe's crisis was structural, and not simply a matter of foolish political management on the part of the great powers. War itself he saw as a product of the imperialist adventures that major states had embarked upon as they sought to weather the crises of capitalism. Lenin could tell a story linking the Spanish–American War (1898), the Anglo–Boer War (1899–1902) and the dramatic consequences of the European war that broke out in 1914. As Lenin wrote *Imperialism, the Highest Stage of Capitalism,* war in Europe was continuing, with long-term results that could not be confidently predicted. What was certain, though, was that questions of domestic and international order were inextricably interlinked. Lenin tried to explain these connections in theoretical terms, though his discussion remains highly contentious and deeply charged.

Lenin specifically saw imperialism as 'the eve of the social revolution of the proletariat'.[6] Capitalism had effectively 'internationalized' the class struggle, in ways that had taken socialists throughout Europe by surprise in 1914. For most socialists, the thought that workers would enlist for a capitalist war was anathema. The appeal of nationalism had proved to be far stronger than class solidarity. Yet close readers of Marx could extend discussions of demagogic populism within states to the ease with which political leaders managed to persuade workers to pit their lives against fellow workers in neighbouring states.

As capitalist competition became more deadly economically, so states would try to maximize their resources by exploiting cheap labour and raw materials overseas. This would inevitably lead to conflict as states found themselves locked in struggles for empire. War itself would also change economies dramatically, leading 'directly to the most comprehensive social-isation', dragging 'the capitalists, against their will and consciousness, into some sort of a new social order, a transitional one from complete free compe-tition to complete socialisation' (p. 649). Thus at both elite and popular levels, transformations were afoot that would make a straightforward resumption of parliamentary politics and market-based capitalism deeply problematic when states had fought themselves to exhaustion.

Lenin supplies a wealth of detail to explain the causal link between what he styles 'monopoly capitalism' and imperialism (pp. 442–53). What this high-lights in both economic and political terms is a concentration of decision making in ever fewer hands. Under monopoly conditions, decisions about production, distribution and exchange have already become so thoroughly centralized that market criteria cease to operate in the fashion envisaged by classical economists. Lenin, of course, sees no problem with this, anticipat-ing a wholly different distributive principle once communism is finally attained. Relative scarcity would no longer be a relevant factor in the alloca-tion of resources; hence individual and collective decision making would not be governed by calculations of marginal utility. In such a situation, decision making would reflect Marx's dictum: 'From each according to his ability, to each according to his need.'[7] The allocation of roles, responsibilities and rewards is unlikely to be contentious in conditions of plenty. Yet administrat-ive decisions will have to be made. And we may assume that questions of marginal utility will continue to be relevant.

Utopia, however, is a prospect for a (more or less) distant future in Lenin's writings. Revolution in the name of communism will not bring its immediate fulfilment. The conquest of the state by Communists actually obliges them to use the state ruthlessly for their own ends. In the aftermath of revolution, argues Lenin, socialists will 'demand the *strictest* control by society *and by the state* over the measure of labour and the measure of consumption'.[8] How long such structures would have to remain in place is a matter of fine judgement. Lenin's expectation in 1917 was that revolution in Russia would trigger wider upheavals in the more developed European states. The outcome was in fact very different. Though there were other revolutionary disturbances, success-ful revolution was accomplished only in Russia. The Soviet Union was left trying to consolidate itself in hostile circumstances both domestically and internationally. A bitter civil war saw massive administrative dislocation and chronic food shortages. If rigid centralization of decision making was neces-sary in revolution, it became even more imperative in the face of institutional implosion. The temporary 'dictatorship of the proletariat' was transformed into the permanent dictatorship of the Communist Party, informed by the daunting (and finally catastrophic) project of reshaping a culture in its entirety.

Controversy still rages about just how far the Soviet Union should be regarded as a Marxist (or even Leninist) state. Lenin's was very much a theory of the state in revolution. His followers (down to Gorbachev) often tried to distance his theory from the form the Soviet Union assumed under Stalin. There is no doubt, though, about Lenin's deep-seated hostility to autonomous institutions within the sphere of civil society. His rejection of pluralism was complete, on both theoretical and political grounds. In his view, difference amounted to deviation from an appropriate path. Lenin assumed that such a path could be specified theoretically. That, in itself, is a controversial, though not necessarily sinister, position. What makes his doctrine so chilling is the easy shift to a view of theoretical opponents as necessarily political enemies. Here are grounds for political paranoia, without invoking the idea of a paranoid personality such as Stalin. Even the most doctrinaire of us can tolerate theoretical opponents if we regard them as benign or irrelevant. Class analysis of theoretical disagreement raises the stakes significantly. If class division is the root cause of differences of political view, then there is no scope for discursive agreement. Hypothetical 'bridging' positions are not available. A regime governed according to these assumptions may be more or less brutal; but it could not be an open society. In this scheme of things, the gap between theoretical conviction and political cynicism is very narrow indeed.

The view from the right was no more flattering for parliamentary politics. The dominant progressive ideologies of the nineteenth century, liberalism and socialism, both had roots in the Enlightenment belief in the historical emergence of a rationally defensible political order. To be sure, they depicted radically different paths to a reasonable politics; and their assumptions about how that politics would ideally work were starkly opposed. From the perspective of the first decades of the twentieth century, however, ideologies which had been assumed to be at opposite poles of the political spectrum began to exhibit strong affinities. Liberalism and socialism were products of the cult of science, aiming to subject all facets of a way of life to rational scrutiny. No one could doubt the power of the industrial technology that had transformed life prospects in the nineteenth century. One way or another (it was assumed), this capacity to change the world could be harnessed for the unprecedented betterment of humankind. The image of massively powerful industrial states locked in imperial competition and conflict put a very different gloss on a complacent picture. And experience of the First World War itself brought these doubts to the fore for ordinary soldiers who had little interest in economic or political theory. A technology that could lead to the slaughter of thousands for the sake of a few hundred metres of territory did not look like the apogee of progress. Certainly elites that had sacrificed troops on this scale would find their authority shaken.

Political and economic traumas were obvious. At a deeper level, philosophers, psychologists, novelists, dramatists and commentators more broadly had begun to question the conception of the individual that had informed the development of liberalism in particular. John Stuart Mill, for example, had no doubt that individuals could take stock of their conduct, learn from experience, respond to criticism and plan for the future. No doubt this is an idealization. Mill was as aware as anyone that we do not always act rationally. We might put the best gloss we can on our conduct in public, while recognizing that we might have been motivated by envy, greed or lust. From the 1880s, however, the disturbing prospect was raised that all our actions might be rationalizations of more fundamental drives. The received scientific view in the nineteenth century depended upon assumptions about impartiality and objectivity. Nietzsche and others raised the prospect that all judgements might be expressions of partial perspectives.[9] The cult of 'scientific' objectivity might serve the scientist very well as an individual who wants to be taken seriously. But suppose his knowledge claims are simply projections of interest – plausible, for sure, and cast in a highly sophisticated language? We do not have to assume that all statements have the same status to be concerned that none of them could possibly be objective. What exactly were social and political scientists trying to claim? They seemed not to be advancing ordinary opinions. Yet, if objectivity is an unattainable ideal, it is by no means clear what we should make of (so-called) experts.

Nor was moral conduct quite as straightforward as conventional wisdom had assumed. Freud and an emerging school in psychology would identify the subconscious as a source of action and decision, relegating moral precepts to a problematic status. Moral choice could no longer be seen simply as a matter of doing the right thing. Each of us would be given grounds to mistrust at least some of our attitudes. Here, again, we are dealing with matters of degree. We can each accept that motivation is a complex matter. None of us can be quite sure of our deepest reasons for holding certain beliefs or pursuing specific objectives. What is novel (and disturbing) in psychoanalytic language is that the unity of the self is being challenged. In Freud's case, childhood sexuality is a key to the explanation of personality. Yet these are not necessarily matters that we are ordinarily aware of at all. Subconsciousness exists for us only after it has been theoretically characterized. From that moment, however, whether we endorse the idea of the subconscious or not, we have at least to consider the possibility that we may not (perhaps cannot) mean what we say. We are torn between different accounts of what we are 'really' doing, with no clinching grounds for preferring one theoretical explanation to another. Theories of these kinds can be destabilizing in ordinary circumstances; in a context of political and cultural crisis, they can also be thoroughly subversive.

Implications for parliamentary politics can be particularly troubling. Debate between groups holding distinctive positions is at the heart of the idea. Political programmes and ideas may well support certain interests rather than others, but the thought that they merely reflect those interests narrows the scope for principled agreement. Marxist class analysis focuses on this specific point. If the factors that drive political argument are broadened, embracing national, ethnic or racial identity, struggles for power or status or personality clashes, then principled justifications of specific forms of political order begin to look precarious. When parliamentary politics is going well, these concerns will not dominate everyday perceptions of public life. We can comfortably think of parliamentary politics as (among other things) a competition between elites in good times. Authorities begin to look exposed, however, if it is felt that nothing else is at stake than the spoils that power confers.

This is precisely the move that Vilfredo Pareto made in his *Socialist Systems* (1902). He focused specifically on the humbug (as he saw it) at the heart of socialism. Far from offering people a prospect of liberation from class-inspired government, socialist parties were just another emerging elite struggling to dominate a political order. For Pareto it is axiomatic that all political competition is simply 'the struggle between one aristocracy and another'.[10] Ideology is irrelevant here. A democratic context will make popular appeal a key factor in political success. Political leaders will be encouraged to project themselves as champions of the people. Propaganda will be fashioned to meet the demands of the problem to hand. Politicians may believe they are acting from principle, but in fact they will be trying to mobilize resources that had proved to be beyond the reach of political competitors. An entrenched elite will grow decadent, corrupt and finally ineffective. A rising elite will expose obvious political shortcomings in the name of an ideal or programme. We can take the sorry comedy at face value, or opt for a more compelling analysis. Political conflict (everywhere and always) is merely a competition between elites focused on perceived advantage. Pareto accepts that there are apparent changes of government, dressed up sometimes as radical breaches with old habits and customs. All that happens, in fact, is that one aristocracy is replaced by another. A new elite, for a time, may be more vigorous and effective. It will not help to have lofty ideals. Politics is (potentially deadly) struggle. The point is to be victorious, at whatever cost.

Pareto developed his view of elites through close study of parliamentary politics in Italy in the 1890s. Among his early publications was an analysis of the pattern of activity in the Italian parliament.[11] Despite the rhetoric of political debate and contrasting political programmes, what Pareto saw instead was that factions would shift position in order to consolidate support for particular sectional projects. Often this meant in practice that a faction leader would exchange support in parliament for a guarantee that government patronage would be put at his disposal in order to 'buy' electoral votes for his group. The parliamentary deputy would effectively act as a middle man between government spending channels and prominent constituents whose projects and interests would dominate local politics. Government conducted in this style could not be programmatic. The ruling bloc in parliament would 'absorb' as much support as possible from factions, making offers that could not be refused to faction leaders who made a nuisance of themselves. This is a game of political compromise played according to grubby rules. Isolating an individual from government-inspired contracts, or offering to support a challenger at an election, could spell disaster for a deputy. He was viewed by his influential constituents as a conduit to government. If he could not facilitate deals, he was dispensable. The upshot was stable government of a kind, but not strong government. Governments had to rely upon shifting coalitions of factions, all of which would have a narrow view of their political role. In Pareto's view, this was not simply an example of bad parliamentary practice; it was a style of doing political business generated by the parliamentary system itself. It could not be reformed. Governmental weakness was endemic to parliamentary politics.

Pareto had endorsed much of the Marxian critique of parliamentary representation, while categorically rejecting the Marxian solution. Parliamentary deliberation was inevitably a species of horse trading among private (perhaps predominantly class) interests. His point, however, is that a congeries of private interests could not mobilize sufficient interests around the basic goals that states had to accomplish. A state needed to be strong in relation to potential competitors. Indeed, the satisfaction of the private interests within a state could not be guaranteed if governments simply tried to broker a line of least resistance between interests. Weak government would ultimately undermine private interests. The state would be a prey to internal and external forces, unable to pursue consistent policies. Pareto's is a plea to free the state from the constraint of representative interests.

Pareto gave no clear indication in his writings as to how strong government might be attained, though at the end of his life he was sympathetic to the rise of Mussolini and the fascists in Italy. He saw parliamentary government as the end of a natural cycle. He describes the modern parliamentary system as 'the effective instrument of demagogic plutocracy'.[12] Writing in 1921, two years before his death, he could not envisage democratic politics of any kind surviving what he terms the 'vicissitudes of plutocracy' (p. 92). Government in organized societies, he argues, is 'regulated in the main by two agencies: consent and force' (p. 93). An era of consent, as he saw it, was coming to a close, to be followed inevitably by a sustained period of authoritarian government.

Theory began to catch up with practice as authoritarian politics made headway throughout Europe. Italian fascism, in particular, announced itself as a thoroughly modern phenomenon, unlike earlier authoritarian regimes and difficult to locate on the political spectrum. Exploiting language drawn from Sorel and revolutionary syndicalism, the movement could appeal to critics of capitalism whose previous sympathies had been with the left. Mussolini himself had for a time used Marxist language, before the question of Italian involvement in the First World War led to a splintering and reorientation of anti-capitalist thinking. Contrasting conceptions of the state finally clarified ideological positions, with fascists of all stripes urging governments to use force to impose order on a potentially chaotic world. Matters came to a head in Italy between 1919 and 1922. The success of the Russian Revolution in 1917 had shaken the confidence of establishments throughout Europe. Revolutionary turmoil in Italian factories brought the prospect of Bolshevism closer, precipitating (what many may have regarded as) an unholy alliance of defenders of capitalism and implacable critics of liberalism and parliamentary politics. The middle ground that liberals and reformist socialists had previously occupied lost all credibility in the space of two years. The spectacle of liberal political leaders encouraging Mussolini to form a government illustrates just how far a preoccupation with order had come to dominate political debate.

From the perspective of the right, just as from the left, parliamentary politics was collapsing under its own weight. Liberalism was seen as the flaw at the heart of the system, undermining the foundations of any conceivable political order. What had happened in Italy in 1922 was regarded as a foretaste of the fate of other parliamentary regimes. The choice was between Bolshevism or a species of explicit authoritarianism. There was no scope for limited government or a merely instrumental view of the state as a means to serve the interests of society. Political order was a necessary condition for any other satisfaction that human beings might collectively attain. And it had to be imposed by force.

These were not new ideas. They had been a feature of European political thought since Hobbes's *Leviathan* (1651). What was novel, however, was the administrative and technical capacity of the state in a modern context. Total control and surveillance of a society was simply not an option in the seventeenth century. It remains a moot point, of course, whether it is theoretically conceivable at all. It was nevertheless clear by the early twentieth century that populations could be mobilized and manipulated in unprecedented ways. Temptations were available to elites that looked irresistible in the light of the manifest weakness of the liberal constitutional state.

These arguments were drawn together with devastating effect in Carl Schmitt's *The Concept of the Political* (1927).[13] Schmitt is a controversial figure, not least because he joined the National Socialist Party in Germany in 1933 and for a time presented himself as something of an apologist for the Nazi regime. His ideas, however, capture the crisis of the 1920s with ruthless clarity, and remain disturbing to us precisely because we no longer feel we can take the normative foundation of our societies for granted. Like Pareto, Schmitt based his theoretical critique of liberalism on close study of parliamentary politics in practice.[14] He was haunted by the erosion of a specifically public sphere by the multifarious interests of society. Governments had been reduced to service status, ministering to the needs of powerful private interests. In the process, the liberal distinction between public and private realms had been effectively undermined. Private interests were in a position to dominate public debate so thoroughly that it was no longer possible to distinguish their preferences from the wider good of the state. The relationship between the 'general will' and the 'will of all' in Rousseau's analysis had been inverted, such that a public interest could not properly be characterized at all.[15] Liberal theory, in Schmitt's view, portrayed society as a plurality of interests, more or less compatible, with no prospect of an encompassing good that might bind a society together.

Schmitt's basic premiss is that social order is always under threat, from either internal dissension or external powers. This predicament is a limiting condition for any viable politics. It will not lose its relevance as societies become more sophisticated or interdependent. Liberal theories were built upon a progressive conception of history, picturing a future in which social and economic values would predominate. Schmitt dismisses such views as naïvely (and finally dangerously) utopian. Organized societies never cease to define themselves in opposition to one another. In political terms, this will reduce to an existential confrontation between 'friend and enemy'.[16] We can describe human relationships in all sorts of other ways. We may want to focus on the contrasting values that individuals or communities may profess, their different conceptions of beauty, their capacities to exploit and manage human and natural resources. These different criteria can connect us in all manner of cross-cutting ways; but they cannot overcome or replace the basic need to impose order on a territory. Note that Schmitt does not discuss the normative criteria that may distinguish political 'friends' from political 'enemies'. His point is more basic. We cannot think of communities at all unless we picture them locked in territorial competition and opposition. We cannot persuade communities to endorse our values or to subscribe to a common cause unconditionally. They may (contingently) support us on this or that issue. Yet nothing can guarantee *our* continuance as a community unless *we* resolve to defend ourselves and assert ourselves against others.

The point to stress, for Schmitt, is that political order must be considered as a good in itself. Within a political order we may be conditionally attached to a variety of goods. We may temporarily devote our energies and resources to certain objectives rather than others, secure in the knowledge that political order gives us the space to make choices. Our attachment to political order itself, however, should be beyond choice. Where we can agree to join a private association on certain terms, our allegiance to the state must be unconditional. Without that commitment, none of our enjoyments would be secure. While it might make sense to regard our endorsement of particular policies as conditional (Schmitt is cautious on this point), we cannot treat political order as a possible good alongside others. In this view, liberalism and democracy are both based upon conceptual confusion. Extra-legal values are invoked to judge the legitimacy of political order. We may regard liberalism (or democracy) as the best political means to attain humanitarian policies or maximal wealth. For these values to work politically, all right-thinking people would have to endorse them. And that can be discounted. Schmitt argues forcefully that political order cannot be a lowest common denominator of views in a pluralist society. No such lowest common factor exists. Political order needs to be imposed precisely because opinions in a society will naturally fragment. Consensus cannot be deep enough to function politically. In its absence, a community must use the force at its disposal to shape the parameters of a shared life.

Schmitt uses extreme cases to highlight the concept of the state and the political. Liberalism had tried to domesticate politics by focusing on the civil practices of moral and economic exchange. Instead of recognizing force and conflict as inescapable phenomena among human beings, liberals translate these notions into 'competition in the domain of economics and discussion in the intellectual realm'.[17] These activities, however, presuppose the existence of an established political order. Liberals, here as elsewhere, get the cart before the horse, treating the fruits of political order as instances of properly political activity. Yet only force (or the threat of force) can create and maintain political order. In quiet, comfortable and prosperous times we can forget this hard truth. But we also know that only states can declare war on each other. And when this happens, we cannot choose (as individuals) not to be at war. We are committed, no matter how deep our reservations may be. We can be compelled by the state to kill complete strangers and to put ourselves in harm's way. Nothing in the repository of liberal political concepts can quite prepare us for this extremity. It is an existential fate rather than a choice. In an important sense, for Schmitt, liberalism is an anti-politics. It should not surprise us that a politics so conceived would appear to be ineffective.

Schmitt's is a harsh view of politics, committing everyone to take sides unconditionally. Within these terms of reference, it should not surprise us that Schmitt (as a German patriot) felt that he had to support the Nazi state. Between 1933 and 1936, indeed, he enjoyed status and authority through the Nazi regime, though after 1936 he became an object of suspicion in some Nazi circles and progressively withdrew from public life. His political theory, however, must be read as a body of ideas distinct from the regime. There is no doubt that it inclined him to support Hitler and his coterie, though in later life he was anxious to distance himself from the more odious aspects of the regime. Schmitt's political entanglements do him no credit. Yet he had provided a defence of authoritarian politics that demands attention, fitted to the exigencies of a mass-based society. Whether we like it or not, an authoritarian strand persists in the European political tradition. In some guises it is compatible with democratic politics, and it is certainly appealing to electorates in times of crisis. It has to be grasped theoretically, both as a response to circumstances and as a normative body of ideas.

The totalitarian state was most fully theorized by Giovanni Gentile, to whom we owe the term in its modern form. A philosopher of genuine distinction, Gentile was a prominent figure, along with Benedetto Croce, in the resurgence of interest in philosophical idealism that flourished in Italy in the early decades of the twentieth century. As a philosophical school, idealists opposed materialism and positivism. There was no pretension among them to present a shared political position. Gentile and Croce, for example, who enjoyed a rich philosophical collaboration before 1922, actually split with the advent of fascism. Instructively, though, Croce, who presented himself for most of his life as a vigorous champion of political liberalism, had initially been guardedly sympathetic to Mussolini and the fascists, as a possible means of imposing order and effective government in face of the chaos and corruption that marked the immediate post-First World War years in Italy. Croce denounced fascism after the regime-inspired assassination of Matteotti, a socialist parliamentary deputy who had been an outspoken critic of the fascists in government, in 1924. The crisis sparked by the assassination was a defining moment in the development of a distinctively fascist state. Thereafter the fascist government progressively dispensed with the parliamentary trappings that had brought Mussolini to power. Croce responded by styling himself a public critic of fascism, albeit through the printed page rather than active involvement in political resistance. Gentile, by contrast, embraced the regime, serving as Minister of Education in Mussolini's first cabinet until 1924, and generally providing intellectual justification for a regime that professed to be inaugurating a radically new order in Italy.

Gentile was thus always close to the fascist regime. Though fascist doctrine shifted between 1922 and 1943, not always in ways that Gentile welcomed, he enjoyed authoritative status as the regime's 'official' philosopher. This, to be sure, is a dubious privilege. It has done little to enhance Gentile's philosophical reputation. He remains a tainted source, despite wide appreciation of his philosophical range and originality. His historical significance, however, is beyond dispute. He was not only a major influence on Mussolini, but also the actual author of some of the writings on fascism that appeared under Mussolini's name.[18] Political scientists examining fascism as a phenomenon have been reluctant to take it seriously as a body of ideas. To some extent this is understandable, since fascism prided itself as a philosophy of life and action, rather than as a narrow political theory or ideology, drawing eclectically from movements that challenged liberalism and socialism in a variety of guises. Yet Gentile's conception of totalitarianism is a distinctively fascist contribution to political theory. For all that the concept remains deeply troubling, it clearly has a resonance beyond the fascist era.

Gentile's political philosophy exploits standard objections to theories focused on the individual, but with a novel twist. He could accept, with Hegel and the nationalists, that individuals were in an important sense products of their communities. But where Hegel stressed established social structures, and nationalists a primordial cultural or ethnic community, Gentile highlighted the active role of the state, creating unity rather than passively reflecting it. It was not enough to value the traditions and practices that had shaped a way of life. Citizens had to identify with the organized projection of those values by the state, treating the state as the public embodiment of their personalities. Thus, where liberalism had sought to contain the state through constitutional procedures in the interest of the freedom of individuals, Gentile invited individuals to see their personal interests and values as inseparable from the state. There was no room for a distinction between public and private spheres in this scheme of things. Everything that we may value as individuals is evanescent, vulnerable to accident and misfortune; but the state can elevate the ordinary things we do to a higher status, permanently involved with the collective political life of fellow citizens over continuing generations.

The potential for a properly organized state to mould the attitudes of citizens was thus limitless. In an important essay of 1929 (*Origins and Doctrine of Fascism*) that continues to frame discussions of fascist theory, Gentile saw the mobilizing role of the state as the distinctive feature of fascist doctrine.[19] Above all, he insists on the 'totalitarian character' of fascist doctrine, concerning itself 'not only with political order and direction of the nation, but with its will, thought and sentiment'.[20] The state, for Gentile, could strive to shape any aspect of a way of life. It did not have to match a preconceived theoretical model in order to be regarded as legitimate. The state created the attitudes and values that enabled citizens to assess their public life. The idea of a political or social construction, newly fashionable in contemporary political theory, was taken by Gentile to an extreme. If, epistemologically, there is nothing outside the mind by which it can be judged, it follows that political orders establish their own terms of reference.[21] They may be more or less successful, but they cannot be illegitimate.

Gentile explores the implications of the priority of the state ruthlessly. Because 'the state is conceived as prior to the individual', individuals cannot possibly be in a position to lay down criteria for the proper pursuit of public objectives.[22] They cannot 'contract', actually or hypothetically, to institute a state. The status of being an 'individual' is conferred on citizens by the state. They have neither capacities nor concepts of themselves outside that political and social framework. Gentile terms the relationship between 'state' and 'individual' in fascist theory a 'necessary synthesis'.[23] Neither is conceivable without the other, but (specific) individuals necessarily fulfil a subordinate role. Individuals are integral components of a wider social and political entity. Taken in isolation, they are of no significance whatever. Each of us can be replaced, our roles and responsibilities assumed by others. The state, however, is irreplaceable, in both phenomenological and normative terms.

The significance of political leadership is stressed throughout Gentile's political writings, in terms that are sometimes difficult to take seriously. The role of the *Duce*, for example, embodying the will of the people, giving direction and significance to people's lives, is intelligible only in the heady political atmosphere of the 1920s and 1930s. We should hesitate, however, before congratulating ourselves on our good sense. Democratic politics, even in stable parliamentary contexts, has often elevated the personal qualities of leaders unrealistically, using the personality of a leader to convey a style or set of priorities. Modern political campaigning invites voters to identify with leaders. Leaders are also expected to set agendas. These are very much political practices adapted to the peculiar demands of mass politics, where electorates (taken in the round) cannot be assumed to have the time or expertise to pass considered judgements on policies. We expect politics to be driven by elites, for better or worse. Fascist theory and rhetoric had grasped the significance of leadership in mass contexts long before liberalism and socialism. Gentile, in particular, was happy to see a strong leader adapting policy to circumstance, even at the cost of apparent contradiction. It is precisely the responsibility of a leader to make those adjustments. They cannot wait upon elaborate discussions and brokerage between groups and factions. Politics is not simply a matter of grasping opportunities, but of creating them, imposing a style. Fascist political ambition far exceeded the bounds of modern elite leadership, but the role of the citizen remains passive in both contexts.

Gentile's philosophy of politics and the state is most fully worked out in *Genesis and Structure of Society* (1943), completed shortly before his assassination in 1944. What emerges is a powerful defence of the priority of the political over any other attachments. In language adapted from Hegel's *Philosophy of Right*, he describes the state as 'the universal common aspect of the will'.[24] Other spheres of organized social life – the economy and religion, for example – assume significance in relation to criteria that are finally political in origin. Outside political life, institutions and practices are inconceivable. Gentile goes so far as to portray religious sentiment as 'immanent in serious political action' (p. 152). In this world of ideas, everything is subsumed under politics, not least because politics creates and sustains a structure of order that is a necessary condition for human flourishing of any kind.

Political order is here conceived in the broadest possible terms, epitomized in a speech of Mussolini's given on 28 October 1925 that became notorious in fascist propaganda: 'Everything for the state; nothing against the state; nothing outside the state.' In *Genesis and Structure of Society*, Gentile is more subtle. Again following Hegel, he treats human personality as intrinsically tied to a conception of institutional order. Rights are conferred on individuals by the state, just as the development of social capacities and self-awareness is dependent upon an array of complex social institutions and practices. In Gentile's phrase, 'the concept of an individual' is immanent in 'the concept of society' (p. 98). At one level we can accept this thought, as Hegel did, without endorsing the idea of a totalitarian state. What is missing in Gentile's account is precisely Hegel's elaborate discussion of civil society in the *Philosophy of Right*, leaving individuals conceptually unadorned in relation to an all-embracing idea of the state.

The institutional detail of a totalitarian state need not detain us here. From a theoretical perspective, the point to stress is that state and society are treated as indivisible entities, demanding central management and control. Liberal theory, in particular, had adapted to the demands of mass society with immense difficulty. Fascism embraced that challenge, and was able to present itself as a vibrant movement shaking tired cultures out of their complacency. The appeal in contexts of economic and international crisis is now too obvious to ignore. The political experiment, of course, was disastrous. Yet a challenge had been thrown down to political theory in the most dramatic circumstances. Worrying numbers of citizens in liberal and democratic states had welcomed a political doctrine that insisted on their permanent subordination to wielders of power. This was a challenge to entrenched assumptions in European political thought. Raw politics had been resurrected, with all its frightening implications. Constitutional politics was effectively in the balance.

9 Politics Chastened

In 1939 Europe was plunged into war again after a respite of barely twenty years. Precipitating circumstances looked significantly different from 1914, with stark ideological divisions superimposed on traditional balance-of-power rivalries. Obsessions with political order in particular states had made peace in Europe more vulnerable, in the process threatening the stability (and even existence) of specific states. The response to the political and economic crises of the 1920s and 1930s had made public and economic life throughout the continent more problematic than ever. If stability and order are regarded as necessary conditions for human flourishing, then states had failed at the most basic level.

From a broader perspective, the two world wars of the first half of the twentieth century are best seen as failures of the European system of states, rather than straightforward consequences of aberrant policies. Neither parliamentary politics nor capitalist economics could be taken for granted. Europe as a continent had been structurally (and perhaps permanently) weakened. Superpower confrontation between the United States and the Soviet Union dictated the alignment of states, with far-reaching consequences for the day-to-day conduct of politics in both Western and Eastern Europe. European political elites had been shaken out of their complacency in the most brutal fashion. Yet politics had somehow to be relaunched when peace was restored in 1945.

Responses varied in scope. Altiero Spinelli, Ernesto Rossi and other anti-fascists in Italy launched a federal movement for the reconstruction of Europe as a whole. Condemned to internal exile on the remote island of Ventotene for subversive activities against the fascist regime, Spinelli and Rossi urged citizens throughout Europe to recognize that the system of states, with the ever-present threat of war, committed political elites to central control and management in ways that would necessarily threaten the freedom and interests of ordinary citizens. In the *Ventotene Manifesto* (1941–2), they depicted the authoritarian fascist state as a model for states on the brink of war.[1] The language might change. Authoritarian states could be described in a variety of styles. But the structural reality (for ordinary citizens) was that political elites would feel compelled to organize all social, economic and political activities as if a state were permanently threatened. In these circumstances, rights could easily be portrayed as a luxury to be set aside in

127

the interest of national security. The economics and politics of defence would dominate political priorities. The rhetoric of nationalism would offer beguiling comfort to citizens who were effectively being treated as instrumental means to a larger good.

Spinelli and Rossi were adamant that the system of states had to be transcended in the name of both peace and democracy. They campaigned instead for the establishment of a federal union on a continental scale, a United States of Europe modelled specifically on the United States of America, though with political priorities that would match the distinctive concerns of Europe as a continent. In the circumstances of Europe in 1945, this was a political vision beyond the capacity or imagination of elites and citizens. To many it seemed to share the utopian excesses of the schemes that had brought Europe to the verge of ruin. The continent looked no more viable as a collective entity than did the separate states of Europe. What the vision highlights, however, is the widespread feeling that political expectations had to shift radically at all levels. The political experiments of the 1920s and 1930s had been shown to be dangerous and morally bankrupt. But political models drawn from the late nineteenth century looked no more reassuring. The challenge to the theory and practice of politics in Europe was immense.

Expectations had to be drastically scaled down. In their different ways, communism and fascism had both treated ordinary political activity as a problem to be solved, offering satisfactions to citizens that could not be attained in a world of compromise, bargaining and accommodation. With the benefit of hindsight, however, the cost of utopia looked unacceptably high to citizens who had variously experienced war, the Holocaust and drastic reductions in civic freedoms, all in the pursuit of an 'ideal' way of life. The politics of total transformation soon lost its appeal. Conventional politics may be a muddle; but it must be treated as a muddle that cannot be qualitatively transcended. The great ideological projects of left and right were now regarded by growing numbers of theorists and citizens as mere pretexts for authoritarian rule. Above all, there was deep suspicion of the idea of a theoretical blueprint that could replace the various compromises that shape politics in practice. Utopia was rejected on both theoretical and practical grounds.

Arguments against utopia were variously couched. Karl Popper, the distinguished philosopher of science, was inspired by the political catastrophe in Europe to try to rebut the very idea of a perfect society. Two highly polemical books, *The Open Society and its Enemies* (1945) and *The Poverty of Historicism* (1957, previously published in article form in 1944–5), focused on two flaws at the heart of utopian thought.[2] He rejected the claims, central to the doctrines of Hegel and Marx as he understood them, that theoretical analysis of the course of historical development yielded any grounds for predictions regarding the future. He accepted, of course, that we can test economic, social and political hypotheses at a micro-level, specifying relevant conditions in which we could anticipate particular outcomes. What he rejected was the idea that historical change in the round could ever be an appropriate subject for theoretical prediction. Coupled with this, he rejected the idea that society as a whole could be an object of study. In Popper's view, a society is an aggregation of individuals pursuing various goals from specific perspectives. The interaction of such individuals will lead to complex outcomes, which can be studied in determinate circumstances, but not from the perspective of society as an entity. In this account, the idea of a society is a theoretical fiction, more or less useful (or more or less useless). The proper focus for a social science should rather be individuals in their diversity.

These are contentious views, which arouse controversy to this day. Popper's attempted refutation of historicism, the view that there are specific laws of historical development, has a logical simplicity and power that still demand attention. In a preface to *The Poverty of Historicism* he reduced a complex argument to five principal propositions. He claims, in the first place, that 'the course of human history is strongly influenced by the growth of human knowledge'.[3] Even Marxists, insisting that ideas are the products of material conditions, would have to accept this point if Marxism is to be considered any sort of contribution to knowledge. Secondly (and crucially) Popper argues that 'we cannot predict, by rational or scientific methods, the future growth of our scientific knowledge' (pp. vi–vii). This would amount to claiming to 'anticipate today what we shall know only tomorrow' (p. vii). It follows from this (thirdly) that 'we cannot, therefore, predict the future course of history' (p. vii). This means (fourthly) 'that we must reject the possibility of a *theoretical history*', and (fifthly) that 'the fundamental aim of historicist methods is . . . misconceived' (p. vii, Popper's italics).

Popper saw this as a devastating and irrefutable argument. The political implications are clear. Any elite that set itself up in authority because it had grasped a theoretical truth about the development of history could be dismissed as bogus. No such expertise is possible. Nor could an elite close off avenues of theoretical or practical research in the name of knowledge claims entrenched in a political ideology. These knowledge claims could only be regarded as provisional, useful for the moment in the light of experience, but with no pretensions to permanence or certitude. We could indeed have confidence in knowledge claims only if we left open the possibility that they might in fact be refuted. Knowledge, in any sphere, should be regarded as provisional and conditional. Recognizing these limits commits us to an open and tentative politics.

Popper's development of these ideas in *The Open Society and its Enemies* is deeply problematic. The book is conceived as a critique of totalitarianism, focusing on the doctrines that have been used to buttress different styles of totalitarian regime. Popper endorses the theoretical position he had advanced in *The Poverty of Historicism*, adding sustained criticism of historical figures who have contributed in any measure to the emergence of what might be described as a collectivist politics. These are not necessarily defences of totalitarianism in its modern forms, barely conceivable before the advent of mass-based industrial societies, but theoretical positions that justify the logical or normative priority of society (or groups of any kind) to the individual.

Popper singles out Plato, Hegel and Marx for special treatment. His scholarship (it must be said) is not always careful, and he admits that he adopted a harsher and more emotional tone than we would normally expect to find in a historical treatment of political ideas.[4] That Plato, who created a style of philosophical criticism which is still indispensable to political theory, should be castigated as a proto-totalitarian seemed preposterous to some scholars. Others objected to the reduction of Marx's rich analysis of the relationship between ideas and economic context to a series of historical prophecies that have turned out to be false. Popper's criticism of Hegel is even more dismissive, attributing direct responsibility for totalitarianism to Hegel's doctrines. He asserts without qualification that 'the formula of the fascist brew is in all countries the same: Hegel plus a dash of nineteenth-century materialism' (ii. 57). Scholars have deplored the selective quotation and failure to engage constructively with Hegel's complex discussion of the logical and historical presuppositions of individual agency. To describe Hegel as an advocate of a 'new tribalism' does scant justice to his subtle account of the interdependence of state and civil society (ii. 25). The fact remains, however, that Popper touched raw nerves in collectivist theory. The modern debate between (so-called) liberals and communitarians has gone beyond Popper's terms of reference.[5] Yet it is recognizably a reiteration of a debate that Popper had contributed to in the bitter aftermath of the Holocaust and the war.

Popper focused specifically on the folly at the heart of any theory that sought to mobilize populations around the idea of a collective good. *The Open Society and its Enemies* can be read as a direct rebuttal of totalitarianism in all its forms, with little to say about the style of parliamentary politics that seemed to be vindicated in the post-war settlement. Hayek, however, adopted a broader strategy, treating totalitarian thinking as an incipient threat to the practice of parliamentary politics itself. An economist by background and training, Hayek used the idea of a market as a model for social co-ordination among strangers. Shifts in prices reflect changing relationships between supply and demand. Individuals make their choices in terms of their own priorities, with no need for authoritative agencies (such as governments) to intervene in a process that actually has no ideal outcomes. Preferences change, prices adapt, suppliers respond. The model is simple. Governments, of course, have a role. Free markets are not *natural* products. They depend upon a legal framework, transparent flows of information, a balanced money supply, a means of seeking redress for wrongdoing, and many other practices and institutions. What governments cannot do, in this scheme of things, is to specify priorities for individuals. The market as a mechanism presupposes a wide area of individual discretion and freedom. Governments have a vital (but limited) role in maintaining appropriate conditions.

It is easy to appreciate the implications of Hayek's individualist philosophy for totalitarianism. What was more disturbing to the conventional wisdom in parliamentary democracies, however, was Hayek's analysis of the way in which liberal opinion had absorbed so many of the collectivist assumptions that informed socialism. In *The Road to Serfdom* (1944) Hayek focused on the threat to freedom from even notionally benign intervention by governments.[6] Attempts to maintain a 'just price' or 'fair wage' within the context of a competitive economic system, for example, actually involve distortions of the market in line with the preferences of planners.[7] But these preferences enjoy no special status. They are simply the priorities of a select group who happen to be in positions of power and authority. There is no 'ideal' distribution of benefits and rewards in a complex society. In democratic contexts, politicians are under pressure from voters, producers and consumers. Interested parties will have very specific views about the levels of governmental support their activities deserve. They will focus their efforts on influencing key decision-makers however they can. The outcome is a politically expedient rather than a rational decision, responsive to vested interests rather than the demands of justice.

Planning requires bureaucracies. And in bureaucracies the quality of decision making depends upon the flow of information up and down the hierarchy. As information flows, so it is sifted. Members of a professional bureaucracy will have their own interests and axes to grind. They will be exposed to personal and professional pressures, striving to please and flatter some key players and to marginalize others. They will also be exposed to wider pressures, much as politicians are. Nobody has a dispassionate or detached perspective in this process. Far from constituting a preferable alternative to the (perceived) anarchy of a market, Hayek sees planning as a necessarily distorted process, loaded in favour of the interests of entrenched groups. These are not problems that more (rational?) planning can resolve. Experts may be called in, but they will have their own pet projects and views. Information flows will continue to be distorted, generating an ever more cumbersome administrative apparatus with increased opportunities to shape policy, formally and informally.

We can assume that a decision-making process of this kind would be slow. It would also be unlikely to reflect the interests of citizens. Co-ordination from the centre presupposes authorization for activities that are radically devolved in market systems. Authorization takes time. By the time it is granted, circumstances may have changed. Typically, bureaucracies bring last year's conventional wisdom to tackle this year's problems.

The unintended consequences of decisions will also take time to work through the system. Anomalies will arise, demanding more attention and further distortions. Citizens (we can assume) will soon recognize the shortcomings of the system and try to devise their own means of managing what may well appear to them to be absurd situations. Formal planning generates black markets. Clientele networks develop, along with a cynical line in political humour.

Elaborate welfare states, in Hayek's view, though well-intentioned, contained the seeds that might later develop into full-blown totalitarianism. In *The Road to Serfdom* Hayek sounded a warning shot, striving to alert a complacent political generation to the perils they were drifting towards. He recognized that conventional wisdom tended in precisely the opposite direction. One reading of the political disasters of the 1920s and 1930s suggested that elites had to take good care of the working masses in order to stave off any flirtation with political extremism. Hayek opposed such thinking, on both economic and political grounds. Persistent government intervention (micro-management) would, in his view, ratchet up public spending over successive business cycles, leading to an inexorable rise in inflation. At the same time, the scope for individual initiative would be progressively narrowed, effectively undermining the source of the dynamism of Western political cultures. Hayek thus combined the economics of Adam Smith with the classical liberalism of Constant and Tocqueville to forge a potent political doctrine, specifically adapted to meet the challenge of mid-century mass-based politics.

Hayek's fullest positive statement of his position is in *The Constitution of Liberty* (1960).[8] In this text he defends liberal (and limited) politics from first principles. He sets schemes of political co-ordination and control in the broad context of the survival of social orders in uncertain contexts. All societies face open futures, with neither the power nor the resources to guarantee their continued flourishing. A political order may be seen (among other things) as a problem-solving device, designed to maximize the co-operative potential of strangers. Note that strangers cannot be expected to subscribe to common goals. We do not know what is most important to them. Nor should we assume that their values will be stable over time. An elite may try to mould a society in its own image, but only by incurring immense economic and political costs. The attempt to micro-manage an entire society is actually self-defeating. The more we try to focus the energy and initiative of citizens on prescribed goals, the less flexible the society as a whole will become. Hayek sees the economic, technical and political dominance of Europe from the early modern period as a product of a set of practices that had enlarged the scope for individuals to address their own problems. The Renaissance, Reformation and Enlightenment thus constituted a complex series of interconnected (but specifically unpredictable) processes. No one could have planned a sequence of development on this scale, though with hindsight we can grasp something of the way it has emerged. If individual initiative is seen as the dynamic core of this activity, then political steps to channel that initiative could have dire consequences. Hayek's cardinal assumption is that individuals (and societies) face unpredictable (and potentially threatening) futures. We simply do not know (and cannot know) what problems we will have to confront in the future. It follows, on this view, that as individuals (and societies) we should endorse institutions and practices that enable us to be maximally responsive. In evolutionary terms, an open society is far more likely to maintain itself and flourish over the long term than a society organized around a set of centrally imposed values.

Hayek treats liberty as a grounding assumption, on both moral and prudential grounds. He accepts the Kantian idea that individuals should be treated as ends in themselves, rather than as means towards some other good, but also contends that we have strong practical incentives to enlarge the sphere of individual freedom whenever possible. What this might require in legislative terms will depend upon circumstances. Hayek is at his most perceptive in discussions of the relationship between liberalism and democracy. He is unhappy with the conventional idea that we just happen to live in 'liberal democracies', as if no conceptual problems were involved in running the two doctrines together. The 'doctrinaire democrat', for Hayek, is a principled advocate of 'popular sovereignty' (p. 106). Democrats believe in majority rule, thus enabling a minority of potential voters to speak for the people as a whole. Hayek has no problems with pragmatic recourse to majority decisions, provided limits are specified to the range of issues that might be so decided. Majority rule as a free-standing principle, however, is 'unlimited and unlimitable' (p. 106). If the 'people' (always a mysterious entity) have expressed their 'will' according to a democratic decision procedure, then nothing (in pure democratic theory) could justify resistance or opposition. Majorities, of course, are arbitrary, shifting with fashion and circumstance. Hayek's fear is that the 'ideal of democracy' leads to 'the justification of a new arbitrary power' (p. 106). With the benefit of hindsight (and experience of elaborate and costly electoral campaigns aimed at voters whose direct involvement with political issues is limited), this is an open invitation to elites to mobilize popular opinion for their own ends. Democrats, in this view, may (or may not) be attached to the principle of individual liberty. We simply do not know how political opinions and fortunes will develop over time. In mass-based democracies, elites may offer electorates more than governments can reasonably provide in order to gain popular support. The upshot could well be that liberty will be sacrificed for welfare, as Tocqueville had earlier feared. In modern democratic contexts, Hayek accepts that we cannot dispense with popular elections. He insists, however, that if democracy is to function effectively, it must be limited by liberal principles. Without such a limiting condition in place, popular democracy is but a short step away from what we might style 'soft' totalitarianism, preferable (no doubt) to earlier brutal versions, but none the less a deadly threat to liberty and all that goes with it.

Institutional and policy details need not detain us unduly here. In broad terms Hayek tries to maintain a distinction between the state as a framework of rules and government as a means of pursuing specific objectives. He accepts that the state is (always and necessarily) a coercive apparatus, and strives accordingly to limit its activities to matters that are indispensable to individuals in the pursuit of substantive goals, whatever they might be. In this view, it is certainly not a proper use of the state to direct individuals to particular objectives rather than others. For Hayek it is of paramount importance that an individual should be 'subject only to the same laws as all his fellow citizens . . . immune from arbitrary confinement and free to choose his work', and that he should be 'able to own and acquire property' (p. 20). Interference by the state in these spheres would necessarily be coercive; and since the substantive priorities that individuals set themselves cannot be assessed against an ideal criterion, any attempt to use the resources of the state to persuade individuals to accommodate their interests to collective goals would be unjustified.

Coercion can, of course, be justified in order to maintain a framework of public rules. Without a legal order, strangers cannot co-operate together, individuals cannot plan their future activities with a reasonable assurance that procedures and practices will be honoured, and each of us would have to devote time and resources to security matters that would always remain beyond our control. Life would be an uphill struggle. Public trust (what modern theorists have described as 'social capital') would be eroded. This would not necessarily amount to a 'state of nature'; but certainly we would be loath to look beyond family and friends for services that could not be provided immediately. Coercion to sustain a viable public order actually enlarges the scope for individual activities, provided a line is drawn between rules and procedures on the one side and substantive goals on the other.

Hayek is best known as a staunch defender of economic liberalism in its modern form, arguing for the withdrawal of government from market activities wherever possible. Indeed he became a highly influential figure in Britain and the United States in the 1970s, as conservative governments sought to limit the role of the state and to 'privatize' key functions. His political philosophy, however, should be considered in broader perspective. His conception of limited government is driven by normative criteria. He combined scepticism about the normative status of substantive preferences and choices with a strong commitment to the conditions that would have to be satisfied for individuals to exercise their discretion and talents optimally. To be sure, maintaining a distinction between formal and substantive criteria is not without its own difficulties. But without some such distinction, it is easy to see how the state might engulf all social and civil arenas. Simply by recognizing moral and cultural diversity, we commit ourselves to limiting the way in which the state may be used to buttress certain values rather than others. Governments have both carrots and sticks at their disposal to focus the minds of citizens. Either way, though, government would be intruding on individual conduct with no conceivable theoretical warrant. In these circumstances, in fact, government policy would be fashioned to suit the interests of the influential and powerful, much as Marx had argued. Yet, for Hayek, the Marxist remedy is worse than the liberal disease. A properly liberal theory of the state would not be exposed to the same objections. Whether political elites and electorates would accept these constraints is quite another matter.

Both Hayek and Popper deployed strong individualist assumptions in their attempts to undermine the theoretical credentials of political collectivism. Michael Oakeshott, by contrast, while endorsing their deep suspicion of utopian politics, defended a conception of agency and practice that was able to draw from the resources of the Hegelian tradition, without elevating the state or collectivity to an all-embracing role. Oakeshott extended a critique of rationalist politics to a critique of rationalist philosophy more broadly. He had profound reservations about the pragmatic problem-solving approach of Hayek and Popper, stressing instead the priority of established practices in any defensible conception of human agency. In Oakeshott's view, the role of the philosopher is not to resolve the practical dilemmas which bedevil us every day of our lives, but rather to clarify the conceptual confusions that prevent us from thinking clearly about ourselves.

Oakeshott's political theory first gained widespread influence with the publication of *Rationalism in Politics and Other Essays* (1962), a collection of ten essays written between 1947 and 1961, each concerned in various ways (as he puts it in the preface) with 'understanding and explaining' human conduct.[9] He takes practical life in its many and varied forms, each a product of traditions of conduct, standards and institutions that constitute a way of life. He does not focus on one practice as the ideal form for all others, or one society as the ideal model to be followed, but asks, rather, what it means to engage in activities of any kind. He insists, in particular, on a distinction between philosophical and practical approaches to politics, aware that political philosophers in the classic tradition had often shifted in the course of argument from one perspective to the other. Order, liberty, equality or whatever value might be variously stressed as keys to human well-being and fulfilment. Philosophers advancing arguments in this style would see themselves as contributors to practical political debates. Oakeshott is more circumspect. He treats normative arguments very much as parochial preferences, urging philosophers to focus on the basic presuppositions of normative engagements rather than the substantive goals that theorists might seek to advance.

Oakeshott presupposes in *Rationalism in Politics and Other Essays* the sophisticated view of knowledge and experience which he had elaborated in *Experience and its Modes* (1933).[10] The crucial point to recall from his earlier statement is that he sees knowledge as a *factum* rather than a *datum*. Our knowledge is an achievement based upon assumptions we make. These assumptions will differ in our various fields of enquiry. In *Experience and its Modes* Oakeshott distinguished, in particular, history, science and practice from one another. In history we presuppose a world of discrete events which are alleged to have taken place in a past we can no longer examine directly; in science a world of mechanical quantitative relationships between entities which we can neither see nor touch; in practice a world of given social relationships which we are ceaselessly (but necessarily unsatisfactorily) trying to transform into something better. In none of these fields can it be claimed that what we are said to know corresponds with a world out there (in the past, in the natural environment, enshrined in tablets of stone). What we know, instead, must be seen as a product of the world of ideas in which we are working. The assumptions we make furnish us with more or less plausible (but contestable) judgements. Truth is a function of the coherence of a world of ideas. A world of ideas will change, of course, as new arguments are advanced. But it is never possible to leap outside a world of ideas in order to assess its overall adequacy against an external standard. The reservations we have about a world of ideas are themselves a consequence of the contradictions and fissures within it. Our intellectual endeavours are bent on making a given world of ideas more coherent. Coherence is the only criterion of truth we have.

Knowledge in specialized fields is thus conditional upon specific constitutive assumptions. A crucial implication which Oakeshott insists upon in *Experience and its Modes*, and further develops in *Rationalism in Politics and Other Essays*, is that constructive dialogue between distinct modes of knowledge is impossible. A mode of discourse operates between designated conceptual parameters. To attempt to cross constitutive conceptual boundaries is to lapse into irrelevance or absurdity. The divisions between modes of discourse or experience are in fact sharper than the divisions between natural languages. For while we can make reasonable translations from French into Italian, we cannot intelligibly 'translate' knowledge couched in one idiom into knowledge couched in another. The scientist cannot learn from the historian, or the politician from either. The modes of science, history and practice are categorially distinct. Only philosophy is exempt from these modal limitations because it is occupied not with a world of substantive facts, events or desires, but with the conditions of intelligibility that make any kind of discourse possible. All other modes of discourse are committed to a species of conceptual limitation in order to function.

Oakeshott treats politics as an activity as an integral part of the practical realm. Yet political discourse always has a tendency to overreach itself. We are tempted to present what is good for ourselves as good for others. The need to secure the co-operation of others if we are to attain our own ends encourages us to present the things we happen to want as somehow objectively desirable. For the most part, we are entirely innocent when we deceive ourselves in these ways. Philosophers themselves have sometimes succumbed to the false allure of their own pet projects, defending their idiosyncratic conceptions of fulfilment as necessary conditions for human well-being. It may be, indeed, that the temptation to political and moral overstatement is irresistible to us. But it remains a philosophical error. The challenge of political philosophy for Oakeshott is precisely to disentangle the confusion of idioms which we have habitually employed in considering our practical affairs. If a principal task of philosophy is to establish appropriate criteria of intelligibility in the various modes of experience, the practical mode has consistently proved to be the most difficult to contain within its designated sphere. History, science and the arts have often been misleadingly justified in practical terms. More fundamentally still, argues Oakeshott, the way we live and regard ourselves has been distorted by a failure to recognize the conceptual limits of practical life.

Oakeshott invites us to consider, for example, our understanding of 'rational conduct'.[11] To act rationally, we might assume, would be to set aside habit, custom or prejudice and to regulate our conduct solely in terms of the goals we have determined for ourselves. A basic presupposition of rationality, in this scheme of things, is that our goals can be separated analytically from the activities we happen to be engaged in. But when we begin to reflect intelligently on our various pursuits, it is with a mind already informed by the practices and procedures that constitute those pursuits. We cannot think 'rationally' about cricket, chess, cooking, carpentry, politics and so on unless we already know something about them. We may be casually inducted into these pursuits in the first instance. Yet it would be unwise to ask our advice until we had gained some 'know-how'. To treat a condition of pure innocence, where all acquired knowledge is discounted, as a paradigm case of rational reflection is pure folly.

Lurking behind the error, in this case, is a widely held but wholly misleading conception of mind. The mind is not an entity that subsequently acquires 'beliefs, knowledge, prejudices' (p. 89). The mind is what it does. It is inseparable from the judgements we make in the course of our thinking and doing. It is not 'an apparatus for thinking' but is thought itself (p. 90). It follows that we cannot step outside our thought in order to check its rationality. Whatever we think and do is informed by specific assumptions. These can be reviewed as we develop a more sophisticated awareness of what we are doing. But it makes no sense to seek an independent rational standard for conduct as such. We may be said to act rationally when our conduct 'exhibits the sort of intelligence appropriate to the idiom of activity concerned' (p. 110).

The implications of this position for our understanding of political and moral discourse are far-reaching and radically subversive. Oakeshott contends that, at least since the Renaissance, respect for practical judgement has tended to be undermined by an obsession with technique. Practical judgement is refined in the course of our experience of various arts, crafts and pursuits. It may be passed on in some measure by a master to his apprentice, or by a supervisor to her research student. But it 'cannot be formulated in rules' or committed in preceptive form to a textbook (p. 8). We cannot learn to cook from a cookery book, or to drive from close study of the Highway Code. Books of this kind may be useful to us once we know something about cooking or driving. But we need to be shown how to do these things in the first instance, and subsequently improve upon our initial incompetence only with practice.

Why should practical knowledge have been so undervalued in modern times? Oakeshott offers no more than a tantalizing abridgement of a highly contentious view. He argues that Western culture in the last 400 years has become afflicted with a kind of collective impatience. We crave to better ourselves, and to better ourselves in a hurry. We no longer have the time to devote to the acquisition of specialized skills, and instead seek short cuts in technical manuals of one kind or another. Above all, we need to be assured that forced instruction will fit us for our tasks once and for all. What cannot be learned quickly is dismissed as an irrelevance. If judgement is set aside, all we have left to rely upon is technical certainty.

Politics in this rationalist idiom is always 'a matter of solving problems', of applying 'reason' to politics in much the same way as an engineer tackles the business of construction and repair (p. 4). Just as the technical skills of the engineer are held to be universal in scope and application, so too the 'politician' who knows his business will be able to apply his instrumental criteria in any circumstance or situation. He will rely not upon received political wisdom ('prejudice'), but upon the most up-to-date technical manual ('science'). On closer inspection, however, it will be evident that the rationalist politician understands neither politics nor science. His basic conception of what it means to engage in any sort of practice is so wide of the mark that anything that has been accomplished is bound to appear unsatisfactory to him. He cannot accept accommodation and compromise, because what he seeks is perfection. Yet even to envisage perfection in his terms is to conceive of human life as completely other than it could possibly be.

The rationalist analysis of politics, in Oakeshott's view, is thus untenable in theory and unrealizable in practice. Yet its hold on modern discourse is almost complete. It is manifested most obviously in the predilection for abstract formulations of political doctrines and programmes. A political party or movement without its ideology is now considered to be lamentably ill-equipped for the cut and thrust of argument and debate on a public stage. The 'politics of the book' has replaced the kind of practical understanding and discrimination that was once entrenched in an older (and narrower) political class (p. 22).

What the 'book' offers in a modern context is clear. New classes have risen to power and influence without the benefit of a traditional political education, addressing an enlarged citizenry whose ignorance is even more complete. In these circumstances both rulers and citizens desperately need 'a crib, a political doctrine, to take the place of a habit of political behaviour' (p. 25). Some of the best political 'cribs' have been written by thinkers of genuine distinction (Machiavelli, Locke, Mill, Marx), who have managed to abridge complex traditions of political conduct in pocket-size form. But the flexibility of a living tradition is lost in the very best abridgements; and in the worst, political argument gives place to the raucous exchange of slogans.

In Oakeshott's view, then, the intrusion of a rationalist frame of mind has seriously corrupted political thought and practice. Yet the damage wrought by rationalism extends far beyond the conduct of public affairs. What we are dealing with is 'an identifiable error, a misconception with regard to the nature of human knowledge, which amounts to a corruption of the mind' (p. 31). And because it is the mind itself which has been corrupted, it is difficult to see how we might best take stock of our situation and remedy our shortcomings. Following rationalist precepts in all walks of life ('living by the book') leads 'not only to specific mistakes, but . . . also dries up the mind itself', generating an 'intellectual dishonesty' which renders intellectual effort to improve affairs more dangerous than the malaise itself (p. 31). The rationalist is a liability not only because his projects are ill-advised, but because he fails to recognize what he is doing. He cannot accept that all prac- tices are rooted in traditional modes of conduct. If he sees a problem, he seeks always to wipe the slate clean and to start again. Yet the supposition that we can simply 'start again' is the root of our difficulties.

Oakeshott insists that all conduct (in fact) is in an important sense tradition-bound. This does not mean that we must simply accept the patterns of conduct we happen to have inherited. Traditions are not static; and even a veneration of the past contains within it intimations of how we should respond to the vagaries of circumstance. A tradition 'is neither fixed nor finished; it has no changeless centre to which understanding can anchor itself; there is no sovereign purpose to be perceived or invariable direction to be detected; there is no model to be copied, idea to be realized, or rule to be followed' (p. 128). But there is 'a principle of continuity', with authority 'diffused between past, present, and future; between the old, the new, and what is to come' (p. 128). Even as we strive to chart new directions, we are enmeshed in a complex web of practices and attitudes which both constrain and facilitate our dealings with one another.

Underpinning Oakeshott's conception of political thought and practice is a deep theoretical scepticism. We rely on traditions of conduct, not because they are the best we can conceive of, but because they serve (at least some of) our purposes. There can be no theoretical resolution of the many conflicting ends we may happen to desire. In these circumstances, the best that we can hope for is that our way of life might enable us to make (essentially contestable) choices for ourselves. We should not expect governments to devise practical 'solutions' to problems that cannot (in principle) be solved. Oakeshott focuses, instead, on conditions that would have to be satisfied for any of our (necessarily co-operative) activities to be (at least minimally) effective. He stresses throughout his writings the idea of the rule of law and stable expectations. In a later work, *On Human Conduct* (1975), he system-atized his reflections on agency and practice, distinguishing between 'civil association' and 'enterprise association'.[12] A civil relationship, in Oakeshott's terms, is not directed to the attainment of substantive goals. It is (he says) human relationship viewed 'in terms of the (formal) considerations which compose a practice', the rules (implicit and explicit) that enable us to assess appropriate means in complex social engagements (p. 121). 'Enterprise association', by contrast, is 'concerned with the satisfaction of chosen wants' (p. 121). We may (or may not) join private associations for the pursuit of specific goals. We seek certain kinds of employment and join social clubs where we might expect to meet like-minded people. The point to stress, for Oakeshott, is that we can always leave such associations if we become indifferent or hostile to their goals. It is open to us to resign from specific employment or to refuse to renew our subscriptions. The goals of enterprise associations will not be shared by a whole community. But, crucially, nobody should be obliged to join them. The position is quite otherwise with the state. None of us chooses to be born under the jurisdiction of specific political authorities. We have to abide by (political) laws and rules irrespective of our particular preferences and predilections. To be forced to pursue substantive goals that are contestable will strike many of us as intrusion on our liberty and discretion. Yet we can perfectly well recognize that some co-operative rules and procedures must be in place if we are to flourish. Oakeshott high-lights the contrast between formal rules and substantive goals, the former indispensable to social life, the latter optional among citizens who may have very different priorities. In Oakeshott's view, the authority of the state in the long term depends upon a recognition of conditions that are vital to all citi-zens, and not simply to those who happen to share the same interests.

Oakeshott's political scepticism thus operates on two levels. He defends a strictly limited function for the state, and a similarly limited role for political philosophy. We simply lack the theoretical resources to transform the human condition. Instead, theory can expose the myriad sources of conceptual confusion that set elites and citizens in pursuit of unrealizable objectives. Oakeshott warns of political folly, but offers no panaceas. He urges us to focus on the very satisfactions of varied lives rather than the illusory promise of heaven on earth.

Oakeshott's politics is conservative by implication, though it remains open-ended. In arguing that conceptions of practice are implicit within traditions, he is not committed to the view that acceptance of any tradition can confer authority upon a practice. We cannot understand our practical lives outside traditions of conduct; but it does not follow that all traditions of conduct are equally valid. Oakeshott's starting point is not necessarily the arbitrary traditions we happen to have grown up with. He recognizes (with modern anti-foundationalists) that our practical judgements cannot be supported by an abstract deontological criterion.[13] Traditions, however, are not incommensurable. They contain within themselves different possibilities for conduct and achievement.

In seeking to provide definitive answers to practical dilemmas, some traditions will irredeemably stunt prospects for human well-being and achievement. Oakeshott, like so many of his contemporaries, was haunted by the impact of the various versions of collectivist politics that had dominated the twentieth century. Yet he could not rest content with a straightforward reassertion of the priority of the individual over the community. He saw individuality as a specifically social product. But it would not flourish in any and every community. In focusing on human beings as the creators of meanings and values, he is clear that he is validating certain sorts of communities and not others. At the heart of any defensible view is a politics of self-restraint. Elites and citizens ignore that necessary limitation at their peril.

For all their polemical zeal, Popper, Hayek and Oakeshott set themselves modest political goals. In different ways, they sought to expose the hubris at the heart of the rationalist follies of the first half of the twentieth century. They each had distinctive views of the style and scope of a balanced politics, embracing diversity within certain (more or less closely specified) parameters. From a philosophical point of view, however, the focus of their work was largely negative, creating the theoretical space for a sober appraisal of the limits of political possibility.

In some quarters it was accepted that normative political philosophy in the classical style was neither possible nor desirable. Indeed the death of political theory was proclaimed by political theorists themselves.[14] In reality normative theory continued, though it was conducted in a cautious (sometimes narrowly academic) style. Citizens and elites had largely accepted that 'high' politics was a dangerous game. Attention switched instead to a 'low' political agenda, focused on distribution, rights and provision of space and opportunity for citizens to fashion their lives.

Political priorities ranged across a narrower spectrum. Isaiah Berlin, for example, in a classic inaugural lecture at Oxford in 1958, insisted on a distinction between 'positive' and 'negative' liberty.[15] The focus of the essay was on the way in which the idea of liberty had been used and abused within and beyond the liberal tradition in political theory. Drawing very much on Constant's critique of Rousseau, Berlin argued that the diversity of views in any conceivable society in modern times precluded the pursuit of a 'common good' for citizens in the modern state. Citizens may (or may not) favour redistributive policies for the poor, they may be more (or less) comfortable with a state that celebrates a unique cultural or religious heritage, more (or less) enthusiastic about the subordination of their positive interests to the perceived needs of the wider polity. These may be worthy goals, but they are contentious. Right-thinking people will come down on different sides in any dispassionate consideration of their merits. It certainly could not be supposed that differences on these issues were consequences of malice or folly. Berlin objected (specifically) to the idea that rational reflection could (in principle) resolve these disputes, thus (indirectly) authorizing the state to be used in all manner of ways to encourage us to endorse the appropriate positions. The idea that 'real' freedom could be identified with the pursuit of substantive goals was anathema to him. The state could, of course, intervene coercively in order to achieve certain objectives. But it would not thereby make us more free. Freedom, for Berlin as for Constant, is the absence of constraint, the space to pursue our ends, whatever they may be. This freedom can be abused. It is perfectly proper to constrain felons of various kinds. In these circumstances we restrict freedom as a means of attaining other goals. Whether this is justifiable in a given context is a matter of judgement. But it will always be a restriction of freedom.

The priority of liberty was broadly accepted, though not always on Berlin's terms. John Rawls, in his magisterial *A Theory of Justice* (1971), defended a conception of equal citizenship within a liberal constitutional state.[16] The text sparked a resurgence of interest in normative theory, deploying Kantian contractualist argument in order to justify the broad redistributive provisions of a welfare state. Rawls used the idea of a hypothetical 'original position' to model terms of co-operation that individuals would accept if they were unaware of the role or status they would enjoy in a society.[17] Rawls's supposition is that none of us would be prepared to risk our liberty for the possible enjoyment of other goods. But we would nevertheless recognize that we could not flourish at all if we were not guaranteed access to 'social primary goods', construed as resources we need no matter what specific goals we might seek in life. Thus we could all accept that we need some measure of education and welfare, though we might continue to argue about the appropriate distribution of such resources.

Rawls assumes from the outset that we are each free and equal persons. Whatever terms of social co-operation we might deem acceptable would have to be compatible with that status for each and every one. How far this injunction should apply, whether to all human beings on the planet or merely to fellow citizens in a democratic state, was a matter that occupied Rawls in later revisions of his thought.[18] The point to stress here, however, is that (in normative terms) Rawls will not allow us to treat fellow human beings simply as means in the pursuit of our ends. Whatever fortuitous advantages we may enjoy, we are obliged to take into account the free and equal status of the people we deal with on a day-to-day basis. We may employ people on mutually agreeable terms, though not enslave them. We must assume that they have priorities in their lives, just as we have. Whenever we limit their options, it must be in terms of social benefits which they can regard as necessary or appropriate to continued (mutual but not necessarily equal) enjoyment of a scheme of social co-operation.

The contrasting claims of liberty and equality became key themes in normative debate, especially in Anglo-American political theory. On the one side Nozick advanced a rights-based argument for a minimal state, while Dworkin explored the egalitarian implications of a commitment to rights.[19] Even where abstract or 'atomistic' individualism was rejected, communitarian theorists continued broadly to support the rights consensus in liberal democratic polities, though they argued from different premises, stressing the contingent achievement of respect for rights in specific political cultures.[20] It was unusual to reject the values associated with individualism, though MacIntyre (among others) urged that individualist cultures are conceptually flawed, failing to recognize the primacy of social roles in any viable community.[21]

Radical political movements challenged the narrow terms of reference of liberal political theory. An efflorescence of counter-cultural ideas in 1968 drew broadly from Marxist, Maoist, anarchist and environmental sources. The waves of protest and student-led revolt, however, extending from San Francisco, through Paris, to Prague, focused in tangible terms on defence of the rights of individuals against the social, economic and political power of hegemonic institutions. The political achievements of 1968 were evanescent. Young people scorned authority, dressed imaginatively, and conjured up the possibility of a qualitatively better style of life. Western cultures were genuinely opened up to wider influences. Yet critics of establishments settled into positions of authority in the institutions they had despised, largely content that significant social and cultural change could be attained within the structure of liberal polities.

10 Politics Fragmented

At the end of the twentieth century the political world looked more uncertain than at any time since 1945. The dramatic fall of the Berlin Wall (1989) symbolized the end of an era. The ideological rhetoric that underpinned superpower confrontation seemed anachronistic in a world dominated by a single hegemon. Theorists talked (yet again) about the end of ideology. Francis Fukuyama pictured a world which would progressively endorse a liberal democratic consensus in politics and capitalist relations in economics.[1] Whether or not this vision should be regarded as utopian, it nevertheless envisaged a theoretically stable era in which there would be broad consensus on basic terms of social co-operation. Theorists would focus on micro-issues, not the basic institutional structure of society. And to be plausible at all, it had to be assumed that marginal groups would derive sufficient benefit from the institutional system to forestall sustained opposition to the *status quo*.

The global economy presented the spectre of highly integrated financial markets in cosmopolitan cities, surrounded by hinterlands that were becoming ever more conscious of their distinctive identities in relation to wider national cultures. Integration and disintegration were continuing apace, often in adjacent communities. Received terms of political discourse barely reflected the changes taking place. A state built around a conception of the 'common good' could not accommodate the array of groups and cultures contending for political, economic and social space in given territories. Political and economic hubs no longer coincided so readily. Governments did not enjoy even the illusion of economic control, as almost instantaneous capital flows threatened to overwhelm even the best-placed treasuries. A global economic system had emerged without corresponding institutions to manage the vagaries of economic co-operation across the planet. Political elites strove to manage complex interdependence as best they could, with no guarantees that the myriad participants would respect the concerns of others. No political power had the resources to impose its will unilaterally. And weaker players were scarcely able to make their voices heard. For all the optimistic rhetoric that marked the end of the (so-called) cold war, the political world seemed dangerously out of control. States found their effective power and autonomy constrained, at a time when democratic electorates were becoming ever more demanding in a multitude of (often incompatible) ways.[2] Some theorists even claimed that the era of the nation-state had run its course, to be replaced by a new and uncertain system of global politics.[3]

Just how far states have changed their nature is a much disputed issue that cannot be pursued further here. What is clear, however, is that the focus of political discussion has shifted significantly. Interests of various kinds would traditionally channel their energies towards influencing key decision-makers in various spheres, often grouped together as a more or less closely integrated network. It made sense to speak in terms of a 'power elite', gathered in and around government. With the dispersal of power, informal networks have become more important, extending beyond political borders. Theories of democratic accountability in these circumstances are rendered deeply problematic, not least because democratically elected politicians are not in a position to dominate relevant agendas. We continue to use a traditional political language and work through a façade of institutions. Politicians are elected, laws are framed, but governments increasingly operate in a world removed from electorates. The idea of a political manifesto looks touchingly naïve. Who could be held accountable for a political programme that could not (in principle) be put into practice? Governments are integral parts of wider discursive networks. No one calls the shots.

The subversive implications of a stress on discursive contexts was developed most forcefully by Michel Foucault.[4] In wide-ranging studies of disciplines, discourses and social practices, Foucault focused on the contingent assumptions that informed various spheres of activity. Conceptions of the person and mental illness, for example, would change over time, leading to radically different strategies for dealing with specific aspects of human conduct. These strategies would often be justified in terms of scientific or other authoritative views, enshrining truths about human beings and their relationships with one another. In reality, for Foucault, the 'disciplinary' foundations of various social practices reflect, rather, a complex network of social and cultural power relations. Discourse, in this view, projects a conception of the way things stand ('the order of things') which effectively buttresses certain interests rather than others.

The implications for minority groups can be devastating. Practices at the heart of certain minority cultures may be treated as folly, madness or sheer wickedness by establishments. And given the economics of the propagation of knowledge, marginal cultures may be more or less invisible, failing even to register in the range of concerns on public agendas. Gender, racial and sexual issues have historically been evaded by mainstream (male-dominated) establishment discourses, at best relegated to a 'private' sphere beyond public attention, at worst ignored. But the designation of something as a public or private matter cannot be decided in normatively neutral terms. A normative language will be a product of a hegemonic discourse. It can be challenged, but not from the perspective of 'truth'. Groups and cultures will have different views on these questions. Whichever prevails in public discourse will be a matter of politics and power.

Foucault diagnoses abuses of power, but is much less clear about what should replace 'constrained' social relations. We cannot picture complex social relations without the dynamic of power. A 'frictionless' society is undesirable in theory and barely conceivable in practice. We cannot fix any set of practices in concrete. Contingency frames all our activities. Change in any society is unpredictable, hitting the interests and values of groups and individuals in various ways too complex to calculate. We cannot have a theory of how things will change or how we should respond to change. Foucault focuses, instead, on the damage done to groups and individuals at the margins, seeking to undermine the theoretical constraints that prevent them from articulating their interests effectively. This, to be sure, is a normative engagement, though it does not require elaborate theoretical defence. We should not ask Foucault for a theory of the 'good life', because it would inevitably amount merely to a conception of the good viewed from a particular perspective.

Foucault takes the fragmentation of politics seriously. He breaks down concepts like 'state' and 'society' into the discursive networks that sustain sets of practices. His theory reflects the prominence of civil society in a modern context, where associations of various kinds contend for space and shape the character of public life. Where traditional political theory and political science would focus on government as an institutional structure, Foucault talks in terms of 'governmentality', the deeper social and psychological practices that enable structures of power and authority to work.[5] In important respects, authoritative networks are more intrusive even than the totalitarian state. Individuals are socialized to see themselves in specific terms, internalizing moral and social ideas that make them amenable to the requirements of hegemonic groups. The idea of 'conscience', for example, enables individuals to 'police' their own activities, reinforcing values and practices that effectively prevent them from advancing subversive ideas and proposals.

Foucault thus defends a politics of resistance, but not in the name of a specific doctrine or ideology. He disdains political mobilization precisely because it depends for its success on the imposition of views from a notional centre, encouraging passivity and conformism. If power is dispersed in modern contexts, so, too, is protest. Foucault is acutely aware of the threat to individuality and diversity stemming from bogus moral and political solidarity. His critique of political ideologies is aimed at both right and left.

A politics of dispersed resistance runs the real risk of being politically ineffective. In a late newspaper article, Foucault accepts that we might all have an obligation to confront governments, though we cannot urge their permanent replacement by an alternative scheme as a remedy for the myriad misfortunes of being governed.[6] At a minimal level, however, he maintains that we should 'speak out against every abuse of power', not least because 'we are all members of the community of the governed' (p. 474). Governments presume to concern themselves with the 'welfare of societies', yet set themselves up as the judges of what that might involve (p. 474). Foucault insists that we have 'an absolute right to stand up and speak to those who hold power', though he is deeply sceptical of the traditional language of rights. We are all (as he puts it) 'just private individuals', but we cannot allow governments to speak for us, 'to reserve a monopoly for themselves' of authoritative pronouncement (pp. 474–5). This amounts to a minimal exercise of 'international citizenship', despite the obvious absence of an international polity (p. 474).

Foucault's appeal to a right to judgement for 'private individuals' is intriguing in light of his celebrated critique of the self. No one had argued more forcefully that the self is a social product. The fact that we make personal judgements is not a problem (what else could we do?). But why should we attach normative authority to judgements that are framed and determined by contingent factors? The perspective from which we make our judgements is just one among others. We may be repelled by the values and choices of others, but what normative significance should we attribute to that reaction? These issues take us to the heart of problems that have bedevilled normative theory for the last 300 years. In different ways theorists have confronted the status of normative judgements, treating them as products of historical circumstances or economic relations or as mere preferences. What Foucault challenges is the very idea of a self that could make authoritative judgements. Yet he also shows vividly that they are inescapable.

Postmodern theorists (drawing extensively on Foucault and Nietzsche) accepted that the paradox could not be resolved. Grand theory was treated as a species of myth, more or less comforting, but with no epistemological or moral status. Human beings simply tell themselves stories. Sometimes they take them very seriously indeed, presuming to impose their stories on others. Intellectual establishments devote time, effort and resources to narrative plausibility, striving to buttress a specific view of the world with whatever imaginative materials are to hand. Political philosophy, from this perspective, is an elaborate narrative game, with possibly serious political consequences. Imposing a set of stories on a whole population is necessarily intrusive. Assuming that the stories themselves have a special status affords a pretext for more drastic measures, moulding populations to fit the requirements of hegemonic groups. From a Foucauldian (or postmodern) position, however, these are not illusions that can be dispelled. A theory of discourse cannot replace discourse. We simply have to accept that we are story-tellers. Our political options are limited. Recognizing the contingency of our stories might encourage us not to impose them on others. But even that strategy presupposes that we can distance ourselves from narrative messages. We may not be disposed to listen to everything that people may be inclined to tell us. How do we draw lines?

Postmodern theory allows only an exiguous role for theory. Theory can highlight what is going on in normative argument, without privileging any substantive arguments. A theoretical warrant for any particular choice or preference is actually ruled out. What we are left with, instead, is raw politics itself. Theorists may favour an inclusive rather than an exclusive politics, without having anything authoritative to say on any given issue. Postmodern theory provides a strategy for reading normative argument, rather than engaging in normative controversy. We are given procedural grounds for preferring an open politics, but very little help when we actually confront hard cases.

Conventional normative theory was assailed by a variety of objections to the very idea of a theoretical foundation to discursive positions. Communitarian theory argued that embedded roles and traditions furnish a frame of reference for normative debate. Individuals are construed as products of their cultures, acquiring a critical vocabulary and reflective capacity in a specific society. Their sense of themselves is seen to be inseparable from a wider social context. We have already encountered versions of these arguments in Burke, Hegel, Oakeshott and others. The point to stress in a modern context is that politically radical positions could be endorsed by communitarian theory, provided the arguments themselves are not accorded status or authority beyond a given cultural world.

Everything hinges in these discussions on the way in which cultural identities are characterized. A stock objection to some versions of communitarianism has been that the conception of culture doing the work is a theoretical abstraction, reflecting a yearning for cultural and moral coherence that (so it is claimed) has been lost in the modern world. The argument may be that human flourishing depends upon feeling at home in the world (in a Hegelian or Aristotelian sense), and that typically liberal ways of characterizing social co-operation underplay the significance of the cultural preconditions for the initiation of co-operative projects in the first place. In essence this is a conceptual reworking of certain standard objections to social contract theory (typically, but misleadingly, attributed to Hegel).[7]

If we focus, instead, on the way in which cultures are constituted, the picture looks significantly different. Cultures, like traditions, are the product of bewilderingly complex (and necessarily open-ended) interactions. Sociologists and anthropologists argue fiercely among themselves about the process of culture formation. Yet political philosophers defending communitarian positions sometimes seem inclined to invoke a conception of culture as if it were uncontentious. Some of the most influential figures (Charles Taylor, for example) adopt an expressivist view of culture, stemming originally from Herder, that would be rejected out of hand as a piece of Romantic nonsense by most modern sociologists.[8] Yet, conceptions of culture are actually rhetorical devices in complex normative situations. The idea of 'culture' or 'community' can no more be taken as a foundation for argument and judgement than the 'individual' or 'self'. These terms may be treated as political trumps in polemical contexts, but they are always open to challenge.

In the 1990s 'identity' began to enjoy the prominence in political debate accorded to 'class' in earlier decades. A resurgence of interest in nationalism in Eastern Europe was an understandable response to years of Soviet hegemony. But in Western Europe, too, identity politics flourished, challenging the self-understandings of citizens in solidly established states. In the United Kingdom, for example, citizens in Scotland and Wales were increasingly uncomfortable with the easy assumption that England should dominate British political life, while in Italy the terms in which the state had been unified in the nineteenth century to reflect a proclaimed Italian national culture began to look strained.[9]

Identity politics thus enjoyed a variety of forms. The implosion of the Soviet empire triggered a round of state-building in difficult circumstances that made the nineteenth-century idea of the nation-state almost irresistible to elites that found themselves exposed without theoretical or rhetorical resources. Paradoxically, the 'triumph' of liberal capitalism at a global level was not matched by a liberal consensus in reconfigured states. Instead, liberal reformers were often marginalized, as programmes of structural institutional and economic reform encountered problems.[10]

The emergence of strong normative arguments in defence of minority cultures was more challenging to the conventional idea of a nation-state. Kymlicka (among others) champions the concept of 'ethno-cultural justice', urging a liberal case for the recognition of diverse cultures as a key to individual fulfilment and well-being.[11] Conventional liberal theory has no problem with the thought that we all require cultural resources in order to flourish. What is more disconcerting (at least to liberals with a strong commitment to equal citizenship) is the claim that hegemonic cultures in nation-states seldom accord adequate space or resources to the distinctive development of minority groups. In this light, the French revolutionary ideal of the 'liberty, equality, fraternity' of all citizens could look decidedly awkward (say) to cultures that distinguished sharply between male and female roles or viewed the state as a means of advancing specific religious goals. While liberals traditionally defend a concept of the state as a neutral arbiter between contending groups and cultures, advocates of 'ethno-cultural justice' argue, to the contrary, that political elites will always distribute resources in a partial fashion, even when they are sensitized to the interests of minorities. Cultural elites decide detailed questions of language policy, curriculum design, schedules of public holidays, etc., which inevitably marginalize groups that do not have ready access to the media and authoritative bureaucratic channels.

Responses to this dilemma are complex. Brian Barry has argued forcefully that the attempt to merge liberal and communitarian positions is conceptually flawed, effectively discounting liberal decision procedures in contexts where they may be regarded as contentious.[12] We appeal to liberal principles precisely when values clash. Crucially, liberal principles are not treated as 'values', but as formal means of resolving complex issues from a (notionally) neutral perspective. It is not fatal to the liberal position if in fact liberal elites display cultural bias. They can be alerted to this and urged to try harder. But it makes little sense to try to treat cultural (or other) groups 'fairly' if the concept of 'fairness' has been rejected at the outset as an independent principle.

It is now a vexed question even among liberals whether principles enjoy an independent status at all. The foundational arguments that were once the stock-in-trade of liberal theory are now regarded with profound suspicion. Rawls's defection from foundationalism in his later work is the most celebrated (and arresting) case of a phenomenon which is wider and deeper, going to the heart of what we might mean by normative political philosophy.[13] Rawls continues to espouse a comprehensive liberal doctrine, but he is anxious to show that terms of political co-operation can be defended independently of the particular comprehensive doctrine he happens to endorse.

Other theorists – Rorty and Gray have been prominent here – defend the institutions and values they happen to have grown up with, but for purely contingent reasons.[14] Rorty's liberal ironist can delight in the cultural diversity which confronts him, enriching the heritage through complex description rather than analysis. Sentimental stories may be said to enhance possibilities for self-understanding. They do not furnish rules to live by. Rules which purport to be theoretically defensible are in fact simply arbitrary conventions that facilitate mutual enjoyment. But they do not facilitate everybody's enjoyment. The pretence that arbitrary conventions are necessary conditions for a just society is one of the principal foundational illusions that the liberal ironist is concerned to dispel.

Gray's position (at least in his more recent writings) is more straightforward. He simply asserts that attachment to liberalism is a function of loyalty to a (purely contingent) national tradition. Liberals may express their loyalty in terms of doctrinal commitments. But once they recognize the fragility of the assumptions they have made (regarding progress, rationality, personal autonomy and so on), they are bound to accept that the sources of their attachment are cultural rather than philosophical. There may well be decisive practical reasons for endorsing liberal institutions and practices as the best means of preserving and developing the advantages that accrue from flourishing civil societies. Yet such a defence could never be more than conditional, and certainly could not assume the guise of a deontological theory.

Far from helping us to resolve difficult cases, political philosophy conducted in a certain style is being portrayed here as an integral part of the problem. At one level, arguments against normative theory look very strong indeed. If terms of reference differ radically, arguments across cultures simply miss their mark. The point can be pressed further. Arguing for the priority of values over arguments commits us to the stronger position that arguments framed by radically divergent values are 'incommensurable'.[15]

It is never quite clear what precisely is being claimed in these discussions. Conflicts of value make mutual comprehension difficult. Some commitments are mutually exclusive. It is difficult to be a soldier and a pacifist at the same time. Individuals balance their commitments in relation to their values, and recognize the necessary loss in some of the choices they make. They also revise their choices in the light of experience. Something further is being claimed, however, when it is suggested that values are 'incommensurable'. From the simple fact that we cannot understand or accommodate a position now, it does not follow that we might not do much better next week or next year. Problems arise, demand attention, and may be more or less successfully solved. There are no guarantees. But it is simply not an option to argue that theory has nothing to contribute in these cases, though it would be naïve to assume that theory alone will ever be sufficient to address our ills. Theory is dangerous when it overreaches itself; but that is not a warrant for giving up on theory altogether. We know that acute conflicts of value can lead to a breakdown in discursive politics. It would be quite another matter to claim that at certain points discursive politics will break down everywhere and always.

The political implications are profound. Advocates of 'strong' identity politics discount the possibility of building effective discursive or institutional 'bridges' between cultures. Within this view of the world, there is little scope for elites to engage in constructive dialogue internationally. Huntington's influential *The Clash of Civilizations and the Remaking of World Order* (1996) stresses the deep fissures between major cultures that condemn states to a policy of containment.[16] Essentially, Huntington offers a conceptual and ideological defence of a 'realist' view of international politics. He assumes from the outset that 'civilizations' are beyond significant discursive amendment. We are thus placed in situations where we simply have to take sides. In the aftermath of the catastrophe in New York on 11 September 2001, it is easy to see how appealing this language is to politicians and citizens confronting new styles of conflict. Yet it is also a counsel of despair, suggesting that this is an existential dilemma that can only be endured.

The situation is also complex in multicultural states. Groups may assert unique claims for special treatment, based on heightened awareness of the things that make them different from dominant cultures. Arguments are couched in terms not of universal justice or entitlement, but rather of practices that matter to 'us' but may be anathema to others. What can liberals make of demands that women should be circumcised or forced into virtual seclusion? Are governments obliged to recognize and support faith-based schools irrespective of the practical tenets of the faith in question? Clearly lines have to be drawn, but it is difficult to specify limits that will be acceptable to all cultures.

Where does this leave us as we confront political problems on a global scale, yet within value systems that are fragmented both within and between

states? To some citizens and commentators the challenges seem too daunting for constructive thought. Parekh, for example, claims that 'multicultural
societies throw up problems that have no parallel in history'.[17] Yet there is
nothing new about striving to reconcile 'the legitimate demands of unity and
diversity' (p. 343). Long-standing empires have done it effectively, though
not without incurring political costs that we are no longer prepared to pay.
The nineteenth-century ideal of a homogeneous culture underpinning a
state has made the task more difficult. But it can hardly be claimed that we are
in uncharted territory. Parekh himself gives a nuanced account of the
resources of the various theoretical traditions on which we can draw. He is
right to suggest that 'no political doctrine or ideology can represent the full
truth of human life' (p. 338). No system of ideas, of whatever kind, could
embrace everything that mattered to us. Certainly political ideologies are
poor creatures. Parekh insists that we cannot work exclusively within liberal
(or any other specific) terms of reference. Yet the arguments he deploys come
largely from liberal theory sensitized to cultural diversity. What he is trying to
do is political philosophy of a rather traditional kind. It really does not matter
whether we call it liberal, post-liberal or whatever. The point is that he cannot
avoid the normative arguments that modern liberal theorists typically
address.

Note, for example, Parekh's frank acknowledgement that a multicultural
society must maintain certain normative standards if it is to flourish. 'No
multicultural society can be stable and vibrant unless it ensures that its
constituent communities receive both just recognition and a just share of
economic and political power' (p. 343). The point could have come straight
out of Rawls. What 'just recognition' might amount to is not specified, though
it would not be misleading presumably to think in terms of the social bases of
self-respect. Similarly, a claim to 'a just share of economic and political
power' could invoke Rawls's 'difference principle' or something like it. In relation to this book it is not necessary to defend any particular conception of
justice in these cases, but only to insist that a conception of justice must be
assumed if we are to make any sense of the ordinary business of co-operating
in complex situations. We cannot defend pluralism on *any* terms. The good
sense that is filtered through political cultures will be sufficient for most
purposes. But 'good sense' is a product of practical reason exercised on
myriad occasions by countless individuals. Sometimes, with the best will in
the world, we are unsure how we should respond, what we should do next. On
these occasions, as agents, we have to think harder. As philosophers, we may
be encouraged to model what is going on when difficult choices are made. We
do not put philosophy into practice in any straightforward sense; yet practical life throws up the dilemmas that oblige us to think philosophically.

Multicultural politics shifts our focus of attention, but we are not doing
anything qualitatively different. Parekh stresses the need for a dialogue
between cultures. We can deepen our personal experience by taking seriously

other possible ways of living. All this is unexceptionable. Yet dialogue will only be constructive if it is conducted on reasonable terms. We can hold conversations behind the barrel of a gun. We can also charmingly allow people to give vent to their feelings and then blithely carry on doing what we were minded to do anyway. Dialogue can be loaded, token, dishonest or serious. How we approach dialogue tells us a great deal about the way we regard others. It may be seen as an indicator of what we suppose we owe them. And indeed, sometimes we will not be sure precisely what we do in fact owe them. Dialogue is a charged term. We need to think about its appropriate limits. How these should be specified, whether in terms of categorical rules or ideal situations, is much less important in the context of this book than simple acknowledgement that normative criteria apply.

Attention to the dynamics of social interaction within societies complicates matters further. Cultures, no matter how we style them, are not self-contained entities. They are products of social engagement over time and are always contested. Claiming and characterizing an identity is (among other things) a move in complex political contestation. Public arenas may be dominated by men, marginalizing options for women. Not everyone can speak for a group with the same authority. Establishing whose voice should be heard is both a political and a normative issue. In a real sense, 'culture' is no less a theoretical abstraction than 'community', 'society', 'class' or 'state'. How these terms are understood will reflect a balance of normative and political argument.[18]

In relation to Kymlicka's notion of 'ethno-cultural justice', for example, great care needs to be taken in specifying the relevant territorial or cultural space. Groups and individuals may defend that space in radically divergent ways. The language issue has been especially explosive. To identify a shared language as a key component in cultural membership, as Kymlicka often does, makes it extremely difficult to treat minority language users as full citizens if the legitimacy of the state is identified in ethno-cultural terms. Safeguards can be built into a notion of ethno-cultural justice, defending basic rights, mobility and so forth, but citizens will not be able to identify equally with the dominant culture. Hungarian speakers in Romania can readily be portrayed as a threat to the legitimacy of the unitary Romanian state if they demand the right to educate their children in their native language. And, of course, this issue resonates powerfully in some Western European polities, not least in Wales.

Absence of (even an idea of) transcultural justice leaves the distribution of burdens to the unpredictable outcomes of political discussion and conflict among variously placed groups. Establishments (as Foucault has shown) have formal and informal resources to marginalize awkward and intransigent voices. Power remains an issue in any normative theory. And we can all accept that (no matter how it is measured) it will never be distributed equally. In these circumstances, it is imperative that distributive decisions are based on more than raw convictions. What might count as a fair and attainable principle will remain a contentious matter. To assume that any such principle could reflect only the values of specific groups, however, undermines prospects for a distribution that could be regarded as reasonably acceptable to all interested parties. The point is not that we can easily establish strict neutrality or impartiality, but rather, that giving up on any transcultural distributive principle as a regulatory ideal damages the interests of the worst-placed groups.[19]

The problem emerges acutely in recent feminist writings. It has become customary to focus on liberalism (for example) as a male-friendly ideology, insensitive to women's experience and manner of dealing with moral issues. Gilligan, in a ground-breaking study, combined normative argument with developmental psychology to show in detail how women simply approach issues in a distinctive way.[20] Feminists could use the language of 'difference' (just as multicultural theory has) to highlight a particular and gender-specific scale of values. Co-operation rather than conflict may be regarded as 'natural' to women, encouraging an inclusive and consensual decision-making culture. The merits of this approach are clear. Procedural practices in institutions can be shown to exclude women, despite liberal legislation enshrining the principle of equality of opportunity. And liberal insistence on (at least some form of) a distinction between public and private spheres makes it profoundly difficult to remedy social and institutional values through orthodox legislative means.

Yet perceptions of women's roles remain highly contested and socially constructed. We can alert ourselves to traditional male dominance in the specification of roles, without extricating women from complex webs of social power relations. How 'selves' are formed and framed continues to be controversial and varies historically and culturally.[21] If likely outcomes for women are intrinsically uncertain, the need to appeal to formal principles is unavoidable in hard cases. Notions of agency and autonomy, for sure, need to be adapted to gender-specific circumstances. But a political or cultural consensus will never be a sufficient guarantee of reasonable treatment for women. It is precisely reliance upon 'common sense' and conventional politics that has warranted the historical exclusion of women from public life. Enfranchising women goes some way towards shifting priorities in public debate. It would be naïve, however, to assume that democratic politics will always yield normatively defensible outcomes. Paradoxically, the harshest critics of liberal politics reinforce the indispensability of a style of normative theorizing usually associated with liberalism.

For all the problems we encounter trying to characterize normative argument, we all employ it at one level or other in our practical engagements. Traditional political philosophy distinguished government and state as a relevant focus for issues affecting a whole community. Yet (as we have seen) it can no longer be assumed that the state enjoys the kind of institutional supremacy attributed to it in orthodox theory. As sites of power are dispersed, so the challenge to effective political argument and persuasion among citizens becomes more demanding and tortuous. Formal political institutions and roles may lose some of their authority. One response among citizens may be to seek alternative routes for expressing normative concerns. Single-issue movements have arisen as umbrella ideologies look ever more remote from the interests of citizens.

An alternative is to treat the changed nature of the state as an opportunity for political assertion and mobilization across a wider range of institutions. The idea of 'civil society' has enjoyed renewed prominence since the 1990s, highlighting the autonomous institutional networks that impinge most directly on citizens and constrain the formal policy options of political elites. To be sure, this is a highly demanding style of politics, presupposing knowledge and resources distributed in specialized concentrations throughout a society. David Held (among others) has argued for democratic political theory to be adapted to the very different demands of global order, empowering individuals and groups to articulate demands and hold elites to account on broader fronts.[22] In this scheme of things, the politics of profession or work-place fills a void left by the conventional politics of a governmental hierarchy. Significantly, a politics so conceived must be cosmopolitan in scope, reflecting the interdependence of states, cultures and economies.

The theoretical wheel moves full circle. Confident predictions that the 'Enlightenment project' has run its course, that the very idea of justification is redundant in a postmodern epoch, that a whole cycle in political philosophy has closed, fracture on the hard reality of the need to orchestrate collaborative projects among distant strangers in a global context. Traditional political ideologies may well seem less compelling, sometimes even barely relevant to the circumstances of people's lives. But the contrast between coercion and consent remains. We are still bound to try to fashion reasonable terms of social co-operation, though our theoretical resources may well be stretched in modern contexts.

Dissatisfaction with the way the world is remains, along with unalloyed enjoyment of myriad engagements. Philosophies of public life (in the broadest sense) have been exposed, but largely in terms of counter-positions that have been developed over the last 300 years. The *Communist Manifesto*, for example, looks like a decidedly dated text to some modern readers. Yet, it has been used by Hardt and Negri as a model for the analysis of empire as a phenomenon in the contemporary world.[23] The terms of reference here are intriguing. Exposing humbug is a necessity for us as theorists and citizens. Faced with a cacophony of conflicting voices, we have to try to discriminate. If state-based ideologies look stale to some eyes, there is a clear imperative to think in global terms. The globalization of markets furnishes evidence that would not have surprised Marx himself, though the scale and speed of connections doubtless adds dimensions that could not have been anticipated in 1848. The simple thought that we cannot understand national economies without invoking a global capitalist context has been accepted almost universally. The constraints on political elites are as obvious now as they were to Marx, though we may analyse the interdependence of capitalism differently. These are very much variations on familiar themes, rather than brave new beginnings in uncharted territory.

From a historical perspective, we may view political philosophy and theory as a series of (more or less effective) attempts to model our experience of normative argument. A lot is at stake for all of us. Life chances hinge on the authority of certain views. We all press our views, however, as interested parties, anxious to present our own pet projects as somehow ideally desirable. Normative argument (and political theory with it) is thus 'tainted' by the variety of perspectives we ordinarily encounter. But it remains indispensable. In one sense it simply follows from the thought that things could go better or worse for us. We cannot give up on this idea without incapacitating ourselves as critical agents. Yet we also have very good grounds for doubting the credentials of a whole series of arguments that have been habitually advanced.

Normative argument presupposes two distinct claims. One is the logical point that thinking involves presuppositions which we may regard as foundational. They will be relatively stable and abstract, compatible with a variety of argumentative moves. It would be misleading, however, to equate 'foundations' with values. We can all recognize the contingency of values. Yet, if we treat thinking itself as contingent, we make it unintelligible as an engagement. Thinking hard presupposes that our next argumentative moves are not arbitrary.

The second claim is that thinking hard about moral or political questions can clarify our predicament, even if we are sceptical about the capacity of practical reason to transform our basic situation. We are 'thrown' into circumstances that demand a theoretical response. Despite our (eminently justified) reservations about our intellectual resources, we still have to think hard in some contexts. There is nothing mysterious about this engagement. We all find ourselves doing it on occasion, no matter how ill-equipped we might feel we are. A minimal role for theory is to model what is going on in these situations.

In practice no one disputes that normative dilemmas arise. There is a temptation in contemporary theory, though, to explain the dilemmas away, as if our failure to agree on normative matters could be treated as a necessary limit to our powers of practical reason. Yet we can imagine better and worse ways of modelling normative dilemmas. Equating all choices with personal preferences is unlikely to be helpful when we are really in a fix, struggling to balance contending (and possibly incompatible) demands.

The point here is to take seriously the perspective of the troubled agent, rather than to retreat to a more detached interpretative perspective. The thought is not that theory can resolve the agent's dilemma, but that the dilemma can be modelled in ways that convey the seriousness of what is at stake. Modelling is not neutral. Different ways of framing a context of decision and choice will filter out certain argumentative strategies as unhelpful or redundant. But there is no suggestion that we can deduce options from first principles.

The principles in question here are necessarily 'thin', embracing a range of widely different (yet sustainable) ways of life. And if they are described as 'foundational', it must be clear that the foundation is too weak to sustain thick institutional detail. Thin universal principles may nevertheless be robust enough to do normative work for us. Rawls gives us an intriguing glimpse of what may be involved in the concluding paragraph of the introduction to the paperback edition of *Political Liberalism*. He sets his own work in the context of the 'extreme violence and increasing destructiveness' of the twentieth century, 'culminating in the manic evil of the Holocaust', and asks himself (in the light of that catastrophe) 'whether political relations must be governed by power and coercion alone'.[24] Here, if anywhere, the ineffectiveness of a reflective politics had been most dramatically illustrated. Note that Rawls is not concerned simply with the fact that politics had gone so horribly wrong. His wider worry is the very possibility that 'a reasonably just society that subordinates power to its aims' might be discounted (p. lxii).

This takes us to the heart of an issue that has dominated political thought. On one side we have the thought that 'people are largely amoral, if not incurably cynical and self-centered' (p. lxii). If this is the case, asks Rawls, following Kant, would it be 'worthwhile for human beings to live on the earth'? (p. lxii). It is not clear how we should take this question. We are lumbered with human beings on the face of the earth, 'thrown' into situations that are often deeply precarious and threatening. Yet Rawls is remarkably robust. 'We must start [he says] with the assumption that a reasonably just society is possible, and for it to be possible, human beings must have a moral nature, not of course a perfect such nature, yet one that can understand, act on, and be sufficiently moved by a reasonable political conception of right and justice to support a society guided by its ideals and principles' (p. lxii). We should focus here on the force of the sentence. Rawls says that we *must* make these theoretical commitments, not merely that we *should* (all things considered). Without these commitments, we cannot begin to think normatively, and we have already granted that normative thinking is unavoidable.

Rawls's position, of course, is one among many. But he highlights forcefully the need to invoke broad conceptions of what is possible for human beings before we go on to look at more specific questions. Rawls is emphatic on this issue. He is assuming that a society is a system of social co-operation (more or less fair) extending over a complete life. He is also assuming that the agents involved in such schemes of social co-operation are aware of themselves and their dealings with others, though they may articulate that involvement in all manner of intriguing ways. No matter how agents conceive of themselves, however, we must assume that they have 'a capacity for a sense of justice and a capacity for a sense of the good' (p. 19). We have to assume that all human beings have these 'two moral powers', and not simply the citizens of polities such as our own (p. 19). Of course, human beings may not always conceive of themselves in these ways. They may suppose that they are marionettes in God's hands or the products of strictly demarcated property relations. These notions may comfort them and make various aspects of their lives more or less intelligible. But they disguise the fact that they are exercising the 'burdens of judgement' in conditions of uncertainty, anxious to preserve social co-operation on at least minimally sustainable terms. In order to understand what they are thinking and doing, we actually have to construe their engagements in another idiom. We would not want to accuse them of being victims of false consciousness, because we all filter our experience through symbols and myths. Where we differ from them is in invoking the constructive symbolism of the social world. Our disenchantment changes things radically for us. They think they are doing God's will, and we think they are doing the best they can for themselves in determinate circumstances. We can take a permissive view of the way in which social experience is construed in different contexts. But we cannot avoid meta-ethical assumptions about the 'burdens of judgement' and the 'circumstances of justice'.

The history of modern political thought is very much a series of (often starkly contrasting) responses to this basic dilemma. The universal citizen of French revolutionary rhetoric has begun to seem deeply intolerant at the beginning of the twenty-first century. The quintessentially 'modern' and secular French state has enormous difficulty accommodating religious symbolism in public contexts such as schools. Political rhetoric has failed to keep up with the reality of a multicultural (and post-imperial) identity. And even in polities that find pluralism less threatening, obvious cultural differences are often associated with strong reassertion of traditional values. A politics of nostalgia goes hand in hand with the emergence of cosmopolitan cultures in great cities.

Even if the radical contingency of values and institutions is granted, we are still left with the problem of explaining what it means to make hard choices in contexts where binding decisions have to be made. For the most part, we can accept that reasons which are regarded as compelling within a culture may have little purchase beyond it. But cultures are not self-contained. It is precisely when terms of reference are challenged that more basic forms of justification are called for. In these cases, we have to give reasons for our choices which extend beyond the values we happen to have. We do not have to presuppose that stark moral or theoretical dilemmas can always be resolved satisfactorily, only that we have to appeal to (something like) practical reason whenever we are asked to give a public justification of our preferences.

Theorists carry on asking the standard question ('What do we owe to each other?'), but it is less clear who the question is addressed to.[25] Specifying what can count as politically relevant difference significantly complicates the original liberal theory of citizenship. Gender and culture are seen as prisms that render universal principles deeply problematic. Yet criteria still have to be specified for access to public goods. As groups challenge the distortion implicit in hegemonic discourse, they still have to justify their claims in public arenas. Normative theory has to answer the contention that in a profound sense we simply cannot understand each other. In these circumstances, there is a real risk that power will replace right as a legitimate distributive criterion. Normative theory remains indispensable to a decent politics. Its grounding principles, however, are more contentious than ever.

Suggestions for Further Reading

Good studies covering the range of texts and thinkers in the history of political thought abound. David Boucher and Paul Kelly (eds), *Political Thinkers: From Socrates to the Present* (Oxford: Oxford University Press, 2003), deals clearly with major figures and is helpful on further reading. Iain Hampsher-Monk, *A History of Modern Political Thought: Major Political Thinkers from Hobbes to Marx* (Oxford: Blackwell, 1992), is also a sound introduction to selected theorists. Murray Forsyth, Maurice Keens-Soper and John Hoffman (eds), *The Political Classics: Hamilton to Mill* (Oxford: Oxford University Press, 1993), and Murray Forsyth and Maurice Keens-Soper (eds), *The Political Classics: Green to Dworkin* (Oxford: Oxford University Press, 1996), focus instead on specific texts. J. S. McClelland, *A History of Western Political Thought* (London: Routledge, 1996), is wider-ranging and patchy, but written in a lively and accessible style. Terence Ball, *Reappraising Political Theory: Revisionist Studies in the History of Political Thought* (Oxford: Oxford University Press, 1995), includes sensitive discussion of recent methodological debates. Quentin Skinner's seminal 'Meaning and Understanding in the History of Ideas', *History and Theory*, 8 (1969), sparked a generation of debate on the relationship between theory and history. David Boucher, *Texts in Context: Revisionist Methods for Studying the History of Ideas* (Dordrecht: Martinus Nijhof, 1985), addresses key contributions to the debate. Among older studies, Sheldon Wolin, *Politics and Vision* (Boston: Little Brown, 1960), and John Plamenatz, *Man and Society: A Critical Examination of Some Important Social and Political Theories from Machiavelli to Marx*, 2 vols (London: Longman, 1963), continue to be rewarding. Students coming to political theory for the first time should perhaps begin with Peri Roberts and Peter Sutch, *An Introduction to Political Thought: A Conceptual Toolkit* (Edinburgh: Edinburgh University Press, 2004), or John Morrow, *The History of Political Thought: A Thematic Introduction* (Basingstoke: Macmillan, 1998).

An understanding of modern political thought requires some familiarity with arguments and issues raised in the French Revolution. William Doyle, *The French Revolution: A Very Short Introduction* (Oxford: Oxford University Press, 2001), is admirably clear. Other standard studies include William Doyle, *The Oxford History of the French Revolution* (Oxford: Oxford University Press, 1989), and François Furet, *Revolutionary France: 1770–1870* (Oxford: Oxford University Press, 1992). Geoffrey Best (ed.), *The Permanent*

Revolution: The French Revolution and its Legacy, 1789–1989 (London: Fontana, 1988), is exceptionally useful for students primarily interested in political theory. J. L. Talmon, *The Origins of Totalitarian Democracy: Political Theory and Practice during the French Revolution and Beyond* (Harmondsworth: Penguin Books, 1982; first published 1952), is a polemical critique of the revolutionary tradition which is now attracting renewed attention. On specific theorists, see Murray Forsyth, *Reason and Revolution: The Political Thought of the Abbé Sieyes* (Leicester: Leicester University Press, 1987), and Murray Forsyth, 'Emmanuel Sieyes: *What is the Third Estate?*', in Murray Forsyth, Maurice Keens-Soper and John Hoffman (eds), *The Political Classics: Hamilton to Mill*.

There is a wealth of literature on Kant's moral and political thought, often written from a technical philosophical perspective. For Kant's life, Ernst Cassirer, *Kant's Life and Thought*, trans. James Haden (New Haven: Yale University Press, 1981), is a model of clarity. Allen W. Wood, *Kant's Ethical Thought* (Cambridge: Cambridge University Press, 1999), is painstaking and demanding, but richly rewarding. Kant's politics is covered exhaustively in Howard Williams, *Kant's Political Philosophy* (Oxford: Blackwell, 1983). *Perpetual Peace* is the focus of Georg Cavallar, *Kant and the Theory and Practice of International Right* (Cardiff: University of Wales Press, 1999). More advanced students should not neglect the engagement of contemporary philosophers with Kant's ethics: see Barbara Herman, *The Practice of Moral Judgement* (Cambridge, Mass.: Harvard University Press, 1993); Onora O'Neill, *Constructions of Reason: Explorations of Kant's Practical Philosophy* (Cambridge: Cambridge University Press, 1989); and John Rawls, *Lectures on the History of Moral Philosophy*, ed. Barbara Herman (Cambridge, Mass.: Harvard University Press, 2000).

For the history and politics of the American Revolution, see Edmund S. Morgan, *The Birth of the Republic, 1763–89* (Chicago: University of Chicago Press, 1992). For broader theoretical background to the thinking of the revolutionary period, see J. G. A. Pocock, *The Machiavellian Moment: Florentine Political Thought and the Atlantic Republican Tradition* (Princeton: Princeton University Press, 1975). Hannah Arendt's parallel reading of the American and French revolutions, *On Revolution* (London: Faber, 1963), is provocative and challenging. Among studies focused more specifically on the *Federalist Papers*, see Morton White, *Philosophy, 'The Federalist' and the Constitution* (Oxford: Oxford University Press, 1987), and David F. Epstein, *The Political Theory of the Federalist* (Chicago: University of Chicago Press, 1986). Wider constitutional issues are addressed in Terence Ball and J. G. A. Pocock (eds), *Conceptual Change and the Constitution* (Lawrence: University Press of Kansas, 1988).

Developments in political thought in the nineteenth century must be seen in relation to wider currents of thought. The emergence of historical awareness, in particular, is crucial: see Bruce Haddock, *An Introduction to*

Historical Thought (London: Edward Arnold, 1980); Maurice Mandelbaum, *History, Man and Reason: A Study in Nineteenth-Century Thought* (Baltimore: Johns Hopkins University Press, 1971); and Hayden White, *Metahistory: The Historical Imagination in Nineteenth-Century Europe* (Baltimore: Johns Hopkins University Press, 1973). For the cult of science in the nineteenth century, see W. M. Simon, *European Positivism in the Nineteenth Century: An Essay in Intellectual History* (Ithaca, NY: Cornell University Press, 1963). The optimistic current in French thought is covered in Frank E. Manuel, *The Prophets of Paris* (Cambridge, Mass.: Harvard University Press, 1962). Wider cultural currents are vividly portrayed in J. W. Barrow, *The Crisis of Reason: European Thought, 1848–1914* (New Haven: Yale University Press, 2000).

Burke's specific reaction to the French Revolution has always attracted attention: see Michael Freeman, *Edmund Burke and the Critique of Political Radicalism* (Oxford: Blackwell, 1980); Frank O'Gorman, *Edmund Burke: His Political Philosophy* (London: Allen & Unwin, 1973); C. B. Macpherson, *Burke* (Oxford: Oxford University Press, 1980); Alfred Cobban, *Edmund Burke and the Revolt against the Eighteenth Century* (London: Allen & Unwin, 1960); and Charles Parkin, *The Moral Basis of Burke's Political Thought* (Cambridge: Cambridge University Press, 1956).

For Joseph de Maistre, see Richard A. Lebrun, *Throne and Altar: The Political and Religious Thought of Joseph de Maistre* (Ottawa: University of Ottawa Press, 1965); Richard A. Lebrun (ed.), *Joseph de Maistre's Life, Thought and Influence: Selected Studies* (Montreal: McGill–Queen's University Press, 2001); and Domenico Fisichella, *Il pensiero politico di De Maistre* (Bari: Laterza, 1993).

There is no secondary literature in English on Cuoco. Readers of Italian should look at Antonino de Francesco, *Vincenzo Cuoco: Una vita politica* (Bari: Laterza, 1997), and Fulvio Tessitore, *Lo storicismo di Vincenzo Cuoco* (Naples: Morano, 1965).

Constant's case for a modern constitutional state is vigorously defended in Stephen Holmes, *Benjamin Constant and the Making of Modern Liberalism* (New Haven: Yale University Press, 1984). See also Beatrice C. Fink, 'Benjamin Constant on Equality', *Journal of the History of Ideas*, 33 (1972). The wider context of discussions of liberty is explored in Larry Siedentop, 'Two Liberal Traditions', in Alan Ryan (ed.), *The Idea of Freedom: Essays in Honour of Isaiah Berlin* (Oxford: Oxford University Press, 1979).

Hegel's defence of the constitutional state is more complex, raising fundamental questions about the nature of historicity. The Knox edition of the *Philosophy of Right* has been used in this book. Allen W. Wood's edition, *Elements of the Philosophy of Right* (Cambridge: Cambridge University Press, 1991), can also be strongly recommended. Recent Hegel scholarship has been very good indeed. For Hegel's life, see Terry Pinkard, *Hegel: A Biography* (Cambridge: Cambridge University Press, 2000). Among critical studies, see Allen W. Wood, *Hegel's Ethical Thought* (Cambridge: Cambridge University

Press, 1991); Michael Hardimon, *Hegel's Social Philosophy: The Project of Reconciliation* (Cambridge: Cambridge University Press, 1994); Manfred Riedel, *Between Tradition and Revolution: The Hegelian Transformation of Political Philosophy* (Cambridge: Cambridge University Press, 1984); Shlomo Avineri, *Hegel's Theory of the Modern State* (Cambridge: Cambridge University Press, 1972); Alan Patten, *Hegel's Idea of Freedom* (Oxford: Oxford University Press, 1999); Robert Pippin, *Idealism as Modernism: Hegelian Variations* (Cambridge: Cambridge University Press, 1997); and Charles Taylor, *Hegel* (Cambridge: Cambridge University Press, 1975).

There has been a proliferation of studies of nationalism in recent years. From a vast literature, see John Hutchinson and Anthony D. Smith (eds), *Nationalism* (Oxford: Oxford University Press, 1994); John Hutchinson, *Modern Nationalism* (London: Fontana, 1994); Ernest Gellner, *Nations and Nationalism* (Oxford: Blackwell, 1983); Peter Alter, *Nationalism* (London: Edward Arnold, 1989); Benedict Anderson, *Imagined Communities: Reflections on the Origin and Spread of Nationalism* (London: Verso, 1991); Liah Greenfeld, *Nationalism: Five Roads to Modernity* (Cambridge, Mass.: Harvard University Press, 1992); E. J. Hobsbawm, *Nations and Nationality since 1780: Programme, Myth, Reality* (Cambridge: Cambridge University Press, 1990); Anthony D. Smith, *Nations and Nationalism in a Global Era* (Cambridge: Polity, 1995); David Miller, *On Nationality* (Oxford: Oxford University Press, 1995); Margaret Canovan, *Nationhood and Political Theory* (Cheltenham: Edward Elgar, 1996); and Andrew Vincent, *Nationalism and Particularity* (Cambridge: Cambridge University Press, 2002).

Individual nationalist theorists have attracted less attention. On Herder, see F. M. Barnard, *Herder's Social and Political Thought: From Enlightenment to Nationalism* (Oxford: Oxford University Press, 1965); Isaiah Berlin, *Vico and Herder: Two Studies in the History of Ideas* (London: Hogarth Press, 1976); and Robert T. Clark, Jr, *Herder: His Life and Thought* (Berkeley and Los Angeles: University of California Press, 1969).

For Mazzini we have Denis Mack Smith, *Mazzini* (New Haven: Yale University Press, 1994), for the life; Nadia Urbinati, 'A Common Law of Nations: Giuseppe Mazzini's Democratic Nationality', *Journal of Modern Italian Studies*, 1 (1996); C. E. Vaughan, 'Mazzini', in his *Studies in the History of Political Philosophy before and after Rousseau* (Manchester: Manchester University Press, 1925), vol. 2; and Bruce Haddock, 'State and Nation in Mazzini's Political Thought', *History of Political Thought*, 20 (1999). For wider context, see Bruce Haddock, 'State, Nation and Risorgimento', in Gino Bedani and Bruce Haddock (eds), *The Politics of Italian National Identity: A Multidisciplinary Perspective* (Cardiff: University of Wales Press, 2000).

There has been a renaissance of interest in Tocqueville's thought among both historians and political theorists. Sheldon S. Wolin, *Tocqueville between Two Worlds: The Making of a Political and Theoretical Life* (Princeton: Princeton University Press, 2001), is characteristically subtle and wide-ranging, combining careful reading of the gamut of Tocqueville writings and papers with critical engagement with his ideas. Larry Siedentop, *Tocqueville* (Oxford: Oxford University Press, 1994), is a short but stimulating introduction. The following can also be thoroughly recommended: Cheryl Welch, *De Tocqueville* (Oxford: Oxford University Press, 2001); James T. Schleifer, *The Making of Tocqueville's Democracy in America* (Chapel Hill: University of North Carolina Press, 1980); and Jack Lively, *The Social and Political Thought of Alexis de Tocqueville* (Oxford: Clarendon Press, 1965).

For Bentham, see P. J. Kelly, *Utilitarianism and Distributive Justice: Jeremy Bentham and the Civil Law* (Oxford: Clarendon Press, 1990); David Manning, *The Mind of Jeremy Bentham* (London: Longman, 1968); F. Rosen, *Jeremy Bentham and Representative Democracy* (Oxford: Clarendon Press, 1983); and R. Harrison, *Bentham* (London: Routledge, 1983). Advanced students should not neglect H. L. A. Hart, *Essays on Bentham* (Oxford: Clarendon Press, 1983).

John Stuart Mill remains a staple figure for political theorists, attracting consistently high levels of scholarship. From a vast literature, see J. C. Rees, *John Stuart Mill's On Liberty*, ed. G. L. Williams (Oxford: Oxford University Press, 1985); John Gray, *Mill on Liberty: A Defence* (London: Routledge, 1983); Roger Crisp, *Mill on Utilitarianism* (London: Routledge, 1997); W. Thomas, *Mill* (Oxford: Oxford University Press, 1985); Joseph Hamburger, *John Stuart Mill on Liberty and Control* (Princeton: Princeton University Press, 1999); C. L. Ten, *Mill on Liberty* (Oxford: Oxford University Press, 1980); John Skorupski, *John Stuart Mill* (London: Routledge, 1990); Isaiah Berlin, 'John Stuart Mill and the Ends of Life', in his *Four Essays on Liberty* (London: Oxford University Press, 1969); Alan Ryan, *The Philosophy of John Stuart Mill* (London: Macmillan, 1970); and John Skorupski (ed.), *The Cambridge Companion to Mill* (Cambridge: Cambridge University Press, 1998).

Leszek Kolakowski, *Main Currents of Marxism*, trans. P. S. Falla, 3 vols (Oxford: Oxford University Press, 1978), is a masterly guide to the socialist tradition. David McLellan, *Karl Marx: His Life and Thought* (London: Macmillan, 1973), is a solid guide to the range of Marx's writings. The most rigorous philosophical study of Marx's theory of history is G. A. Cohen, *Karl Marx's Theory of History: A Defence* (Oxford: Oxford University Press, 1978). On Marx's politics, see Shlomo Avineri, *The Social and Political Thought of Karl Marx* (Cambridge: Cambridge University Press, 1968); Bertell Ollman, *Alienation: Marx's Critique of Man in Capitalist Society* (Cambridge: Cambridge University Press, 1971); Terrell Carver, *Marx's Social Theory* (Oxford: Oxford University Press, 1982); and Alan W. Thomas, *Karl Marx* (London: Routledge, 1981).

The idea and character of totalitarianism remain hotly contested issues, not least in relation to the emergence of Eastern European states from the tutelage of the Soviet Union. The most arresting study of the phenomenon in relation to political ideas is Hannah Arendt, *The Origins of Totalitarianism* (London: George Allen & Unwin, 1967, 3rd edn). For broader discussion, see Simon Tormey, *Making Sense of Tyranny: Interpretations of Totalitarianism* (Manchester: Manchester University Press, 1995). Margaret Canovan, *Hannah Arendt: A Reinterpretation* (Cambridge: Cambridge University Press, 1992), is the best guide to Arendt's thought.

For Lenin, see Neil Harding, *Lenin's Political Thought*, 2 vols (London: Macmillan, 1977–81), and Robert Service, *Lenin: A Political Life* (London: Macmillan, 1995).

Carl Schmitt remains a troubling figure, though his critique of liberalism touches a nerve in modern political theory. See Joseph W. Bendersky, *Carl Schmitt: Theorist for the Reich* (Princeton: Princeton University Press, 1983); Renato Cristi, *Carl Schmitt and Authoritarian Liberalism: Strong State, Free Economy* (Cardiff: Cardiff University Press, 1997); Paul Gottfried, *Carl Schmitt: Politics and Theory* (Westport, Conn.: Greenwood Press, 1990); John P. McCormick, *Carl Schmitt's Critique of Liberalism: Against Politics as Technology* (Cambridge: Cambridge University Press, 1997); and David Dyzenhaus (ed.), *Law as Politics: Carl Schmitt's Critique of Liberalism* (Durham, NC: Duke University Press, 1998).

H. S. Harris, *The Social Philosophy of Giovanni Gentile* (Urbana: University of Illinois Press, 1960), did most to sustain Gentile's reputation as a serious political philosopher in the English-speaking world. A. James Gregor, *Giovanni Gentile: Philosopher of Fascism* (New Brunswick, NJ: Transaction Publishers, 2001), is a shorter, and less rigorous, introduction.

Popper, Hayek, Oakeshott and Berlin are all readily accessible as philosophers and political theorists. For discussion, see Bryan Magee, *Popper* (London: Fontana, 1973); Jeremy Shearmur, *The Political Thought of Karl Popper* (London: Routledge, 1996); Geoffrey Stokes, *Popper: Philosophy, Politics and Scientific Method* (Cambridge: Polity, 1998); John Gray, *Hayek on Liberty* (Oxford: Blackwell, 1986); Norman P. Barry, *Hayek's Social and Economic Philosophy* (London: Macmillan, 1979); Andrew Gamble, *Hayek: The Iron Cage of Liberty* (Cambridge: Polity, 1996); Chandran Kukathas, *Hayek and Modern Liberalism* (Oxford: Oxford University Press, 1989); Alan Ebenstein, *Friedrich Hayek: A Biography* (Chicago: University of Chicago Press, 2003); Paul Franco, *The Political Philosophy of Michael Oakeshott* (New Haven: Yale University Press, 1990); W. H. Greenleaf, *Oakeshott's Philosophical Politics* (London: Longman, 1966); Anthony Quinton, *The Politics of Imperfection: The Religious and Secular Traditions in Conservative Thought from Hooker to Oakeshott* (London: Faber, 1978); Terry Nardin, *The Philosophy of Michael Oakeshott* (University Park, Pa.: Pennsylvania State University Press, 2001); Bruce Haddock, 'Contingency and Judgement in Oakeshott's Political Thought', *European Journal of Political Theory*, 4 (2005); Claude J. Galipeau, *Isaiah Berlin's Liberalism* (Oxford: Clarendon Press, 1994); and John Gray, *Berlin* (London: HarperCollins, 1995).

John Rawls has been the focus of more discussion than any other contemporary political theorist, in terms of both exegesis and critical engagement. A clear introduction is Chandran Kukathas and Philip Pettit, *A Theory of Justice and its Critics* (Cambridge: Polity, 1990). Brian Barry, *The Liberal Theory of Justice* (Oxford: Clarendon Press, 1973), is a sustained critical analysis of leading ideas from *A Theory of Justice*. Michael J. Sandel, *Liberalism and the Limits of Justice* (Cambridge: Cambridge University Press, 1982), is a close criticism of Rawls from a communitarian perspective. Thomas Pogge, *Realizing Rawls* (Ithaca, NY: Cornell University Press, 1989), pursues implications in the wider international arena. Students coming to analytical political theory for the first time would do well to begin with broader texts. See Will Kymlicka, *Contemporary Political Philosophy* (Oxford: Oxford University Press, 1990); Jonathan Wolff, *An Introduction to Political Philosophy* (Oxford: Oxford University Press, 1996); Andrew Vincent, *The Nature of Political Theory* (Oxford: Oxford University Press, 2004); Raymond Plant, *Modern Political Thought* (Oxford: Blackwell, 1991); and Jean Hampton, *Political Philosophy* (Boulder, Colo.: Westview Press, 1997).

The presuppositions of normative theory have been challenged most forcefully by Foucault. For discussion, see Jon Simons, *Foucault and the Political* (London: Routledge, 1995); Michael Clifford, *Political Genealogy after Foucault: Savage Identities* (London: Routledge, 2001); John S. Ransom, *Foucault's Discipline: The Politics of Subjectivity* (Durham, NC: Duke University Press, 1997); Gary Gutting (ed.), *The Cambridge Companion to Foucault* (Cambridge: Cambridge University Press, 1994); Roy Boyne, *Foucault and Derrida: The Other Side of Reason* (London: Unwin Hyman, 1990); Jeremy Moss (ed.), *The Later Foucault: Politics and Philosophy* (London: Sage, 1998); and Barry Hindess, *Discourses of Power: From Hobbes to Foucault* (Oxford: Oxford University Press).

For broader themes in twentieth-century political thought, see Terence Ball and Richard Bellamy (eds), *The Cambridge History of Twentieth-Century Political Thought* (Cambridge: Cambridge University Press, 2003). The problematic impact of intellectuals is covered in Mark Lilla, *The Reckless Mind: Intellectuals in Politics* (New York: New York Review of Books, 2001), and Richard Wolin, *The Seduction of Unreason: The Intellectual Romance with Fascism from Nietzsche to Postmodernism* (Princeton: Princeton University Press, 2004).

What is perhaps most marked in the contemporary literature on the status of normative argument is a failure to engage across disciplines. One of the major attractions of approaching normative argument through history of political thought is precisely that theory and history are brought together. The recent literature on multiculturalism has also forced a dialogue between disciplines, though results have not always been encouraging. Responses to Brian Barry, *Culture and Equality* (Cambridge: Polity,

2000), highlight the striking political implications of contemporary theory. See Paul Kelly (ed.), *Multiculturalism Reconsidered* (Cambridge: Polity, 2002), and Bruce Haddock and Peter Sutch (eds), *Multiculturalism, Identity and Rights* (London: Routledge, 2003). These are contemporary versions of long-standing arguments between universalists and particularists. And there is no end in sight.

Notes

Chapter 1 Introduction

1 See *The New Science of Giambattista Vico*, trans. T. G. Bergin and M. H. Fisch (Ithaca, NY: Cornell University Press, 1968); and for discussion Bruce Haddock, *Vico's Political Thought* (Swansea: Mortlake Press, 1986).

2 See Bruce Haddock, *An Introduction to Historical Thought* (London: Edward Arnold, 1980).

3 See H. A. Prichard, 'Does Moral Philosophy Rest on a Mistake?', in his *Moral Obligation* (Oxford: Clarendon Press, 1949), 1–17.

Chapter 2 Revolution

1 Alexander Hamilton, James Madison and John Jay, *The Federalist, with Letters of 'Brutus'*, ed. Terence Ball (Cambridge: Cambridge University Press, 2003), no. 1, p. 1.

2 The text of the *Declaration* is reproduced in Thomas Paine, *Rights of Man*, ed. Henry Collins (Harmondsworth: Penguin Books, 1969), 132–4. The quotation is from p. 132. Subsequent page references are given parenthetically in the text.

3 See Emmanuel Joseph Sieyes, *What is the Third Estate?*, ed. S. E. Finer (London: Pall Mall Press, 1963). Subsequent page references are given parenthetically in the text.

4 Thomas Paine, *Common Sense*, ed. Isaak Kramnick (Harmondsworth: Penguin Books, 1976), 65.

5 Ibid. 65.

6 Paine, *Rights of Man*, 187.

7 See Edmund Burke, *Reflections on the Revolution in France*, ed. A. J. Grieve (London: Dent, 1967); and the discussion below, pp. 26–32.

8 See *The Federalist*, 40–6. Subsequent page references are given parenthetically in the text.

9 See Immanuel Kant, *Critique of Pure Reason*, trans. Norman Kemp Smith (London: Macmillan, 1929); 'Critique of Practical Reason', in Immanuel Kant, *Practical Philosophy*, ed. Mary J. Gregor (Cambridge: Cambridge University Press, 1996); and Immanuel Kant, *The Critique of Judgement*, trans. J. C. Meredith (Oxford: Clarendon Press, 1953).

10 See Kant, *Critique of Pure Reason*, 25.

11 See Immanuel Kant, 'Groundwork of the Metaphysics of Morals', in his *Practical Philosophy*, 41–108. Subsequent page references are given parenthetically in the text.

12 See Immanuel Kant, 'Toward Perpetual Peace: A Philosophical Project', in his *Practical Philosophy*, 315–51. Subsequent page references are given parenthetically in the text.

13 Immanuel Kant, 'The Metaphysics of Morals', in his *Practical Philosophy*, 363–603. Subsequent page references are given parenthetically in the text.

14 See Immanuel Kant, 'An Answer to the Question: What is Enlightenment?', in his *Practical Philosophy*, 15–22. Subsequent page references are given parenthetically in the text.

Chapter 3   Reaction

1 See Edmund Burke, *Reflections on the Revolution in France*, ed. A. J. Grieve (London: Dent, 1967).

2 See Michael Oakeshott, *Rationalism in Politics and Other Essays* (London: Methuen, 1962).

3 See Edmund Burke, 'Speech on American Taxation' (19 April 1774) and 'Speech on Conciliation with the Colonies' (22 March 1775), in B. W. Hill (ed.), *Edmund Burke on Government, Politics and Society* (London: Fontana, 1975), 121–55 and 159–87.

4 Burke, *Reflections on the Revolution in France*, 15–16. Subsequent page references are given parenthetically in the text.

5 See John Locke, *Two Treatises of Government*, ed. Peter Laslett (Cambridge: Cambridge University Press, 1988).

6 See Joseph de Maistre, *Considerations on France*, trans. Richard A. Lebrun (Montreal: McGill–Queen's University Press, 1974). Subsequent page references are given parenthetically in the text.

7 See Vincenzo Cuoco, *Saggio storico sulla rivoluzione napoletana del 1799*, ed. Pasquale Villani (Bari: Laterza, 1976). Subsequent page references are given parenthetically in the text.

8 See F. C. von Savigny, 'On the Vocation of Our Age for Legislation and Jurisprudence', in H. S. Reiss (ed.), *The Political Thought of the German Romantics: 1793–1815* (Oxford: Blackwell, 1955), 203–11.

9 Ibid. 205.

10 See P. S. Ballanche, *Essais de palingénésie sociale*, 2 vols (Paris: Didotaîné, 1827–9).

11 See Bruce Haddock, *An Introduction to Historical Thought* (London: Edward Arnold, 1980), 90–105.

Chapter 4   The Constitutional State

1 See Benjamin Constant, 'The Liberty of the Ancients Compared with that of the Moderns', in his *Political Writings*, ed. and trans. Biancamaria Fontana (Cambridge: Cambridge University Press, 1988), 307–28.

2 Ibid. 326.

3 See ibid. 310–11.

4 See G. W. F. Hegel, *Early Theological Writings*, ed. R. Kroner, trans. T. M. Knox (Philadelphia: Pennsylvania University Press, 1971); *Phenomenology of Spirit*, trans. A. V. Miller (Oxford: Clarendon Press, 1977); *Philosophy of Right*, ed. and trans. T. M. Knox (Oxford: Clarendon Press, 1952); *Lectures on the Philosophy of World History*, trans. H. B. Nisbet (Cambridge: Cambridge University Press, 1975); and *Lectures on the History of Philosophy*, trans. E. S. Haldane (London: Routledge and Kegan Paul, 1955).

5 Hegel, *Philosophy of Right*, p. 11. References to the preface of the *Philosophy of Right* (inserted parenthetically in the text) are to page numbers; references to the rest of the text are to the numbered paragraphs of the Knox edition, with an 'R' or 'A' appended to indicate respectively 'remarks' and 'additions'.

6 See G. W. F. Hegel, *Philosophy of Mind*, trans. A. V. Miller (Oxford: Clarendon Press, 1971). The text is part 3 of the 1830 edition of the *Encyclopaedia of the Philosophical Sciences*.

7 Hegel, *Philosophy of Right*, §5. Subsequent references are inserted parenthetically in the text.

8 See Immanuel Kant, 'Groundwork of the Metaphysics of Morals', in his *Practical Philosophy*, 73.

9 Hegel, *Philosophy of Right*, §135R. Subsequent references are inserted parenthetically in the text.

Chapter 5 The Nation-State

1 See J. G. Herder, 'Journal of my Voyage in the Year 1769', in *Herder on Social and Political Culture*, ed. and trans. F. M. Barnard (Cambridge: Cambridge University Press, 1969), 61–113.

2 Ibid. 85–6.

3 Michael Oakeshott, 'The Voice of Poetry in the Conversation of Mankind', in his *Rationalism in Politics and Other Essays* (London: Methuen, 1962), 197.

4 *Herder on Social and Political Culture*, 182. Subsequent page references are given parenthetically in the text.

5 See Bruce Haddock, 'Italy: Independence and Unification without Power', in Bruce Waller (ed.), *Themes in Modern European History 1830–90* (London: Unwin Hyman, 1990), 67–98.

6 Giuseppe Mazzini, 'Carlo Botta e I romantici', in his *Scritti editi ed inediti*, ed. L. Rave et al., 98 vols (Imola: Galeati, 1906–40), i.65.

7 Giuseppe Mazzini, 'Storia della letteratura antica e moderna di Federico di Schlegel', in ibid. 114.

8 Giuseppe Mazzini, 'D'una letteratura europea', in ibid. 177–222. Subsequent page references are given parenthetically in the text.

9 Giuseppe Mazzini, 'Manifesto della *giovine Italia*', in his *Scritti editi ed inediti*, ii.76.

10 Giuseppe Mazzini, 'Istruzione generale per gli affratellati nella *giovine Italia*', in his *Scritti editi ed inediti*, ii.46. Subsequent page references are given parenthetically in the text.

11 See Francesco Salfi, *L'Italie au dix-neuvième siècle* (Paris: Dufart, 1821); Luigi Angeloni, *Sopra l'ordinamento che aver dovrebbero I governi d'Italia* (Paris: Appresso l'autore, 1814); and for wider discussion Franco della Peruta, 'La federazione nel dibattito politico risorgimentale: 1814–1847', in Ettore A. Albertini and Massimo Ganci (eds), *Federalismo, regionalismo, autonomismo: Esperienze e proposte a confronto*, 2 vols (Palermo: Ediprint, 1989), i.55–79; and Bruce Haddock, 'State, Nation and Risorgimento', in Gino Bedani and Bruce Haddock (eds), *The Politics of Italian National Identity* (Cardiff: University of Wales Press, 2000), 1–49.

12 See esp. Giuseppe Mazzini, 'Dell'unità italiana', in his *Scritti editi ed inediti*, iii.261–335.

13 Mazzini, 'Istruzione generale per gli affratellati nella *giovine Italia*', ii.49. Subsequent page references are given parenthetically in the text.

14 Giuseppe Mazzini, 'Dei doveri dell'uomo', in his *Scritti politici*, ed. Terenzio Grandi and Augusto Comba (Turin: Unione tipografico-editrice torinese, 1972), 910. Subsequent page references are given parenthetically in the text.

15 See Mazzini, 'Dell'unità italiana'.

16 See the editor's introductory comments in ibid., pp. xiii–xvi; and *Scritti politici*, 131–2. Note that federalism has continued to be a contentious issue in recent Italian political thought. See Gianfranco Morra, *Breve storia del pensiero federalista* (Milan: Mondadori, 1993); Zeffiro Ciuffoletti, *Federalismo e regionalismo: Da Cattaneo alla Lega* (Bari: Laterza, 1994); and Bruce Haddock, 'The Crisis of the Italian State', in Robert Bideleux and Richard Taylor (eds), *European Integration and Disintegration: East and West* (London: Routledge, 1996), 111–26.

17 See, in particular, the discussion of Cuoco above, pp. 34–9.

18 Mazzini, 'Dell'unità italiana', 309.

19 See ibid. 263. The most celebrated statement of a moderate federalist position in the 1840s in Italy is Vincenzo Gioberti, *Del primato morale e civile degli italiani*, 2 vols (Brussels: Meline-Cans, 1843). For discussion see Bruce Haddock, 'Political Union without Social Revolution: Vincenzo Gioberti's *Primato*', *Historical Journal*, 41 (1998): 705–23.

20 See Mazzini, 'Dell'unità italiana', 266. Subsequent page references are given parenthetically in the text.

21 See Jean-Jacques Rousseau, *The Social Contract*, trans. Maurice Cranston (Harmondsworth: Penguin Books, 1968), 62–4.

22 See Denis Mack Smith (ed.), *Il Risorgimento italiano* (Bari: Laterza, 1987), 422; Giuseppe Mazzini, *Scritti editi ed inediti*, lviii.42–4; and E. J. Hobsbawm, *Nations and Nationalism since 1780: Programme, Myth, Reality* (Cambridge: Cambridge University Press, 1990), 31–2.

23 See Jules Michelet, *The People*, ed. J. P. Mckay (Urbana: University of Illinois Press, 1973).

24 See Bruce Haddock, *An Introduction to Historical Thought*, 90–105.

25 See Mazzini, 'D'una letteratura europea'.

26 Giuseppe Mazzini, *Note autobiografiche*, ed. Mario Menghini (Florence: Le Monnier, 1943), 179.

27 Giuseppe Mazzini, 'Atto di fratellanza della *Giovine Europa*', in his *Scritti politici*, 373–4.

28 See Giorgio Candeloro, *Storia dell'Italia moderna*, 11 vols (Milan: Feltrinelli, 1956–86), ii.224–42 and 371–84; and Mazzini, *Note autobiografiche*, 248–50 and 261. Note that Mazzini had in fact opposed the expedition of the Bandiera brothers.

29 See J. G. Fichte, 'The Closed Commercial State', in Hans Reiss (ed.), *The Political Thought of the German Romantics* (Oxford: Blackwell, 1955), 86–102; and J. G. Fichte, *Addresses to the German Nation*, trans. R. E. Jones and G. H. Turnbull (Chicago: Open Court Publishing Company, 1922).

Chapter 6 Liberty

1 See Alexis de Tocqueville, *Democracy in America and Two Essays on America*, trans. Gerald E. Bevan (London: Penguin Books, 2003). Subsequent page references are given parenthetically in the text.

2 See Wilhelm von Humboldt, *The Limits of State Action*, ed. J. W. Burrow (Cambridge: Cambridge University Press, 1969). Subsequent page references are given parenthetically in the text.

3 See John Stuart Mill, *On Liberty and Other Essays*, ed. John Gray (Oxford: Oxford University Press, 1991). Subsequent page references are given parenthetically in the text.

4 See John Stuart Mill, *Autobiography* (London: Longman, 1873).

5 John Stuart Mill, *On Liberty and Other Essays*, 15. Subsequent page references are given parenthetically in the text.

6 See Thomas Hill Green, *Lectures on the Principles of Political Obligation*, ed. A. D. Lindsay (London: Longman, 1941).

7 Hobhouse was especially critical of the neo-Hegelian Bernard Bosanquet. See L. T. Hobhouse, *Liberalism and Other Writings*, ed. James Meadowcroft (Cambridge: Cambridge University Press, 1994); and Bernard Bosanquet, *The Philosophical Theory of the State* (London: Macmillan, 1965).

Chapter 7 Welfare

1 Jeremy Bentham, 'An Introduction to the Principles of Morals and Legislation', in *A Fragment on Government with an Introduction to the Principles of Morals and Legislation*, ed. Wilfred Harrison (Oxford: Blackwell, 1967), 125.

2 Ibid.

3 Jeremy Bentham, 'A Fragment on Government', ibid. 3.

4 John Stuart Mill, 'Utilitarianism', in his *On Liberty and Other Essays*, 138. Subsequent page references are given parenthetically in the text.

5 See Robert Owen, *A New View of Society*, ed. Gregory Claeys (Harmondsworth: Penguin Books, 1991); and Ghita Ionescu (ed.), *The Political Thought of Saint-Simon* (Oxford: Oxford University Press, 1976).

6 See David Friedrich Strauss, *The Life of Jesus Critically Examined*, ed. Peter C. Hodgson, trans. George Eliot (London: SCM Press, 1973); and Ludwig Feuerbach, *The Essence of Christianity*, trans. George Eliot (New York: Harper, 1957).

7 Feuerbach, *The Essence of Christianity*, 20. Subsequent page references are given parenthetically in the text.

8 See, in particular, Karl Marx, 'Critique of Hegel's Doctrine of the State' and 'A Contribution to the Critique of Hegel's Philosophy of Right', in his *Early Writings*, ed. Lucio Colletti (Harmondsworth: Penguin Books, 1975), 57–198 and 243–57.

9 Karl Marx and Frederick Engels, *Collected Works* (London: Lawrence and Wishart, 1976), v. 31. Subsequent page references are given parenthetically in the text.

10 See Karl Marx and Frederick Engels, 'Manifesto of the Communist Party', in Karl Marx, *The Revolutions of 1848*, ed. David Fernbach (Harmondsworth: Penguin Books, 1973), 62–98. Subsequent page references are given parenthetically in the text.

11 Karl Marx and Frederick Engels, *Selected Works* (London: Lawrence and Wishart, 1968), 182.

12 Ibid. 182–3.

13 Hegel, *Philosophy of Right*, 11.

14 Karl Marx, *Capital: A Critique of Political Economy*, trans. Ben Fowkes (Harmondsworth: Penguin Books, 1976). Subsequent page references are given parenthetically in the text.

15 Karl Marx and Frederick Engels, 'The German Ideology', in *Collected Works*, v. 47.

16 Ibid.

17 Both are available in Karl Marx, *Surveys from Exile*, ed. David Fernbach (Harmondsworth: Penguin Books, 1973). Subsequent page references are given parenthetically in the text.

18 See Eduard Bernstein, *Evolutionary Socialism*, trans. E. C. Harvey (London: Independent Labour Party, 1909).

19 Karl Marx and Frederick Engels, 'Manifesto of the Communist Party', 98.

20 See Antonio Labriola, *La concezione materialistica della storia*, ed. Eugenio Garin (Bari: Laterza, 1965); and Benedetto Croce, *Materialismo storico ed economia marxista* (Bari: Laterza, 1941).

21 See Georges Sorel, *La Décomposition du marxisme* (Paris: Marcel Rivière, 1907); Georges Sorel, *Les Illusions du progrès* (Paris: Marcel Rivière, 1927); and Georges Sorel, *Reflections on Violence*, trans. T. E. Hulme (London: Allen & Unwin, 1925).

Chapter 8 Totalitarianism

1 See Thomas Hobbes's classic analysis of the logic of a 'state of nature', in *Leviathan*, ed. C. B. Macpherson (Harmondsworth: Penguin Books, 1968), 183–8.

2 V. I. Lenin, 'What is to be Done?', in his *Selected Works* (Moscow: Progress Publishers, 1963), i. 121. Subsequent page references are given parenthetically in the text.

3 V. I. Lenin, *The State and Revolution*, trans. Robert Service (London: Penguin Books, 1992), 79. Subsequent page references are given parenthetically in the text.

4 See V. I. Lenin, 'Imperialism, the Highest Stage of Capitalism', in his *Selected Works*, i. 634–731.

5 See Karl Marx, *Capital: A Critique of Political Economy*, vol. 3, ed. Frederick Engels (Chicago: Kerr, 1909).

6 Lenin, 'Imperialism, the Highest Stage of Capitalism', 640. Subsequent page references are given parenthetically in the text.

7 Lenin, *The State and Revolution*, 86.

8 Ibid. 87; Lenin's italics.

9 See Friedrich Nietzsche, *On the Genealogy of Morals*, ed. Keith Ansell Pearson (Cambridge: Cambridge University Press, 1994).

10 Vilfredo Pareto, 'Les systèmes socialistes', in Adrian Lyttelton (ed.), *Italian Fascisms: From Pareto to Gentile* (London: Jonathan Cape, 1973), 78.
11 Vilfredo Pareto, 'The Parliamentary Regime in Italy', *Political Science Quarterly*, 8 (1893): 677–721.
12 Vilfredo Pareto, 'Trasformazioni della democrazia', in Lyttelton (ed.), *Italian Fascisms*, 92. Subsequent page references are given parenthetically in the text.
13 See Carl Schmitt, *The Concept of the Political*, ed. George Schwab (Chicago: University of Chicago Press, 1996).
14 See Carl Schmitt, *The Crisis of Parliamentary Democracy*, ed. Ellen Kennedy (Cambridge, Mass.: MIT Press, 1988).
15 See ibid. 26.
16 Schmitt, *Concept of the Political*, 26.
17 Ibid. 71.
18 See Benito Mussolini, 'The Doctrine of Fascism', in Lyttelton (ed.), *Italian Fascisms*, 39–57.
19 Giovanni Gentile, *Origins and Doctrine of Fascism*, trans. A. James Gregor (New Brunswick, NJ: Transaction Publishers, 2002).
20 Ibid. 21.
21 See Giovanni Gentile, *The Theory of Mind as Pure Act*, trans. H. Wildon Carr (London: Macmillan, 1922).
22 Giovanni Gentile, *Origins and Doctrine of Fascism*, 25.
23 Ibid.
24 Giovanni Gentile, *Genesis and Structure of Society*, trans. H. S. Harris (Urbana: University of Illinois Press, 1960), 121. Subsequent page references are given parenthetically in the text.

Chapter 9 Politics Chastened

1 Altiero Spinelli and Ernesto Rossi, *Il manifesto di Ventotene*, ed. Norberto Bobbio (Naples: Guida, 1982).
2 K. R. Popper, *The Open Society and its Enemies*, 2 vols (London: Routledge and Kegan Paul, 1945); and *The Poverty of Historicism* (London: Routledge, 1991).
3 Popper, *Poverty of Historicism*, p. vi. Subsequent page references are given parenthetically in the text.
4 Popper, *The Open Society and its Enemies*, i, p. viii. Subsequent page references are given parenthetically in the text.
5 See Stephen Mulhall and Adam Swift, *Liberals and Communitarians* (Oxford: Blackwell, 1996).
6 See F. A. Hayek, *The Road to Serfdom* (London: Routledge, 2001).
7 Ibid. 115.
8 See F. A. Hayek, *The Constitution of Liberty* (London: Routledge and Kegan Paul, 1960). Subsequent page references are given parenthetically in the text.
9 Michael Oakeshott, *Rationalism in Politics and Other Essays* (London: Methuen, 1962), preface.
10 Michael Oakeshott, *Experience and its Modes* (Cambridge: Cambridge University Press, 1933).
11 See Oakeshott, *Rationalism in Politics and Other Essays*, 80–110. Subsequent page references are given parenthetically in the text.
12 See Michael Oakeshott, *On Human Conduct* (Oxford: Oxford University Press, 1975), 108–84. Subsequent page references are given parenthetically in the text.
13 See Richard Rorty, *Contingency, Irony and Solidarity* (Cambridge: Cambridge University Press, 1989).

14 See Peter Laslett (ed.), *Politics, Philosophy and Society* (Oxford: Blackwell, 1956).
15 See Isaiah Berlin, 'Two Concepts of Liberty', in his *Four Essays on Liberty* (London: Oxford University Press, 1969), 118–72.
16 John Rawls, *A Theory of Justice* (Oxford: Oxford University Press, 1972).
17 See ibid. 118–92.
18 See John Rawls, *Political Liberalism* (New York: Columbia University Press, 1996).
19 See Robert Nozick, *Anarchy, State and Utopia* (Oxford: Blackwell, 1974); Ronald Dworkin, *Taking Rights Seriously* (London: Duckworth, 1977); *idem, A Matter of Principle* (Cambridge, Mass.: Harvard University Press, 1985); and *idem*, 'Foundations of Liberal Equality', in Grethe B. Peterson (ed.), *The Tanner Lectures on Human Value*, xi (Salt Lake City: University of Utah Press, 1990).
20 See Michael J. Sandel, *Liberalism and the Limits of Justice* (Cambridge: Cambridge University Press, 1982).
21 See Alasdair MacIntyre, *After Virtue*, 2nd edn (London: Duckworth, 1985).

Chapter 10 Politics Fragmented

 1 See Francis Fukuyama, 'The End of History?', *The National Interest*, 16 (1989): 3–18; and Fukuyama's extended defence of the position in *The End of History and the Last Man* (Harmondsworth: Penguin Books, 1992).
 2 See Susan Strange, *The Retreat of the State: The Diffusion of Power in the World Economy* (Cambridge: Cambridge University Press, 1996).
 3 See Jean-Marie Guéhenno, *The End of the Nation-State*, trans. Victoria Elliott (Minneapolis: University of Minnesota Press, 1995).
 4 See Michel Foucault, *Madness and Civilization*, trans. R. Howard (New York: Pantheon, 1965); *idem, The Birth of the Clinic*, trans. A. Sheridan (New York: Vintage, 1973); *idem, The Order of Things: An Archaeology of the Human Sciences*, trans. A. Sheridan (London: Routledge, 2002); and *idem, The Archaeology of Knowledge*, trans. A. Sheridan (London: Routledge, 2002).
 5 See Michel Foucault, 'Governmentality', in his *Power*, ed. James D. Faubion (London: Penguin, 2000), 201–22.
 6 See Michel Foucault, 'Confronting Governments: Human Rights', ibid. 474–5. Subsequent page references are given parenthetically in the text.
 7 See Bruce Haddock, 'Hegel's Critique of the Theory of Social Contract', in David Boucher and Paul Kelly (eds), *The Social Contract from Hobbes to Rawls* (London: Routledge, 1994), 147–63.
 8 See Charles Taylor, *Hegel* (Cambridge: Cambridge University Press, 1975), 3–50.
 9 See Gino Bedani and Bruce Haddock (eds), *The Politics of Italian National Identity* (Cardiff: University of Wales Press, 2000).
10 See Bruce Haddock and Ovidiu Caraiani, 'Nationalism and Civil Society in Romania', *Political Studies*, 47 (1999): 258–74; *idem*, 'Legitimacy, National Identity and Civil Association', in Lucian Boia (ed.), *Nation and National Ideology: Past, Present and Prospects* (Bucharest: New Europe College, 2002), 377–89.
11 Will Kymlicka, 'Western Political Theory and Ethnic Relations in Eastern Europe', in Will Kymlicka and Magda Opalski (eds), *Can Liberal Pluralism be Exported? Western Political Theory and Ethnic Relations in Eastern Europe* (Oxford: Oxford University Press, 2001), 48.
12 See Brian Barry, *Culture and Equality: An Egalitarian Critique of Multiculturalism* (Cambridge: Polity, 2001).
13 See John Rawls, *Political Liberalism* (New York: Columbia University Press, 1996).
14 See Richard Rorty, *Contingency, Irony and Solidarity* (Cambridge: Cambridge University Press, 1989); John Gray, *Enlightenment's Wake* (London: Routledge, 1995); and *idem, Endgames: Questions in Late Modern Political Thought* (Cambridge: Polity, 1997).

15 See Joseph Raz, *The Morality of Freedom* (Oxford: Clarendon Press, 1986), 321–66; W. B. Gallie, 'Essentially Contested Concepts', *Proceedings of the Aristotelian Society*, 66 (1955–6): 167–98; and John Gray, 'Political Power, Social Theory and Essential Contestability', in D. Miller and L. Siedentop (eds), *The Nature of Political Theory* (Oxford: Oxford University Press), 75–101.

16 See Samuel P. Huntington, *The Clash of Civilizations and the Remaking of World Order* (New York: Simon & Schuster, 1996).

17 Bhikhu Parekh, *Rethinking Multiculturalism: Cultural Diversity and Political Theory* (Basingstoke: Macmillan, 2000), 343. Subsequent page references are given parenthetically in the text.

18 See Seyla Benhabib, *The Claims of Culture: Equality and Diversity in the Global Era* (Princeton: Princeton University Press, 2002).

19 See Paul Kelly, 'Identity, Equality and Power: Tensions in Parekh's Political Theory of Multiculturalism', in Bruce Haddock and Peter Sutch (eds), *Multiculturalism, Identity and Rights* (London: Routledge, 2003), 94–110.

20 See Carol Gilligan, *In a Different Voice* (Cambridge, Mass.: Harvard University Press, 1982).

21 See Seyla Benhabib, *Situating the Self* (Cambridge: Polity, 1992).

22 See David Held, *Democracy and the Global Order: From the Modern State to Cosmopolitan Governance* (Cambridge: Polity, 1995).

23 See Michael Hardt and Antonio Negri, *Empire* (Cambridge, Mass.: Harvard University Press, 2000).

24 Rawls, *Political Liberalism*, p. lxii. Subsequent page references are given parenthetically in the text.

25 The phrase is adapted from T. M. Scanlon, *What We Owe to Each Other* (Cambridge, Mass.: Harvard University Press, 1998).

Index